# DOG BEHAVIOUR
# EXPLAINED

## *A Self Help Guide*

*Peter Neville*

# DOG BEHAVIOUR
# EXPLAINED

## *A Self Help Guide*

First published under the title *Do Dogs Need Shrinks?*
in 1991 by Sidgwick & Jackson Limited

This edition produced by Carlton Books Limited for Parragon

ISBN 0 75252 670 7

Printed and bound in Great Britain by Mackays

# Contents

# Contents

# Contents

To Claire, those who play together, stay together

# Acknowledgements

Thanks to Claire and Gill for their behavioural expertise in dangling the prospect of attractive rewards and, less so, for applying the whip as necessary, in the writing of this book. To the irrepressible Bandit, and to the memory of Cass , my Dobermann Colonel, and to Muttley, Pest and Hamish, the other dogs in my life so far. Thanks too to all those veterinary surgeons who refer cases to me . Hearty thanks also to my colleagues in the Association of Pet Behaviour Councellors for all their wisdom and experience and to dogs and their owners everywhere.

# Introduction

*'I know all about the ups and downs, the daily, not to say, hourly changes in mood that seem to be a necessary concomitant of love for us over-sensitive humans. Dogs are not subject to these shifts in mood. When they give their love, they give it for good, true to their dying breath. That is how I should like to be loved.'*         Elisabeth Russell

Dr Neville? I'm sorry to phone you at dinner time but it's my dog . . . no, it's my wife really. She says the dog's got to go. He's done it once too often and she says it's either her or the dog . . . and you're my last resort.'

So yet another meal is allowed to go cold! Gently, I edge my peacefully slumbering, problem-free (when they're asleep) pair of Siamese cats off my lap and go into my office to grab the other phone. As ever, Claire's Bullmastiff, the famous Cass, hauls her 120 lb frame gleefully out of her basket with tail wagging and that ever hopeful 'must be dinner or a walk time' look all over her ugly face. My own dog, the contrastingly unavailable to public view maniac Munsterlander Bandit presently dozing in his bed, opens one eye and wonders who is the real maniac in the house. No gleeful 'let's go' from him. After an insolent stare that only a tough, over-intelligent German could give you, he simply sighs and goes back to sleep while I pick up the phone.

'Now, Mr . . . '

'Wallace.'

'Let's work through this logically so that I can get a better picture. First, what sort of dog do you have, what sex is it and how old is it?'

'Flash is a boy. He's a one-year-old collie crossbreed. We've one other dog, his brother, and they seem to get along okay most of the

1

time, but every so often he just does it again!'

'What is he doing, Mr Wallace?'

'Well, he bites Gordon, our other dog. But it's not *real* biting because he's really only grabbing him around the neck – unless his ears get caught in the way. And then all hell breaks loose. And every time I wade in to separate them, I get bitten. I don't mind so much but my wife does when I'm not there. In fact they seem to fight all the more when I'm away . . . you know what women are like . . . no sense of humour!'

As a fellow man, I haven't got much of one myself when it comes to being bitten by dogs, or hearing about other people who are when I'm mid-way through my dinner.

'How long have Flash and Gordon been doing this?'

'About three months, ever since I started playing cricket at the start of the season. I couldn't bear to part with the dogs . . . but I wouldn't want to lose the wife either.' I bet it was only the thought of having to wash his own cricket whites that prompted his touching show of affection. She was probably happily tucking into her tea and I wished I had left the answer machine on so I could be too!

It's a typical case for the animal behaviourist. A normal, much loved pair of family dogs have started to compete over status within the family. Being of equal backgrounds as brothers and presumably equal size, strength and of equal favour with regard to the Wallaces the dogs have been unable to settle into a nice normal canine social order where one is of higher rank than the other, and the underdog doesn't mind. It's a common problem for brother dogs homed to the same family. Everything is fine for many months until suddenly – adolescence – that most dreaded of all developmental stages strikes. For human teenagers it means spots, self awareness, being treated like a child when you want to be an adult, trying your luck at getting served in bars and, if you're a lad, praying for your voice to break soon and hoping you'll have a hairy chest! With dogs, it's more a question of status and the accompanying rights of rank in the social heap, but when trying it on with an equally developing pack mate, threats don't always work and teeth may be brought seriously into play.

It often happens for the first time when the man of the house is away, so the information from Mr Wallace that problems started when he went off to play cricket at the start of season is actually relevant! The husband is not necessarily the 'top dog' of the group in canine terms, but may be the one who spends more time in formal contact with the dogs and, as a result, has a capping influence on their

2

social competitiveness. But if, initially, dog fights are more likely when Mrs Wallace is alone with Flash and Gordon, they soon become more frequent and less likely to occur at any specific time. The dogs quickly fall from favour with at least one member of the family and relations between the owners are now clearly strained. Last resort I may be, but the fate of the dogs, and possibly even the marriage, may hinge on my successful treatment of the problems.

First I ask Mr Wallace to talk to his vet in the morning, to make sure that there are no medical reasons behind the dogs' behaviour, and to discuss referring the case to me.

The next afternoon I make a house call to the Wallaces to take a closer look at the problem. Two hours later and we've established how and why the dogs are behaving in this manner and developed a programme of treatment involving restructuring of the relationship between the dogs and owners, especially Mr Wallace; and a total change in the method of husbandry for the dogs, whereby democracy has no role at all. I also advise a little added assistance from an anti-male hormone injection to be given to Gordon, the under-dog, by the referring vet. Within a few days, things should be settling down and steadily the dogs should be able to organize their social relations within the Wallace family without more serious incident . . . well, no more than you'd expect from a couple of adolescent males feeling their way into manhood!

Leaving the Wallaces, I casually remarked that the lack of hair along Gordon's back and a little way up his tail looked like a flea allergy.

'Oh, that! He's been chewing away back there since he was about six months old. The vet has given us treatment for fleas, we've sprayed the dogs, the carpets, the whole house . . . even my cricket gear, but he's still doing it! Is it psychological?'

Not content with being a scrapper, Gordon is also a hair plucker. Rare, but not nice for the dog and not nice for the owner to look at. Maybe this case will take a little longer! Any form of self-mutilation is such a bizarre type of behaviour that it's always worth looking closer for interest, as well to try to relieve the suffering of the dog, even though most cases are completely different and usually turn into self-funded research studies that might cause me to start pulling my hair out!

On rare quiet days I often wonder how it came about that I should be a 'pet shrink'. I could never have predicted it even as an animal obsessed child, nor guessed that my working week, weekends and

3

even meal-times would be spent treating aggressive, destructive, car-chasing, nervous, indoor toileting and self-mutilating dogs, amongst others. Even in those twenty years or so since I was a child our society has drastically altered and it is perhaps remarkable that there should be a place for a consultant in canine behaviour at all. Fifty years ago, a dog was an animal that often had to earn its keep as a guard, hunter or playmate for the kids, and it only ever got leftovers from the family table for its dinner, if there were any. If not, it would have go and look for something on the streets or in dustbins. Veterinary care was really only for those dogs fortunate enough to be owned by the wealthy, or quality show specimens, or for out-and-out working dogs of value, such as gun dogs. While many forms of training dogs to task had been practised for thousands of years, treatment from a dog psychologist for the average family mutt was utterly unthinkable and well worth a laugh in the early 1960s.

So times must have changed and likewise our relationship with our dogs and expectations of them for me to do what I do. This book is about what I do, the types of problem that I treat, and the people and dogs I meet for those who, like me, are continually fascinated by the close and complex nature and history of our relationship with the dog. What this book is not, I hope, is another plod through canine behaviour and training, about which many people have said the same thing and to which I could add little. For those interested in the art of canine behaviour therapy and the working life of a dog shrink, its ups, downs, therapies, humour and teeth, this book is for you.

# 1
# Dogs, Cats and People

*'Affection without ambivalence'*                          Sigmund Freud

Dogs have always been appreciated by man for the tasks they can perform. The dog probably started as a tag-along, happy to pick up leftovers and settle somewhere near us at night. It was a symbiotic relationship: we got protection, status and companionship and the dog got a strong pack to be part of, food, protection and friendship. But in the Western world at least, the dog may now be losing its place as man's traditional best friend to the more uncompromising and, in some ways, more parasitic cat. In the USA more cats are kept than dogs, and, probably by the mid 1990s, we in the United Kingdom will have followed suit. The same is set to happen elsewhere in Northern Europe.

One might think that we could breed a type of dog to continue to suit all our modern requirements – after all, throughout history we have been enormously successful in altering the basic design of the dog to suit our various purposes. We have manipulated dog genes to produce huge variations in phenotype (appearance) and function, from Chihuahua to Mastiff in terms of size, Mexican Hairless Dog to the dreadlocked Hungarian Puli in terms of coat and King Charles Cavalier to Bearded Collie to Afghan Hound in terms of function.

The amazing elasticity of the dog's genotype (genetic make-up) has probably been the key to its successful association with us. It has enabled it to come with us in new forms and fulfil new tasks, or old ones in modern contexts, as our own social development has progressed from early agrarian livestock rearing to modern high-tech living. From stock and territory protector against wolves and other dangers, the dog's role has increasingly become one of companion in the human social group, although many insurance companies value the dog's bark and offer cheaper home policies to owners. This is all in marked contrast to the genetically less alterable and behaviourally less manipulable cat. The cat is rarely trainable to any set task and brings few naturally evolved benefits to our den, other than rodent control.

The cat also has no great perception of social hierarchy, and there is no role for us as pack leaders to an animal that hunts alone, beyond provision of food in the den. But we are nonetheless prepared to take on the role of hotel keepers for our cats who, in turn, affectionately view us as mother figures throughout their lives, at least when they are at home.

With dogs there is a price to pay. It is the price of physical dependency in providing necessary exercise, washing and grooming, cleaning the house of hair and mud around them and the efforts of having to be a life-controlling, decision-making pack leader. Forget those duties and the dog will suffer and so, therefore, may the relationship. We feel guilty if we cannot provide the necessary time and effort that dogs need. It is difficult to relax emotionally with pets or people if we feel guilty about not caring for them properly. With the adaptable, self-reliant cat, the physical demands are less: the consequences of, for example, not getting home from work on time are less likely to make us feel guilty. The chances are that he'll be outside in the garden anyway and not sitting at home with his legs crossed, desperately waiting for us.

Our preference for the cat is evolving mainly as a consequence of our own changing lifestyle rather than any failure on the part of the dog, and perhaps our decision to take the easier way out when we choose our non-human companions. That the keeping of both dogs and cats is still so enormously popular demonstrates our overall desire to keep them as companions; it is just that now our expectations of them and our own social and activity patterns are changing rapidly.

# Fitting in

Dogs used to be kept for their speed and skill in hunting, so improving our own survival prospects. Nowadays their physical skill at scent-

6

following is cleverly applied to drug and explosive detection work and their ability to be trained is invaluable to the blind, the disabled, and to the police in apprehending ever-increasing numbers of villains. But while it is true that the number of dogs being kept in the United Kingdom now exceeds 7 million, and in the USA 55 million, fewer and fewer of us have the lifestyle to accommodate, or sometimes even afford, the luxury of a dog simply as a companion, as 'man's best friend'. Those that do fill this role tend to be the smaller or toy breeds which require less effort and fit more conveniently into our urban lifestyle. As in earlier times the larger, tougher guarding breeds are kept to protect us and our property, perhaps indicating that the modern role of the dog is increasingly returning to the 'utilitarian' as it was all those thousands of years ago. It's just that we – not the wolves – are now our own worst enemies.

Protection in the form of a hefty Rottweiler or barking German Shepherd Dog may be necessary for survival in some areas of our cities not sufficiently affluent to afford entry phones at the door. But there is unease at encouraging dogs to be aggressive and our ability as a society to control them. Environmental concern about the use of parks and open spaces, let alone pavements, as dog toilets, added to fears of enteric worm and other diseases transmissible from dog to man via their faeces, means that we have a pet under pressure in our crowded cities. However good they are at protecting us, dogs are becoming more and more unpopular with much of the non-dog-owning public and calls for tighter legislation over ownership, licencing and physical control are heard frequently in the press and from politicians.

# Dog ownership

According to the annual survey of pet ownership trends in the United Kingdom for 1992, published in 1993 by the Pet Food Manufacturers' Association (PFMA), 7.3 million dogs are kept in 5.8 million households compared with 7 million cats in 4.7 million houses. However, there are clear regional variations both in the number and type of pet being kept. In cities the wealthier, younger section of our society is abandoning the medium-to-large dog, and even the smaller breeds, and opting instead for the cat. They can often afford non-canine security systems for their property and so need a pet for more emotional reasons. Along with budgies, though less markedly so, dogs remain most popular with the C2 and DE socio-economic groups, perhaps less likely to be able to afford trendy apartments with entry phones or who find that type of lifestyle less attractive anyway. While pet owning generally is most common in the South West, dog owning is most prolific in detached, semi-detached or terraced rural homes, particularly in the Midlands and the North East of the country and dogs are especially popular with young people in Wales. There, in a survey of 10,000 young people by the Royal Society for the Prevention of Cruelty to Animals ( RSPCA) in 1990, 49 per cent kept a dog – 8 per cent above the national average for the survey. Dog owning is apparently unaffected by increased unemployment; a dog can certainly be a loyal friend to talk to, take exercise with and generally rely on for keeping sane at such a time.

Cats are favoured by socio-economic groups AB and C1 compared with dogs and are increasingly being kept permanently indoors. With that sort of lifestyle, it's no surprise that, according to the RSPCA survey, cats only outnumber dogs as pets for young people in the South East and in London. Dogs tend to be kept by the older age groups, especially the 35 to 44 age bracket and in houses where at least one member of the household, usually Mum, stays at home during the day. A study of pet owner demographics in the United Kingdom published in 1985 by Messent and Horsfield, shows that dog ownership tends to be influenced by the age of the wife and whether she works or not, the presence of children and the type of housing enjoyed by the family. In present economic conditions and especially in the more expensive property zone of the south of England, both partners in marriage/ settled relationships have to work to be able to afford to pay the mortgage and this militates against the keeping of dogs.

Thankfully not all pet owners are alike or easily categorizable and not everyone chooses to keep cats in cities. Fifty-one per cent of all UK households keep at least one pet and are as likely as ever to keep a dog, or sometimes two. In the United Kingdom 80 per cent of owners keep only one dog and 20 per cent have two or more, whereas 34 per cent of cat owners keep more than one cat, perhaps an indication that as a companion to man, one cat cannot give as much as one dog. Many people, like this rurally based, cottage-dwelling pet behaviourist (who happily cannot easily be classified into any socio-economic grade because 'they' don't know where to slot a pet shrink into the scheme of things), enjoy keeping both cats and dogs, and a myriad of other beasts, furred and feathered. I'd like to think it is normal for human beings to want to surround themselves with other creatures and care for them, and that all of us would do so, given the chance.

Perhaps, then, we should view the absence of pet keeping in some sections of society, or its decline in city areas, as an indicator of social depravity and loss of richness in our civilization, demanding better government policy on how we construct our towns and living areas, instead of being simply a collection of interesting facts arising from the information required by the pet food and accessory markets.

It's almost impossible not to treat the dog as a human when he shares our den and our lives so closely, and we can communicate so well with him. His facial expressions and use of vocalizations are similar to our own and, of course, his body language is pronounced and helps us understand his changing moods and desires. As a result of this inevitable anthropomorphasization, says Dr Serpell of the Companion Animal Research Group at Cambridge University, 'we inevitably form much closer and more intense emotional attachments' to our dogs. In return, as the British psychiatrist Alasdair MacDonald said, 'Pets are less threatening and more controllable' than the relationships we may form with our human friends and family. The relationship is so close and similar because 'the combined qualities of warmth, touch, non-threatening movement and sound produce a simple analogue of human attachment behaviour but without the risk of vulnerability of offering emotional contact'.

If we were already close to the dog that lived in or around our social group then, of course, the dog will be the first to enjoy, for the most part, being allowed right into our hearts as well.

Dogs may be under pressure in our cities nowadays, and may be finding it hard to keep their place by our fireside in competition with the cat, but they have stuck with us for thousands of years. As that relationship strains and evolves as our society and lifestyles change, new demands and responses start to emerge, and the resultant sanity of dog and owner is what this book is all about.

## The support industry for dogs

'*A dog starved at his master's gate predicts the ruin of the state'*
William Blake

For whatever reason we keep dogs there is no denying that, for the most part, as a society we look after them extremely well. In the

United Kingdom we spent over £2 billion on all our pets even in 1988 – prompting one daily newspaper to observe 'this is about 58 times the gross national product of The Gambia and 23 times the World Bank's agricultural grant to beleaguered, famine torn Ethiopa in 1987'. In such terms this is morally questionable, but a glance at the huge industries now centred around the pet dog alone indicates its importance in creating employment and generating income in the United Kingdom.

In days past the dog was fed leftovers from the master's table, or scavenged much like its ancestors. The local butcher could usually provide a few scraps or 'pet pieces' at a cheap enough rate for most to improve the general quality of their dog's diet. Now few owners can be bothered to buy and prepare special food for their dogs or, if they can, are less likely to be able to provide a fully adequate, balanced diet. Nowadays it's far more convenient to provide a quality, ready balanced, value-for-money diet by purchasing a specially prepared dog food.

Canned dog food occupies one of the largest shelf facings for grocery items for either man or beast in our supermarkets, and the lion's share of a market which, in 1992, sold a total of 794,000 tonnes of wet, dry and semi-moist dog food, at a retail price of £598.2 million. 45,000 tonnes of dog biscuits and treats also command a £77 million market at the UK till. This is rising rapidly as we feel the need to love, reward, bribe and over-eat with our dogs who, like us, ought not to snack on too many extras between meals if they are to avoid obesity! We pet owners are all used to being bombarded by the pet-food and treat manufacturers advertising on our television screens, doubtless at enormous but justifiable cost. One famous advert, which pictured vast numbers of dogs running through beautiful countryside without so much as a growl at each other or a pause to admire the scenery, even won one of the advertising industry's top design awards. Clearly the way to our pocket through satisfying the dog's appetite is well worth engaging the top people for and we are all far more easily influenced than we'd sometimes like to believe!

Add to all that food the huge array of dog leads and collars made of nylon, Terylene and cotton webbing, leather and even plastic with flashing lights so you can see him the dark, wicker work and moulded plastic dog beds, bean bags, identity tags of plastic, metal and now high-tech microchip implants, poop scoopers, rubber balls, toys and chews, nail clippers, hair brushes and combs, shampoo and even dental floss, breath freshener and special canine toothpaste so that even Bonzo can give you a nice white smile, and it's no surprise just how many industries are contributing to the care and management of our dogs in one way or another.

We've been spending over £500 million per year at the vets since 1988 on all our pets, so dog health is big business for veterinary drug companies. There are now approximately 10,000 vets in the country, though not all in general practice as some work for the government or are in industry or research. There are about 2800 actual practices to choose from and despite the difficulty of entering veterinary school, it is still a largely vocational profession. You can usually rely on your vet for a sympathetic ear and a high level of compassion concerning your dog or any other pet that is all too often missing from our own health facilities. It's not that doctors don't care, it's just that they are overworked and don't often have time for those important touches within a state health system. The National Health Service unfortunately militates against the vet in practice because few of us are aware of the true cost of treatment when we are ill. We simply go to the doctor or into hospital and are made better, without a bill. When our dogs are sick we trot along to the vet, expect the same equipment to be available to diagnose the problem and the same competent treatment, be it via drugs or surgery, to make them better. Then we get a bill and complain!

Vets have a tough time of it in many cases simply because the public has precious little idea of the cost of health care, let alone an appreciation of the skills involved, which include a range of surgical skills for different species that would require a group of specialist consultant surgeons in the human field. So next time your dog is unwell or due for his annual booster vaccinations, take a fresh look at your vet and be grateful that the bill isn't half what it would be elsewhere in Europe or America because of the National Health Service! But if you are still worried by the prospect of even a fairly large bill you should consider insuring your dog or puppy against the costs of unforeseen veterinary treatment. This can cost as little as £35 per year and, although routine vaccination, neutering and other non-essential surgery is excluded, you will always have the peace of mind whenever your dog is unwell of telling your vet to carry out whatever treatment is possible, irrespective of cost. Many pet insurance policies are also prepared to cover some or all of the costs of treating behaviour problems, which is comforting for owners and myself alike.

Canine medicine has made major advances over the past ten to fifteen years as our demand to keep our dogs healthy has risen. In this country the Royal College of Veterinary Surgeons prohibits vets from

11

establishing practices to see only one species, but canine-only clinics are becoming more common in the USA and elsewhere and, like the university referral departments at UK veterinary schools, act as important collectors and disseminators of information as a result of the huge numbers of cases seen. It all adds up to the best possible service for the ill dog. No wonder that dogs are now living longer and it is not uncommon to hear of sixteen- and seventeen-year-olds, when even ten years ago a thirteen-or fourteen-year-old was notable. The world record is, incidentally, twenty-seven years and three months achieved by a gamekeeper's Black Labrador from Boston in England called Adjutant, which lived from 1936 to 1963.

We have a technologically rapidly advancing country, part of the self-help and generally dog-loving community of Europe, and a society that is not only keeping more dogs but is also generating huge support industries for them in all areas from food to private health insurance.

# 2
# Domestication – the evolution of a relationship

*'The wolf shall dwell with the lamb and the leopard shall lie down with the kid; and the calf and the young lion and the fatling together and a little child shall lead them'*                    Isaiah 11:6

Many theories have been proposed as to the origins of the domestic dog, *Canis familiaris*, including suggestions that it is descended, in part at least, from the jackal, as purported by the great ethologist Konrad Lorenz, or even from a now extinct dingo-like canid. However, it is now generally accepted that the wolf, *Canis lupus*, is the original ancestor of our modern dog in all its forms. The dog has 78 chromosomes, the same as the wolf. Other canids usually have fewer, but all are thought to have about 40,000 genes.

Behaviourally, extensive studies have shown similarities between the dog and the wolf – this can be corroborated without a trained scientific eye simply by observing the way individuals in a wolf pack behave towards each other, even in the confines of a zoo enclosure. It is markedly different from the behaviour shown by foxes or jackals. Additionally, many believe that the form of the modern dog could only be so adaptable and expressed in so many different shapes and sizes if the original genetic complement and form of its ancestor were also highly adaptable. While the jackal, fox and many other canids have been very successful at adapting to fill many different niches around the world, the wolf stands alongside man as one of the most successful

13

and highly adaptable mammals ever to walk the earth. For thousands of years the wolf was man's sole rival in the Arctic region, being as adaptable to a wide range of environments and climatic conditions and as efficient a hunter/scavenger in the northern hemisphere. Small wonder that man and wolf have always been competitors for food and resources and that the wolf has been so persecuted by man throughout history.

There are presently no less than twenty-three sub-species of the wolf showing huge variations in appearance from the white coat of the Arctic wolf to the jet black varieties found in North American forests, while the Spanish wolf is brownish grey with rust or yellow tints on the ears and tail. Larger forms, weighing up to 100 kg, predominate in the north while smaller forms, weighing as little as 20 kg, tend to be found further south. Sadly, at least seven sub-species of wolf have become extinct this century and many more are under threat either through continued persecution by man or, more insidiously, through hybridization with feral dogs. As a result the wolf is now rare over much of its former range, especially in Europe. However, moves to protect it are allowing numbers to stabilize or even recover a little in certain areas of Spain, former Yugoslavia and Russia. Our increased understanding of the wolf's true role is also melting the traditional prejudices and misconceptions of child-eating and unfettered savagery that sadly have built up around this magnificent animal.

With such a successful original pedigree, one might almost regard it as inevitable that man could adapt the wolf still further to suit his requirements. 'It takes a Fox to know a dog,' said Desmond Morris of that leading authority on wolf and dog ethology, history and behaviour, Dr Mike Fox. Mike certainly has one of the most frighteningly powerful intellects I have ever encountered, and I am indebted to his many books on the subject for much of the information in the following brief account of the history of the domestication of the wolf and development of the dog as a companion to man.

# From wolf to dog

The earliest known forerunners of the wolf and, subsequently, the present day domestic dog, appeared on earth in the Oligocene period about 40 million years ago, with the arrival of a small, more cat-like predator called *Miacis*. Later in this era, two species evolved from

*Miacis*, one being a bear/dog or wolverine-type animal from which bears are believed to have evolved, the other, called *Cynodictis*, being more dog-like and believed to be the forerunner of all canids. *Cynodictis* had retractable claws and so may have lived in trees. It was the probable ancestor of the cat family too, but also gave rise later to a hyena-like plains-dwelling animal, called *Cynodesmus*. Before *Cynodesmus* became extinct it evolved into a new line of development producing a creature known as *Tomarctus*. It is from *Tomarctus* that the modern-day wolf, coyote, jackal, fox, fennec and dog all evolved.

Some think that all dogs are descended from a smallish subspecies, the Asiatic wolf, living in the Near East, while others believe four basic stocks of wolf contributed from different parts of the world. The North American wolf is believed to have given rise to the Eskimo dog, and these dogs indeed continue to resemble their supposed ancestor today. From the Chinese wolf arose the Chow and perhaps the Pekinese, while the Indian wolf was thought to be the ancestor of many of the fast hunting breeds such as the Greyhound, Saluki and Afghan hound, as well as being the forerunner to the Dingo. The European wolf both individually and through crossbreeding of dogs arising from the Indian wolf side of the 'family tree', is believed to be the originator of most of the common dog breeds today such as the Mastiff, Bulldog, Newfoundland, Great Dane, St Bernard, sheepdogs, Spitz breeds, terriers and gun dogs such as spaniels.

But whether from one sub-species or several, the domestication of the wolf and development into the dog probably started to occur in the Mesolithic phase, 10,000 to 14,000 years ago, and about the same time as the development of a true agrarian lifestyle by man. If this is so, then the dog was one of the first animals to be domesticated, and probably just preceded other scavengers such as the pig and the duck. A little later, easily corralled and fed species, such as the sheep and goat, were domesticated and this enabled man to change from being a full or semi-nomadic hunter/gatherer to leading more of a settled existence.

Wolves were probably attracted to man's temporary settlements, and particularly so in winter or at other times of food shortage, because there was waste to be scavenged. But the initial social coming-together of man and wolf probably occurred as a result of an early man or his children acquiring a young wolf cub which was allowed to remain associated with the family, provided it did not show any aggressive tendencies. This probably occurred many, many times and, in most cases, the cub will either have died or been rejected, left behind or killed by man either to protect himself, or for religious sacrifice or food.

Those pups that survived to adolescence will also, by and large, have become competitive with their human packmates and then been killed or, as with the vast majority of hand-reared wild animals, simply have wandered away from the pseudo-maternal nest to seek their fortunes elsewhere.

But there will have been some individuals which were placid even through adolescence and which stayed alongside their human family and continued to be fed scraps and who perhaps even tolerated close handling without protest. As the wolf grew up, he would have become more territorial and started to bark or howl when danger threatened his group, including their livestock. The family would therefore have perceived benefit in keeping him around and then taken more positive steps to encourage him and look after him. Doubtless, too, the family would have benefited from a little more respect from other families in their immediate society by having apparently friendly relations with what was still a feared wild creature, which will have improved their perception of their own status in the same way as owning a large fearsome-looking dog does for some people today. On hunting trips the wolf may have contributed its vital abilities of scent-following and speed in the pursuance and capture of game, and back home, would soon have been valued for its herding capabilities, either once the desire to kill the stock had been bred out or intervention and direction by the human pack leader had become possible.

There are suggestions that while the wolf's early associations with man occurred probably as a result of a natural attraction of a scavenger to temporary human sites to feed on waste pickings, the closer acceptance of the wolf into the human group, and its associated benefits of improved hunting efficiency, actually fuelled the development of our more settled lifestyle and facilitated the existence of larger social groups of men.

The association between man and wolf undoubtedly contributed to improving a human family's quality of life and survival chances. It would not have been long before they acquired another one and the habit spread through the human group and on to other groups. And when one owner of a particularly pleasant or effective wolf met another owner with a wolf of the opposite sex to his own, the first selective breeding was arranged in an attempt to produce a combination of the two wolves' best characteristics. And then they found it wasn't quite so simple to select for desired traits, and their efforts had to be widened and pursued more intensively! But while man deliberately produced his own type of wolf in genetic isolation, he continued with the systematic destruction of the wild ancestral wolf to the point where so few exist today; man's wolf, the dog, predominates in all its many guises with man in all of the ancestral wolf's old home ranges.

Domestication itself is usually defined as when the breeding, care and feeding of animals is under the control of man and for such an event to occur, many of the wild, self-determining and survival-orientated aspects of the wolf's natural behaviour will have had to have been suppressed and then excluded by being bred out. This almost inevitably means that the first wolves to be taken in by man will have had to have been confined, and then kept in conditions sufficiently suitable for them to breed. Breeding in captivity is, in my opinion, often quite wrongly used as the measure of success of the design of cages and pens and conditions for animals in zoos. Many animals will happily breed in almost any environment, no matter how disgusting or apparently inappropriate. It is reasonable to presume that the first wolves kept by man would breed anyway, irrespective of conditions.

The wolf had always been a successful colonizer of new environments and had the genetic blueprint to facilitate breeding and survival under virtually any conditions imposed by man, and in spite of the withdrawal of their freedom. With that crucial first step achieved, the way was clear for man to breed wolves selectively; in other words, to take away the pressures of natural selection and survival of the fittest, and deliberately breed from animals with desired appearances or behaviour patterns that suited man's requirements, even though individuals bred with those traits would certainly have been less equipped to survive in the wild.

Mike Fox has described as follows the general characteristics that man was deliberately selecting for in his captive wolves in unknowingly genetically engineering the dog: docility, adaptability to different domestic environments, desirable economic characteristics such as rapid growth, fertility, reduction in the time between birth and effective function with retention of certain infantile characteristics (as these would enhance docility), reduction of wild characteristics – both behavioural, such as aggression, and physical, such as size, sharpness of teeth and so on – and, finally, strength and resistance to disease through hybrid vigour achieved by crossbreeding of stock.

Domestication implies a genetic disposition for docility or, more importantly in the case of the wolf, sociability which man is able to exploit and then deliberately select in breeding to make his animal companions non-aggressive, less fearful and easier to handle. Clearly the modern farm species were originally, and still are, strongly selected for production, but docility was also essential if they were to be enclosed and farmed safely. Original selection of the newly domesticated wolf will probably have been based largely on manageability and tolerance of human presence, perhaps even handling, and those without such traits, or which showed undesirable 'natural' wolf traits, would have been driven away, or more likely killed and eaten. It was only after thousands of years of selection for tractable, stable character that we started to manipulate the dog's genetic complement for appearance and to produce all of the 450 or so breeds that we know today.

We can continue to learn much about the early relationship between man and dog by observation of our own species when living more in harmony with nature in a non-technological society. The Efe people of the rainforest in the north-eastern lip of the river Zaire in Africa are of special interest to anthropologists because they still maintain a foraging or hunter/gatherer existence, believed typical of man prior to settling and becoming agrarian about 10,000 years ago. As well as being a window to our own past, the Efe also keep dogs and give us an insight into the the first associations of dog with man. Small to medium size, dingo-like light brown dogs are owned by individual tribesmen and accompany them on hunting excursions in the forest. While the skill of man is employed in detecting and tracking their quarry, which is usually antelope, sometimes monkeys and even, occasionally, elephants, the dogs are encouraged to chase, harry and hold the target once it has been struck by the first arrow. The largest share of the spoils, the hindquarters and the liver, go to the hunter who fires the first arrow, but the next best pickings go to the owner of the holding dog, while the firer of the *coup de grace* arrow waits for the next best portion. Clearly, the value of the dog is appreciated and the dogs are free to wander around the Efe's temporary encampments as they move through the forest. They are handled and treated as part of the family group much as we treat our pet dogs in western culture. Other tribes, formerly more nomadic but now living further north around Lake Turkana in Northern Kenya, go further and, as well as living extremely closely with their dogs, venerate them, to the point of believing that dog faeces placed on an open wound will help it heal. Consequently the Turkana people have the highest incidence of canine derived hydatid disease in the world.

Hydatid worms form cysts in the body and may develop to enormous size, even proving fatal. However, this relationship contrasts with that of the Kelabit people in Borneo. In his marvellous book *Stranger in the Forest*, Eric Hansen describes his first days and nights with four Kelabit men and no less than nineteen hunting dogs.

> The first night I sat cross legged with the other men knee to knee around our banana leaf picnic dinner blanket stacked high with boiled pig meat and steamed white rice. The technique of bone disposal was tricky. We threw the bones over our shoulders to the dogs prowling around in the dark. Like a school of piranhas they would fall upon each morsel with a ferocity that I found alarming. A mere arm's length away the sounds of snarling and snapping jaws was unnerving. Occasionally one of the men would pick up a stick and drive the dogs back a few feet, but they would return within moments. They savaged each other and tufts of unwashed dog hair wafted across the dimly lit dinner scene. Not exactly my idea of a floor show.
>
> The next morning as we walked in single file, the dogs developed an irritating habit of threading their way through everyone's legs before ranging far out into the jungle to pick up the scent of wild game. They would then circle back to the end of the procession, pass through and around our legs and repeat the procedure *ad nauseam*. With nineteen dogs performing this manoeuvre, it was very difficult to walk and I started to lose my temper. The dogs were constantly underfoot at the most inopportune moments. I eventually learned the mistake of getting impatient and learned a painful lesson – don't touch the dogs. One of them had been tripping me up for a few minutes in his attempt to pass me on the steep narrow trail. Each time I stepped to the side to allow him to pass, he hesitated. This continued until I was in the middle of a muddy traverse, and once again the dog was making me stumble. On impulse I grabbed the dog by the scruff of the neck, intending to shove him ahead. Instantly I received a mouthful of teeth to the back of my hand. Four nasty puncture wounds covered with dog slobber. I never made that mistake again; it was two weeks before I could make a fist without pain.

Perhaps in Borneo we are seeing a relationship between man and dog that hasn't evolved to be as close, or as pet-like, as in Zaire where, although the role of the dog is still based on hunting skills, the dogs are viewed as status symbols and with familial affection. Handling is possible, while with the hunting dogs of Borneo, the relationship is clearly more tenuous and less pet-like, and handling or close affiliation unwise. The dogs of the Kelabit people make hunting/stalking forays, whereas the Efe dogs are chasers and graspers after the quarry has been located, though this difference probably only serves to underline the adaptability of the dog when encouraged by man to fulfil certain tasks. Perhaps, as one American psychiatrist put it, 'dogs are caught between nature and culture' with man and their position on the scale between the extremes is governed by our demands on them.

From the wolf's point of view there were clearly many physical, physiological and behavioural changes to be borne in the process of being domesticated. The first selectively bred individuals would have been smaller than their wolf ancestor, even though we have now been able to reverse that trend and select for large size (acromegaly) in producing Wolfhounds and Deerhounds which almost seem too big for themselves. However the popularity of bringing dogs into the home or monastery (in Tibet the Lhasa Apso and Shih Tzu were the guardians of the temples) demanded that smallness was also selected for in many types and gave rise to the toy and small breeds that we continue to find so convenient today. With some we even select for dwarfish-type features (achondroplasia) such as in the Basset Hound of 'Fred' fame.

Most dog breeds have flop ears as opposed to the erect ears of the wolf, although, of course, the ear profile and, indeed, general physical appearance of one of our most popular breeds, the German Shepherd Dog, is very wolf-like. In Europe and the USA especially, though thankfully outlawed in the United Kingdom, the ridiculous cosmetic cropping of the lop ears of some of the larger or guarding breeds such as the Dobermann, Great Dane and Boxer is still practised to produce a fiercer or more wolf-like appearance. Worse still is that ear cropping is actually carried out by veterinary surgeons and demanded by breeders who ought to know better and care more. Many dogs' tails (which are also docked for stupid cosmetic reasons in some breeds, though this thankfully is now illegal in the UK) are shorter and curled over the back, a feature especially pronounced in Spitz breeds such as the Pomeranian, whereas the wolf tail is left hanging down when resting. Important changes have occurred in the skull of the wolf in producing the dog. While there is huge variation in the various breeds of dog, even comparably sized dogs have fewer, smaller teeth than the wolf and smaller jaws with less developed surrounding musculature.

By removing the necessity for the dog to hunt for food itself, the weapons it inherited from the wolf have generally deteriorated, though again, we have been able to improve the strength of the bite, if not the number of teeth, in many baiting or fighting breeds. While the dog's head is usually long and the muzzle slim and on a lower level than the forehead, there is great variation between the brachycephalic breeds with the squashed-in face and often undershot jaws, such as the Bulldog, Pug and irresistibly attractive Bullmastiff, and oligocephalic breeds, such as the Dobermann or Greyhound. Most breeds, most mongrels and the wolf are mesocephalic – somewhere in the middle of these extremes.

Most strikingly perhaps, we have altered the coat of the wolf into so many different shades, patterns, thicknesses and lengths in the domestic dog. One only has to contrast the almost hairless Chinese Crested Dog with the Afghan Hound, the Airedale, the Old English Sheepdog and the Dalmatian to realize how manipulable the genes coding for coat must be, and this is surely a feature continuing from the original variability found in the various wolf types around the world that enabled them to adapt successfully to so many different and varied environments and temperatures.

Of the physiological changes resulting from domestication, the most striking shift has occurred in the reproductive potential of the dog compared with the wolf. The dog reaches sexual maturity much earlier, in some breeds at about seven months of age, compared with two to three years in the wolf, and the dog bitch usually has two seasons per year as opposed to the single cycle of the wolf. Both are economically advantageous changes for man in breeding dogs, but would place a strain on any wild population of wolves and be selected against by Mother Nature.

As with cats, the tail gland has less social significance and is less active in the domesticated dog compared with its ancestors, and the frequency of moulting of the coat is often reduced, though you may not believe it if you own a long-haired dog which seems to shed continuously on the carpets and furniture.

Behaviourally, of course, our dogs continue to show many of their ancestor's traits but we have nonetheless altered them drastically to suit our demands. The first change was that essential criterion of domestication – the need for man not to be attacked and eaten by his new associate! Physical control and confinement will have prevented this to a large extent, but man had to select for individuals which allowed him to approach them, move them and later touch them without risk of injury. So man began to select more placid and tolerant individuals and hone down the wolf's aggressive tendencies.

He was also selecting individuals which showed a reduced flight reaction when challenged or frightened. Flight distance is a critical theme in the development and survival of all creatures and is best demonstrated by the space that antelopes try to maintain between themselves and the lion lurking in the nearby savannah. If the lion decides to attack, that distance defines the time it takes for the antelopes to detect the charge, and build up sufficient speed to avoid being caught and eaten. Hence predators generally only catch the old, sick, young or less observant and so the evolutionary fitness of the surviving antelope population is maintained. Wolves that allowed man to approach them were the ones to be kept and bred from, while those that showed an unrelenting, marked flight response would have been rejected. After a few generations the results of even this elementary selection would have produced wolves far less fit to survive in the wild away from man's care.

But as well as inevitably reducing the size of the wolf in producing the dog, man also selected for infantile behaviour patterns which are not lost, or only partially so, as the young animal grows up. This means that receptive, social patterns are encouraged while more adult, wilder, more aggressive and reactive patterns are selected against and bred out of the domesticated animal. This is known as behavioural neoteny and is probably best exhibited by the modern pet cat, which behaves towards its human owners throughout its life as a kitten, showing rubbing, greeting and social touch behaviour which would ordinarily be lost as it matured as a wild animal.

With dogs, neoteny has enabled us to select individuals and develop breeds with very infantile behaviour patterns because they appeal to us, and allow us to play a continuous parental role which is accepted and enjoyed by the everlasting puppy. Early selection for continuing infantile behaviour in the dog also helped ensure that a wide variety of function and developmental pathways in the dog and many breeds and types could more easily be produced from a willing, puppy-like character of adult dog, than from a fully grown, more reactive and resistant wolf-type. The ancestral wolf is not as fast as the Whippet, it is not as trainable as the Collie. It does not have as sensitive a sense of smell as the Bloodhound or the visual sense of the

22

gaze hounds, but from it, all things canine were possible once the influenceable, less aggressive and highly adaptable puppy-like blueprint had been developed by man. The wolf was well on the way to becoming a dog, and man, with his varied needs in his rapidly developing and different cultures around the world, quickly realized its potential.

# Dogs in history, religion and mythology

There is firm archaeological evidence of dogs living in association with man 10,000 years ago. Canine skulls have been found in Neolithic remains in present day Denmark and Germany, and it is believed that the ancestors of the Dingo, which were true dogs, were brought to Australia by the Aborigines at about the same time. The grave of a man from 8000 BC has been discovered, in what is now Israel, showing evidence of an affectionate, rather than simply utilitarian, relationship between man and dog. The man's arms are touchingly locked around the body of what was presumably his pet puppy. Indeed, the practice of keeping dogs with him seems to have developed in man's settlements simultaneously or spread quickly around the world. Dogs were certainly in evidence in North America by 5000 BC, probably having been introduced by early colonizers from Asia, and there are paintings of Greyhound or Saluki-like hunting dogs on Ancient Egyptian pottery from about the same period.

Babylonian sculptures of Mastiff-type dogs have been dated at about 2000 BC and that time in Mesopotamia was almost certainly one of the major epochs of selective dog breeding. Gaze hounds, Greyhounds, hunting, guard and war dogs were all developed and traded by the Babylonians, and later bred with European dogs to produce much of the variety today.

There are descriptions of dog hunting behaviour left by the ancient Greeks from 50 BC. In ancient Egypt, Anubis was the jackal-headed god of embalming and tombs, presumably for his recognized guarding abilities, and dogs were buried with their masters, perhaps alive along with the master's wives, to ward off evil spirits. Some Greyhound/Saluki-type dogs and Mastiffs were also considered sacred by the Ancient Egyptians and according to Herodotus, a family would shave their heads as a mark of respect if their dog died. The brightest star seen in the skies then was to be found in the constellation now known as *Canis major*. It was then known as Sirius and viewed as a watchful, faithful god and protector by the Egyptians.

Worshipping of dogs was also practised by the Romans, who made sacrifices to the god Procyon represented in the constellation *Canis Minor*, and like the Egyptians, also to Anubis in *Canis Major*. In Tibet, the Tibetan terrier, Shih Tzu and Lhasa Apso were associated with monasteries, and in China, the related Pekinese (also known as the Sun Dog or Lion Dog) was regarded as sacred and the exclusive property of the Emperor and nobility. The penalty for a commoner merely to be caught in possession of the dog that eventually came to be named after the capital of China was death. However, following the sacking of the Imperial Palace in 1860, five of the little blighters were brought to England and presented to Queen Victoria, thus establishing a trend, continued by our present Queen Elizabeth, for keeping lots of small dogs of breeds highly likely to be ankle-biters! Incidentally, Queen Victoria went on to share her death bed with her Pomeranians.

In Greek mythology, when Odysseus (or Ulysses) finally came home after ten years of adventures on his way back from the Trojan War, his wife and children failed to recognize him, partly because he was disguised as a beggar. His dog Argus recognized him immediately, probably because of his smell! This tells us two things. The first is that when the story was written in about 850 BC dogs were already being kept as house pets, and the second is that it was possible for a dog to live for ten years at that time, despite the rudimentary nature of veterinary medicine. Also in Greek mythology, Hades, the realm of the dead, was protected by Cerberus, a frightening three-headed, and therefore six-jawed, Mastiff type dog. One would have thought that one head of two Mastiff size jaws would have been sufficient to guard the dearly departed!

English history and mythology are also full of dogs, and of course one of our most popular breeds, the King Charles Cavalier Spaniel, owes its name to the patronage it enjoyed under Charles I and Charles II. Much of the dog's association in English history centres on its role as a hunter, either officially as a gamebird driver and courser or unofficially as a poacher's assistant, matched by large traditionally gamekeepers' riposte breeds such the Bullmastiff. And if King Arthur isn't already surrounded in enough early English mythology, there is the added mystery of his alleged dog Cabal having left its footprints in stone in Wales, perhaps at the same time as his master was pulling the sword out of another stone and claiming his throne!

We are probably all familiar with the famous Roman mosaic,

*Cave canem* (beware of the dog), from Pompeii, depicting a guard dog on a lead attached to a stud collar and, of course, most dogs still fulfil basic guarding roles for us. A few are kept for specific tasks such as hunting or herding sheep but mainly they are with us as companions, and in many ways have been so altered in the process of domestication as to have little chance of surviving without us.

There are plenty of feral (domestic gone wild) dogs throughout the world from New York to Liverpool to the high regions of Italy but these do not survive long unless able to group with others and form a successful hunting/scavenging unit as did their ancestors. Certainly the most successful feral dogs are medium to large mongrels with short to medium-length coats. Dogs of our artificially maintained pedigree strains soon interbreed, if they survive at all away from our direct care, and quickly start to reverse the process of domestication to adapt to local environmental and social conditions.

Feral, reverting dogs, and indeed feral cats, are the source of much study and public interest nowadays, partly because they give us an insight into just how much or how little we have been able to engineer our favourite pets and how much of the wild, naturally evolved ancestor remains, despite what we may have achieved in altering physical appearances.

These days we are all at least armchair naturalists. The modern media of television, cinema and highly advanced photographic techniques have brought the diversity and complexity of nature into our homes and enthralled us all. As a result we are more educated and no longer regard scavengers as filthy creatures happy to pick at the remains of the dead. Instead we understand how they fulfil the useful role in recycling nutrients. Predators at the top of the food chains such as lions, pike, cats and eagles are no longer seen as ruthless, harmful killers. We can now understand their role in keeping nature fit by feeding on the weak, sick and old and, as a result, can view the scavenging or predatorial side of our pet dog if not with pleasure, then at least with understanding. We still marvel at his fleet movement, sensory skills and sharp reflexes, but we also understand the evolutionary benefit and functional adaptation of these and various other features of the hunter. Highly developed senses and efficient weapons of teeth evolved for good reason and are all part of the divine plan. This opportunity to have the tooth and paw of nature contrasting with faithful loyalty lying benign by our fireside is yet one more reason for the popularity of dogs in human society.

25

# 3
# Learning and Development

*'Dogs are rightly regarded as the epitome of loyalty. Where else shall one find refuge from the endless dissimulation, falsehood and treachery of humans, if not in dogs upon whose honest countenance one can gaze without mistrust'*
Schopenhauer

Domestication is a compromise for many species, protected from the demands of survival in the wild, but controlled, restricted and modified for other purposes. For the dog we are a fellow creature in a social group and usually a pack leader – a Napoleon who makes decisions, orders life, protects the den and other pack-mates and allows access to food.

It is still possible to take a wolf cub, rear it, care for it into adulthood and maintain friendly, bonded relations with it. Indeed, some of the best studies on wolf behaviour have only been achieved because scientists, such as Erik Zimen in Germany, were able to raise wolf cubs, integrate them into their study packs and observe them at close quarters. While the relationship between scientist and such wolves must be based more on the way wolves would behave amongst themselves than the way in which a man would respond to his pet dog, the fact that we can continually, if carefully, socialize with adult pure wolves testifies to the social elasticity and tolerance of the species. It endorses the remarkable special relationship we have been able to forge with the modified wolf, the dog.

It was my own pleasure, though a little sad too, to care for a European Wolf which was brought into an animal shelter I was running in Thessalonika in Northern Greece in 1984. The wolf, a

26

male, had been taken or found as a pup by a gypsy family somewhere in Europe, and had travelled with them as a family pet and guard. They had simply grown tired of him. He was tame, could be handled and embraced and would even walk on a lead. He was, however, rather disinterested in play and never responded at all when passing other dogs in their kennels in the shelter. While most people treated him as another stray or rescue dog initially, such is the reputation of the wolf even now, that few continued to pat him after I'd told them what he was! The only time that I had to be careful with him was at feeding time – a definite case of open kennel door, drop food bowl, slam door very quickly and step sharply back. He growled and spread the contents over the kennel walls and proceeded to lick them clean over the next hour or so! But, to be fair, there were plenty of apparently domestic dogs who behaved similarly in the kennels, so this needn't have been a particular lupine trait! Alas, the wolf died just a couple of weeks after his arrival and while I was getting all too used to sick and starving arrivals dying on me, I remember the acute sadness I felt when he went. Simply by watching him and being with him, he had taught me more about dogs than a hundred books and probably even a hundred dogs could ever do. He was the pure form, the original dog and one could sense in him the unadulterated raw building blocks of all those canine qualities we now admire.

## In the beginning . . .

So just what is it that enables us to enjoy this special relationship with the young wolf, even the older wolf and our own wolf, the dog? The story began with domestication and the selection of many infantile traits in our dogs, as well as for appearance and task fulfilment. And it continues with every puppy, through our relations with it from the time it is born.

After a 63-day gestation period (plus or minus about five days), the mother dog produces a litter of 1–12 puppies depending on the breed but at an average of about 5 or 6. The record is 23 puppies born to a foxhound in America in 1945. The puppies are born with only the basic senses of touch, taste and smell, but can also sense warmth and cold, and feel pain and hunger. They begin sucking almost immediately after birth, so while initial survival obviously depends much on the mothering ability of the dam, each puppy's ability to locate and move towards Mum for warmth and protection and to locate a nipple for nourishment also determines whether it will survive those crucial early hours and days.

Lacking sight at birth, the sense of smell is contrastingly well developed in new-born puppies. Mike Fox has shown that if a mother dog's nipples are coated with aniseed, her puppies will follow a cotton bud soaked in aniseed even 24 hours later if they are hungry or cold. A puppy which hasn't had this early sensitization to the smell of aniseed withdraws noticeably from an unanointed cotton bud placed near its nose. From this simple experiment, we may logically presume that a new-born puppy is born with sufficient neural development to imprint onto the smell of its mother.

More importantly in terms of the relationship between man and dog, the new-born puppy can imprint on to any smells it encounters, including Mike Fox's aniseed and, more subtly, the smell of man. So handling of puppies at birth by people is probably a very important and generally overlooked feature of socialization with man. It could improve the prospect of good responses towards the owners and, perhaps, people in general, when the puppy's eyes finally open after about ten days and they start to tie up a visual image with a smell profile of man, or at least the owners of their mum. This imprinting facility of the newborn wolf must have been a crucial feature in the domestication of the wolf by early man, and it certainly makes it easier to comprehend how and why a tolerant relationship could have developed.

Up to about 14 days of age the puppies sleep for about nine-tenths of the time and spend the rest trying to get close to their mother to feed. With each day, the nervous system develops enabling the puppy to begin to organize movement and direction much better and it actively seeks and competes for a warm sleeping area by its mother.

Although the eyes open at about ten days, vision develops progressively over the next ten to fourteen days. Stronger puppies are then already able to compete better for the maternal resources of food and warmth and may grow faster and survive better than weaker siblings.

Until now the puppies have been unable to eliminate (the behavioural term for passing urine or faeces − always sounds a little terminal to me!) without physical stimulation, usually by licking of the abdomen and genital region by the mother, but now their own activity stimulates things into flowing! This too has an obvious evolutionary advantage in that while the puppies are nest bound they can only eliminate when stimulated by their mother, who is therefore on hand to clean up the waste immediately and prevent the nest from becoming soiled and damp with the associated risk of infection. This initial 'house training' is something which we can use to retrain dogs with indoor toileting problems, but more of that later.

At 28–35 days the puppies are mobile enough to leave the nest, and eliminate voluntarily. By about 35–40 days of age, the puppy is fully equipped to start to react competently with its environment, albeit still one protected by its mother.

# Response and socialization

The ability to coordinate incoming information about the environment and organize a response at 21–28 days allows the pup to react in a more self-determining manner with its litter mates, mother and environment and, to some extent, with its human owners. From now until weaning at about 42 days of age is recognized as a critical socialization period in the puppy's life, as one might expect. It was the famous work of Scott and Fuller in the mid 1960s that identified the importance of this first socialisation period, in the development of the puppy as a social mammal. The puppy, particularly in a wild or feral pack, usually has little option but to be socialized with other dogs under this rearing system. Interestingly, however, it was also shown that puppies brought up in isolation from any litter mates or the mother were not necessarily incompetent as a result at six to seven weeks of age, and could quickly make up lost ground through lack of such early exposure at this time. With all systems in place the puppy would simply need occasional opportunity to interact with other puppies, a mother figure and a different, more stimulating environment to achieve the same level of subsequent sociability and competence.

# Fast learning

By six weeks of age the senses are fully functional and the brain is coping with a vast array of information. Our little puppy is starting out on the most active learning period of his life. It is now, by observation of his litter mates and adult dogs, especially his mother, that he will take in and learn many of the things that he will need to

29

react with his own kind and deal with life's problems when he is more on his own. It is at this time that puppies are attracted to change and novelty and, while protected from any immediate danger by their watchful mother, to approach novel objects, creatures and local environments without fear.

From about four to twelve or fourteen weeks of age, overlapping the first socialization period, comes the second important period to be identified by behavioural scientists. This second period is especially important with regard to the dog's socialization with man and successful incorporation into either man's pack, or a mixed species pack of other dogs, people and even other species such as cats. Scott and Fuller showed that if the growing puppy were denied the possibility of reacting with humans in this second period, it would then come to avoid human contact subsequently and, without such emotional attachment developed, be largely untrainable.

When the puppy is getting more and more mobile and wandering temporarily away from the immediate protection of its mother, the onset of the potential for a fear response to sudden or startling novelty at about eight weeks of age is critical. If this successfully helps the puppy avoid the danger of unwanted contact with unusual environmental happenings or objects or especially with unfamiliar animals, such as man, then its ability to form social and emotional attachments with us will deteriorate quickly. So, to be successful at producing tractable and sociable dogs as pets, it is essential for them to have human contact especially at 6 to 8 weeks of age when fear is largely unknown. Constant contact is, however, unnecessary to produce the desired effects. Two 20-minute periods per week of handling and interaction with humans only during weeks 4 to 12 will produce a puppy well socialized to man, according to Scott and Fuller. The same applies to socialization with other animals such as cats.

So from birth the puppy has become an increasingly social, sensitive, intelligent and trainable creature, up to puberty, starting at any time between 6 and about 12 months depending on the breed, continues to learn about survival, feeding and how to react with other packmates, be they canine or human. That sociable tendency, usually so willingly transferred to the human social set-up, is only really possible because our social unit, the family, is so similar to that of the dog pack, both ancestrally in terms of genetic control of behavioural capability, and more immediately, acquired by the puppy in its own development in the litter and then through socialization with us. It is also modified by our efforts in schooling and deliberately 'training' the puppy from his first day with us and throughout his life, to be basically compliant with our wishes and perform certain actions, stop or come to us when given verbal commands.

# Play

*'He that wrestles with us strengthens our nerves and sharpens our skill. Our antagonist is our helper'*                Edmund Burke

Social play between mother and puppies, among the puppies and between breeder and puppies is also vital in a puppy's socialization and balanced upbringing. Play enables the puppy to refine its coordination and social interactive behaviour in a non-serious, sometimes relaxed, sometimes high energy manner with its litter mates. Each learns how to exchange various signals using body postures, eye contact, relative positioning, vocalization, etc, and so develop the intricacies of canine language and communication. The more the nervous system evolves and the brain develops, the more complex the level of communication can become. For example, facial expressions become incorporated into the puppies' social interactions at about 5 weeks of age with the development of a truer face from the earlier rounded, clone type face of all of the litter. The development of all such communication is vital for the organization of the group in any social animal, including man, and youngsters who do not experience such learning may have severe social behaviour problems later as adults.

In play fighting, the manoeuvres of social interaction and conflict can be learned when bites themselves are inhibited and, with only milk teeth involved, are unlikely to be injurious if emotions do run high. Such interaction has few obvious reinforcers other than the physiological positive effects of endorphin (endorphins are natural opiates which make us feel pleasantly 'high' when taking exercise, or when caressing each other) released during activity, or the mild negative reinforcement resulting from the assertive response of a playmate that the puppy may have bitten a little too hard in play. Play interactions also enable puppies to experiment and develop the sexual posturing of solicitation and rejection, which also have a role in the development of general social behaviour to help them order themselves socially later among the adults of the group. Such interplay includes

31

learning about physical positioning when there is no risk of challenge or conflict, or pregnancy! Indeed it is often essential that puppies do experience these types of interaction for them to be able to function sexually later, both in communication at mating and physically. Hence puppies are seen to mount each other, and the reaction may become more pronounced when they are excited for other reasons when a little older. Play also enables puppies to develop their hunting skills of chase, grab, hold and wrestle with each other, and, using trophies of toys or other handy objects, to compete over possessions and start to define their social standing relative to each other. Begging and more devious forms of soliciting or conniving appeasement must also be learned for growing puppies to be able to fit into the pack and stay welcome and survive, however high-ranking they will become in their future pack. Such experience is essential schooling for them later to able to communicate, socialize and compete with other members of their pack aside from their mother and litter mates, and also to learn how to raise their own offspring as adults. There is little quite so delightful as watching young animals start to play and while most aspects of play can be rationally explained through detailed observation, others seem to have no logical explanation and are purely experimental games for the puppies; simply the freedom and innocence of their emotional expression and the energy of their actions are pleasurable and fascinating. Our own children keep us young in mind and body because we are able to shake off the demands of being adult and can enjoy uninhibited play, perhaps by getting out our old train sets or dolls for the kids! We can experience the same feelings from raising our pets' kids too, with the advantage of being able to find new homes for them once they're old enough!

Puppies play noticeably less with each other with every day after about nine or ten weeks, but some breeds are clearly more playful than others. Size has much to do with it and many of the really big chaps like St Bernards are less likely to invite games of chase or trophy competition compared with, say, even a young Dobermann. Males may be more playful than females because much of their initiating behaviour may include aspects of sexual advance and they often enjoy games of physical competition such as wrestling and tugging because these games have winners and losers, and that helps them decide how high-ranking in the pack they can become. Much of this need for competitive play may be fuelled by testosterone, a male hormone, hence bitches may be less playful as they are less concerned about their social standing. Guns for boys and doll 'mock children' for girls.

Although adult dogs play less frequently than puppies, most dogs will play if invited, and this is one of the main reasons for the success of the dog as a pet. Maintaining many of our dog's puppyish characteristics even as an adult appeals to the nurturing playful parent in us, even if the games we play with our dogs of hide and seek, chasing balls, competitive tug-o'-war, scent following, retrieving, etc, are often comprised of otherwise unfulfilled hunting behaviour patterns. The dog has an air of freedom about him when hunting or playing and for us to be involved in directing the game or interacting with our pets in play, gives us the same enjoyable freedom of expression of emotions. Let the endorphins roll!

# Dog sense

*'Unmissed but by his dogs and his groom'*          William Cowper

The dog's sensory capabilities of sight, smell, hearing, touch and taste vary from our own. Many of the problems we may experience with our dogs result from our communicating on different wavelengths or by differing systems.

## Smell

For the dog, smells are highly important and feature strongly in communication and social order maintenance. The dog has a sense of smell perhaps a million times greater than our own. The dog has about 200 million olfactory cells compared with our 5 million. Spread out, our nasal membrane covers an area the size of a large postage stamp – but in the dog, a surface about the size of a school exercise book receives and dissolves the scent. There is also a much larger area in the brain for processing all this information. While we can just about tell the difference between the smell of onion and apple, some dogs can follow a many days' old scent left by a man wandering across a muddy field in wellies, and know which is the right direction – indicating that the dog is also following an upward smell gradient! The dog, like the cat and the horse, also possesses an organ that we humans do not, the vomero-nasal, or Jacobson's organ, situated in the roof of the mouth behind the front teeth. This allows it to smell-taste chemicals, probably

33

by concentrating weak or important signals into more discernible form. With such capacities evolved to assist tracking of prey and social communication between pack members and others, it is small wonder that we have been able to harness it in scent work by drug or explosive detector dogs, to track criminals or hunt. So when your dog sticks his nose rudely between your legs to say hello, bear in mind it's just his way of shaking hands and making eye contact!

# Sight

The dog's eyesight is very good, but varies enormously between breeds. Obviously the dog's eye level is different from ours. Lower down, at knee height, a herd of cows or crowd of people for that matter must seem very ominous indeed and explain why dogs don't seem to observe all the things we can from on high, and why they sometimes over-react to strange or pronounced sights that we saw some while earlier. They will also often tend to rely on their better sense of smell as their first receiver of information and then look to where the scent has come from.

Structurally the human and canine eye are very similar and both function on the same principle. The light enters the eye through the pupil and is focused by the lens on to a layer of light sensitive cells at the back of the eye called the retina which transmits signals to the brain along the optic nerve. The dog's view of the world is one of hues of grey, black and white images for the most part. This explains why you can see the brown rabbit motionless in the grass, but the dog often fails to pick it out. It perceives a grey rabbit against a grey background, for which the rabbit is doubtless grateful! Dogs, however, are believed to have reasonable vision at the red end of the spectrum.

A dog's night vision is far superior to ours. A layer of reflective cells called the tapetum in the back of the eye reflects light back in, enhancing the image, an adaptation vital for the dawn and dusk hunter. This reflective layer can be seen at night in cats' and dogs' eyes when a beam from a car headlight hits them, or when using flash photography. Human eyes appear red in flash photos as a reflection of the blood vessels at the back of the eye; cats and dogs appear yellow or green because of the reflection off the tapetum.

The way the dog's eyes are positioned on the head, coupled with good musculature for moving the eye in its socket ensures that the dog has a wide field of vision, though this is also affected by the shape of the dog's head. Short-nosed or brachycephalic breeds such as the Pug or Bulldog have eyes situated at the front of the face giving them a better overlap (binocular vision) between the individual eye's field of vision than with longer-nosed breeds.

Breeds such as the Dobermann which have the least overlap between the fields of vision, have relatively poor stereoscopic sight and poorest perception of distance. Thus gaze hounds such as the Borzoi manage to run into ditches and trip over small obstacles and Colonel, my old Dobermann, never learned to catch a titbit thrown to him – he either 'lost it' in mid-air to my other keen-eyed dogs or had to scurry for it after it had bounced off his nose (if one of the others hadn't got there first)! By contrast, man and the cat have excellent stereoscopic vision because of the positioning of the eyes, and the resultant overlap between the individual eye's fields of vision allows them to assess distance accurately.

Although a stationary rabbit 15 metres away against a grey or brown background may be difficult for the dog to see without full colour vision, it will be noticed as soon as it moves. Dogs' eyes are particularly good at detecting movement, probably using monocular vision – the dog switches from using information received from one eye to the other in quick succession to gain as much contrast from the moving image as possible.

By changing the shape of the lens the human eye 'accommodates' to produce a sharp focus for both near and distant objects. It is thought that a dog cannot accommodate as efficiently as man, and thus may see a more blurred image of the world. Its range is similar to that of an old person – about 14 times less keen than the eyes of a child. A great many toy breeds, such as the Pekinese, appear to be very short-sighted and rely more heavily on their sense of smell to investigate objects close at hand.

## Hearing

The dog's sense of hearing is roughly the same as ours for low notes, but whereas we hear little beyond 20,000 Hz, the dog hears well up to 40,000 Hz, hence the popularity of 'silent' (to us, ultrasonic) whistles in dog training. While the ability to hear the squeaks of small mammals would have been required by the wolf if he were to detect and prey on them, the dog's sense of hearing is no match for the cat whose audible range goes up to about 70,000 Hz. Both cats and dogs can move their ears independently and so can get a better directional fix on the source of the noise. While their general range and sense of hearing is similar to ours, the dog can usually discern smaller differences in tone than we can.

## Taste

The dog's sense of taste is rather poor compared with ours, though of course all those dog food and treat manufacturers would have us believe differently. The senses of taste and smell are closely linked (to prove this, try identifying common food items by taste while holding your nose) and acceptability of food for a dog is largely determined by smell. Food may be rejected on grounds of its unattractive smell before it reaches the dog's 2000 taste buds, whereas we tend to taste first and spit substances out if they are unpleasant to some of our 10,000 taste buds. However, as we all know, our dogs definitely do have their likes, dislikes and favourite things when it comes to food.

Clearly the senses of sight and hearing are important to social animals communicating vocally and via body language. We often overlook the dog's pronounced sense of smell because we don't have it ourselves, thus missing out on a whole area of potential communication. Perhaps we will really only be able to 'talk' to our dogs when we evolve an improved sense of smell! But the great similarity and overlap between our respective senses and communication patterns facilitates our close existence. We can communicate our needs, wants, pleasure, displeasure and sociability to the dog in a way that he can interpret, and he can respond and behave in ways through facial expression and body posture that we can understand. It is no surprise that we talk to our dogs so much, or that we often credit them with being 'almost human'. From a very early age, in terms of senses and developing social behaviour, they almost are!

By contrast with the fairly independent, almost hunting proficient 12–14 week-old young cat, the 12-week-old dog is still very much a juvenile and is still learning how to use its senses and growing social skills to discover how it should behave within the social system of the dog pack. In the wild it will now be taught the courtesies of the social order. Instead of its mother feeding or regurgitating food for it, the puppy must learn to wait for its share of the spoils of hunting and that older, high-ranking dogs take precedence in selecting favoured shelter and walkways, and have the right of passage. Taking a puppy from its mother after weaning at the age of six weeks or so and placing it in a human pack is simply to take advantage of its development and redivert its attention to us and our homes at a time when the dog is most willing and able to explore. Assimilation into his adult group, and the process of forming more adult social contact is also directed into the relationship with us and any of our other existing dogs and pets in the home.

## Fine-tuning the man/dog relationship

*'Is thy servant a dog, that he should do these great things?'*
2 Kings 8:13

It is noticeable that dogs which are homed early after weaning at about six weeks, handled frequently and, after vaccination, exposed to as wide a variety of people, other dogs and environments as possible are far less likely to present behaviour problems when growing up, or as adults. Keep a puppy isolated during those crucial periods of 4–6 and certainly 4–12 weeks old and it will inevitably be incompetent with environmental challenge, dogs, people, or both, later. Hence the reason why the Guide Dogs for the Blind Association (GDBA) takes its selectively bred, just-weaned 6-week-old puppies and places them in carefully chosen family homes to socialize with humans as early as possible, be brought up in a stimulating family environment with other animals, often including children and dogs all under the careful eye of an experienced 'puppy walker'. Of course, the pup cannot go out freely onto the streets until it is fully protected against disease by vaccination, but this too is done as early as is safely possible so that the young pup is exposed to life in towns, on buses and among crowds as soon as it can be and comes to treat all those things as normal day-to-day events and experiences.

In short, they have to be bomb-proofed early on, and taught basic obedience and to walk to heel before going on later to be trained more specifically to lead the blind. Training guide dogs began in Germany

37

after the First World War and in the UK with the formation of the GDBA in 1931. The GDBA recognized long ago the importance of breeding selectively for task, and now has a total breeding stock of over forty carefully selected stud dogs kept in a special breeding centre and nearly two hundred breeding bitches kept as pets in family households around the country. There are seven main training centres in the UK producing a total of about six hundred fully trained dogs per annum. Having experimented with many breeds of dog, the GDBA now equally favours the Labrador, and Labrador/Golden Retriever crosses in about equal proportions, with pure Golden Retrievers and German Shepherd Dogs also accounting for about one third of the total between them. But, as well as the need for good breeding, training and, of course, the training of the dog's blind owner in the control and care of his guide, the GDBA also recognized the importance of investing effort early in their pups to maximize the chances of benefiting from their selective breeding process.

One might have expected the police force to adopt similar measures in selecting and socializing dogs to perform their tasks, especially as the practice began as far back as 1859 in the Belgian town of Ghent. The use of dogs by the police was well established in much of northern Europe by the turn of the century and by 1909 more than four hundred German police stations kept trained dogs. Things were then just starting in the UK, with Airedales applied to the task of flushing out vagrants by the Hull Docks Police and it wasn't until 1911 that the Metropolitan Police in London authorized its constables to take their pet dogs with them on night patrol duties. One Pomeranian was even taken on the beat! However, the practice stopped in 1918 and wasn't resumed until 1939, and more properly after the war in 1946 with the formation of the modern dog section, some fifteen years after the GDBA. American police didn't recruit canines until after 1940. But even today, the UK Metropolitan force with about 330 dogs in active police service is one of the few in the country that breeds its own dogs and selects for type and character in the favoured breed for general 'street' duties, the German Shepherd Dog. Ten per cent are more specialized 'sniffer' dogs including Labradors, Collies, Retrievers and Springer Spaniels. Most other forces buy in their dogs or, more usually, take unwanted dogs from the general public at an age when they may already be past being influenced into generally sociable or competent behaviour in society, let alone be responsive to the specific and controlled demands of police work and training. Small wonder, said one informed delegate at a recent talk I gave to a police dog handling unit, that the vast majority (he quoted 94 per cent, though I have no official supportive evidence for this figure) of these dogs are then rejected as unsuitable for police work. He desperately wanted to take on at least a 6-week-old puppy to socialize prior to police training, and better still one from the selective police dog breeding programme available but alas, the head of his unit prohibited it, still firmly believing, as so many dog trainers do, that dog training can only start when the dog is at least 6 months old. I wonder how much it costs society to have all these would-be police dogs assessed, fail basic training and then be passed back to their original owners or sent to the rescue centre. Perhaps we are all too impressed by the small percentage which do succeed and go on to demonstrate their training so marvellously at public displays that no one has dared ask why all police dogs are not produced through a proper selective breeding/ socialization/training programme like the Guide Dogs. That said, I'll just go and check that my tyres are not worn!

In most litters there is a wide range of influences on a young, growing pup, from instinctive and breed-focused behaviours right through to the varying input received and the experiences of each puppy. Sometimes there is large variability between members of a litter in their responses and development rates. Most usually learn their way out of any non-productive or harmful behaviour patterns later, given the right sort of exposure. This constant ability to learn through contact and experience is particularly pronounced in the canids, especially the wolf. Without it, the wolf would never have been able to colonize so many different environments so successfully. His adaptability has been passed to the dog, and we should be grateful to him again, for without this age-old lupine and now canine trait, our dogs would not be trainable or responsive to us today. It helps account for the ability of many dogs not to suffer ill effects from a poor upbringing and socialization, and their ability often to recover and behave normally. However, the effects of a less than ideal upbringing in our young or adult dogs can be very noticeable and lead to behaviour problems which are all the more regrettable because they were avoidable.

# 4
# Do Dogs Need Shrinks ?

*'I'd be a dog, a monkey or a bear or anything but that vain animal who
is so proud of being rational'*                     John Wilmot

So just how do dogs learn to cope with life's challenges and forge the
best way through and, more importantly from the point of view of their
relationship with us, just how do they learn to behave around us or
how can they be trained to perform to our requirements? Learning in
animals and man has been the subject of enormous amounts of
research by scientists and, in this century especially, by psychologists
keen to unravel the nature of human behaviour by studying less
complicated processes in simpler (different?) creatures.   But, of
course, we are all scientists to some degree and learn about behaviour
continuously from the experiences of our own day to day lives, through
observation of our children as they develop, and of our pets as they
react with us in their human-orientated lifestyles. Scientists have a
need to quantify and classify events, and the acquisition of learning
and behaviour patterns is generally considered to occur via two basic
processes: classical conditioning, and trial and error or instrumental
learning.


## Classical conditioning

Classical conditioning was first outlined for us using dogs in 1927 by
the famous Pavlov though, of course, every dog owner continues to see

exactly what he demonstrated at feeding time. Pavlov rang a bell prior to blowing food powder into the mouths of his dogs and after a few experiences, the dogs would salivate in expectation of a feed just on hearing the bell – just as our dogs do when the foodbowl is picked up and clattered. If we accidentally brush the dog's lead and make it jangle, he gets excited in anticipation of a walk – the sound and experience are closely associated or 'paired' and produce a conditioned response.

Most of us will associate certain sounds, voices, music or, most strongly, smells with events past and react positively or negatively when in contact with those things, without making any conscious decision to do so.

Perhaps the saddest example of this is the man I saw in London a few years ago who ran for cover in a nearby doorway and started to shake with fear on passing an auditorium which was showing a film about life in London during the Blitz. The sound of the air-raid sirens was being broadcast onto the street to help attract customers, but the conditioned response it produced in him brought them no extra revenue! This demonstrates how long some conditioned reflexes can persist, and it is probably true that such associations will often have a marked effect on the long-term survival of the person or dog in question.

Response to a strong conditioning stimulus such as availability of food or the prospect of being killed will need to be retained for life. Once a response is conditioned, it can only become lost if it is no longer reinforced or because the stimulus becomes associated with something else. Hence when Pavlov stopped feeding the dogs after ringing the bell, they stopped salivating after several such non-eventful experiences.

Over time conditional and, of course, unconditional responses may weaken and this is vital for an animal to become familiarized with regular or non-threatening features of its environment as it grows up. A dog does not need to react to all the things that excited it and prompted investigation when it was on its first voyages of discovery as a puppy.

Most people who lived through the Blitz no longer run for cover at the sound of the air raid siren because it is no longer associated with the actual risk of being bombed. However, for many, the sound does still evoke something of a conditioned response with a nervous shiver running down their backs.

41

# Trial and error learning

Trial and error learning, as it suggests, is more of a voluntary affair. An animal learns to perform certain types or sequences of behaviour which provide the reward of a solution to a problem or a benefit to him. Because the behaviour is rewarded, repetition is more likely in future.

It is the typical pathway followed in training dogs in basic obedience work, such as teaching the 'sit' and 'down' responses to verbal commands, and reinforced with praise, touch, titbits or the opportunity to mouth or hold toys from the owner.

For learning to occur, the rewards must follow the behaviour sequence immediately to become 'associated'. Hence in puppy training, it is no use waiting even two seconds before rewarding a desired response of, say, sitting to a command – chances are that some event will have occurred in between times and the dog will perceive that event as bringing on the reward. The puppy may stand up again and the sit won't be reinforced by reward at all, so immediate rewarding of the correct response is needed, with repetition to compound the learning.

If the behaviour ceases to be rewarded, then the response may become lost. Ideally rewards should follow every correct response to every command. However, occasional reward is usually sufficient to maintain the response. If the command is complex, or what is required as a response from the dog is difficult, what it does will vary with how it regards the value of the reward. This helps account for the varying performance of different breeds of dog. For example, compare recalling a Beagle while out on a walk with the response of a Retriever. The Beagle, a hunting animal, sees little reward in returning to his owner for praise and a titbit – the rewards of following some good smells are much greater. The Retriever, on the other hand, often delights in interacting with its owner, and willingly returns when called, often without formal training because it is more rewarding.

Sometimes dogs learn to respond in a similar fashion to different stimuli. For example, having learned to bark at their own doorbell, the dog may also bark when other doorbells sound, in game shows on the television for example or, like my old Dobermann, while calling to visit someone and ringing their doorbell! The dog may not bark initially when someone knocks rather than rings, however it is soon recognized as similar after a few experiences.

Learning is about adaptation as well and, for more complex

responses to become learned, sequences may have to be learned in stages through 'shaping'. We break down the processes of shaping deliberately in teaching our dogs more complicated responses, such as the tricks performed by circus dogs. With patience and reward of each correct response along the way, a string of tasks can be performed consecutively. Then, on completion of the sequence, a final reward can be given, rather than at each learning stage.

Such is the ability of some dogs (like Bandit, one of my little dears) for sequential learning, that many teach themselves how to jump onto a table, walk along a counter, poke a paw under the loose corner of the fridge door insulation, open the door, jump down via a nearby chair and scoff the remains of the Sunday joint, and only try to do so on a Monday when everyone is away and there is likely to be a Sunday joint left over! When Bandit has tried it later in the week, long after that period of weekend contact with the family, there has been no joint to be had, so the behaviour sequence was only rewarded on the Monday and became extinguished on quieter days! There is a border line here between sequential trial and error learning, and learning by insight. Insight involves the animal forming an advance hypothesis about how a problem may be solved and a reward achieved. Prior to Pavlov, Kohler showed in 1925 that chimpanzees could work out in advance, without trial and error learning, how to pile up boxes scattered individually on the floor to build a platform from which to reach a food reward suspended from the ceiling. This implies that monkeys at least can infer properties and usefulness of certain items from their shape. These are forms of learning not usually credited to dogs, though it is hard with bright individual dogs, like Bandit, to distinguish between such reasoning and their ability to learn rapidly by observation, imitation, and trial and error.

# Punishment

*'If only men could love each other like dogs, the world would be paradise'*                                                    James Douglas

Get out Bandit!' It's a Monday and for once I'm home – I've just heard the fridge door squeak open! This brings us on to punishment, which most of us over-use in reacting with our dogs and gain little or no improvement in them as a result. Most of us assume that punishment has an instant reforming effect on a dog's behaviour because the dog will perceive disadvantage in its actions, either in the form of our verbal displeasure, or because of the shock and pain of a slap on the backside. Only rarely is this so, and rarer still is it for punishment to instil long term behaviour changes so that the dog never does 'it' again under any circumstances.

Punishment is not the opposite of reward. Reward increases the strength of an animal's response, punishment does not produce a decrease. Worse still, the consequences of punishment may be unpredictable and even dangerous. For example, if I were to smack Bandit on the backside while his nose were in the fridge, I would indeed stop him momentarily from his pursuit of the Sunday joint. However, he may also turn and bite me, and then return to the fridge. If I then punished his aggression, the chances are that he would bite me more severely and repeatedly until I backed away, whereupon he would probably continue to seek the joint. If the punishment were so severe as to cow him, he may vacate the fridge, but because the reward of the joint is still inside, he will simply await a fresh opportunity when I am away to have another go.

Punishment is usually futile if one is trying to encourage a dog to perform a certain task in training. Imagine the stupidity of hitting or choking a dog with a choke chain or shouting at him as a punishment for not sitting to the 'sit' command in terms of his learning and desire to please his pack mate or leader. Yet this is exactly what happens to many of the nation's pet dogs every week as their owners try to teach them to be obedient. Better to work on positive methods and be always the nice, benevolent teacher prepared to repeat the message if the dog is a little slow to comprehend and still reward the desired responses, than be a frightening, unpredictable teacher of whom the dog is fearful, and therefore slower to learn.

Extreme forms of punishment can have permanent 'reforming' effects on behaviour, but the punishment must usually be very severe, cause great pain, and be indisputably associated with a particular stimulus or behaviour sequence for that behaviour sequence to cease. This was demonstrated in dogs using electric shock experiments some years ago, experiments that I'm glad to say would be impossible to justify now. They demonstrated that a conditioned sound stimulus like Pavlov's bell could also be associated with an extremely unpleasant, unconditioned stimulus such as an enormous life-threatening electric shock and that, when sounded again, it would cause the dogs to take extreme avoiding action. Naturally the dogs exhibited panic and great generalized fear as well.

For some dogs, being smacked once by their owner for having their head in the fridge, or even being yelled at is sufficiently traumatic to be totally reformative, but for most, like Bandit, punishment merely becomes an occupational hazard of being an opportunist! Sometimes you make mistakes, so you adapt and make sure that conditions are a little different next time. All that the punishment has produced is a brighter dog with a slightly modified unwanted sequence of fridge raiding behaviour that continues to flow as before, with the sole condition that I must be absent because the prospect of reward remains! How to treat? Put a lock on the fridge! Or as we shall see in 'Problems, Problems', think round the problem and turn punishment into an aversion, where the unpleasant consequences are seen as having come from the fridge or the action of stealing the joint rather than from the owner, or by managing the situation whereby the dog receives greater reward for not performing the fridge-opening sequence and his behaviour is re-routed onto something less annoying.

Sad to say, punishment is far too often used by many so- called dog trainers who are sometimes far too lacking in knowledge about canine learning processes to be effective, kind or ethical. If I sound a little over-reactive, it is not because I claim any great knowledge or ability in dog training. Indeed, I have never trained a dog beyond basic obedience as a pet. While teaching Bandit, I was obviously using the same body movements at each session. Unwittingly I had taught him to respond to hand signals as well as verbal commands, as he demonstrated as a young pup when I raised my arm one day to wave at someone. Bandit sat immediately, and then lay down as I brought my arm down. No credit to me, but all credit to my highly observant dog for teaching me how easy it can be! What I do frequently deal with, however, is the result of heavy handed training – those dogs which have been frightened, traumatized or sometimes even physically abused to the point of the trainers committing offences which would render them liable to prosecution under the Cruelty to Animals Acts.

They would benefit from observing the trainers of other animals, for example, the methods used in training a dolphin to jump over a rope suspended 3 metres above its pool. The aim of the trainers is never to let the animal fail, thus everything it does is correct and is rewarded: a positive approach. The rope begins on top of the water and the animal is rewarded for swimming over it. It is raised very slowly and if the dolphin goes underneath, it is seen as the fault of the trainer for going too fast. The rope is lowered again until the task is completed successfully. Think how much better we could all do with our dogs if we had the patience to go through this errorless technique.

Thankfully many understand that dog training is a lot of fun if presented correctly, and both owners and dogs can enjoy the experience enormously. More owners are able to realize their dog's potential as a dog, complete with directable canine sense of smell and those hunting capabilities that might otherwise have lain hidden behind a sometimes maniacal insistence by unthinking trainers that all dogs must sit, all dogs must go down and even Bloodhounds must retrieve the dumb-bell. A dog can easily understand a vocabulary of twenty words from its name, simple words like sit, stay, hold, bark, etc, to interjected commands such as fetch or drop, as the dog is already responding to a 'come', and alterations of speed of response to any instruction with the command 'hurry'. It just takes time, understanding and the correct approach of rewarding correct responses immediately and abandoning the age-old nonsense about punishing mistakes.

## Dog and Man

There is enormous variability in the type and nature of our relationship with the dog. We can select breeds, as practised by the Guide Dogs for the Blind Association, to suit our individual or specific demands. However, not only do breeds differ, but every dog from every litter is different in character and nature. It is important to avoid too much generalization about behaviour qualities or abilities in individual breeds because, despite such marked physical variability, strain and individual dog variability will often overlap breed characteristics. Hence, we find Rottweilers which won't bark or guard our houses, Greyhounds which won't run, Bulldogs which retrieve game and not every Labrador bred by the GDBA has the right attributes for a guide dog.

The pet dog/human relationship picture is, however, too easily explained by the idea that the dog assimilates into the human group as a subordinate member of a hierarchical system similar to the one that he was evolved to be born into, simply in return for the benefits of protection, shelter and access to food. Nor is it that the dog obeys us in training because he has to do what what his master or pack leader wants of him. Often, despite having chosen the right strain of a supposedly suitable breed for companionship, such as the Golden Retriever, selected a carefully bred and well-socialized friendly puppy, having done all the right things as he grows up, and even having taught him to respond well to our obedience commands, many dogs do not integrate into our families easily, or as we would like. They may consequently have 'behavioural problems' or are just unsatisfying to have around in our homes. Many problem dogs might be difficult because of a readily identifiable inappropriate early environment or lack of opportunity in the second critical socialization period, or through subsequent trauma. Lack of investment on the owner's part in making enough signals or the right type for the dog to be able to accept the social position or behaviour we desire of him may also lead to problems for the dog and his relationship with his owner. But the fundamental reason for many difficulties is that we have false expectations based on an incomplete perception of what a dog is, or can be.

Instead of viewing the dog as a proud predator who will conform to our wishes if we make the minimum of effort, we should view the dog more as one of his ancestors. Yes, a meat-eating wolf in our living room – but few wolves are exclusively predatorial with a peaceful social hierarchy based on acceptance of social position. Wolves are highly successful, social and feeding opportunists which largely scavenge for a living and hunt as a unit when the opportunity arises and hunger demands. Social hierarchy has little importance when there is nothing going on and there is nothing to be achieved through expending energy unnecessarily. Hence most dogs are content to lie around at home when all is quiet. But most at least look up, and some leap to their feet, when someone stands up or accidentally rattles the lead and there is the prospect of something to take advantage of. Like its ancestor over 10,000 dog generations ago, the pet dog is, above all, an opportunist. And living with an opportunist involves applying a slightly different set of rules to living with a status conscious, rule obeying and ostensibly low-ranking dog in the human pack. Opportunism in most of our pet dogs has been muted by selective breeding, may be influenced by careful attention to early handling and because we naturally maintain a pack-leading position by dictating when the dog gets anything. These features of our relationship and the fact that, in many cases, the dog's opportunism may even be trained out of him, does not mean that it has disappeared. It simply lies dormant because the dog perceives benefit in behaving according to our rules. However, as with the fridge-raiding Bandit, opportunism

47

to an unacceptable level is expressed in a larger number of dogs than perhaps we might think. Many  are my clients, many more are rejected by well-meaning and often experienced owners who simply have had enough of trying to reform their dogs. They send them to animal welfare or dog rescue centres where they wait to be opportunistic with someone else! (Not yet, Bandit, you're my reference library!)

# The bond

*'The more I see of men, the more I admire dogs'*
(attr) Madame de Sevigne

Shelves full of books are dedicated to the nature, study and success of our relationship with the dog and, of course, there are endless stories and films about that bond. We often take it for granted that the dog is indeed 'man's best friend', but also full time research  studies are being carried out all over the world to analyse a little closer the fundamental nature of that special relationship.

While it has long been known that the keeping of dogs and cats can lower the blood pressure and heart rates of their human owners and increase survival chances after a heart attack, it has also been reported that the incidence of minor ailments such as backache and the common cold falls in pet owners compared with non-owners. Both British and American researchers have demonstrated that pet owners are dramatically healthier,  physically and mentally, than non-pet owners and are better at communicating and socializing with other people too. The elderly especially benefit from increased self-esteem, cheerfulness and morale and are likely to have more human friends if they keep a cat or a dog. Hospital visiting schemes, whereby selected dogs are taken into wards to see and react with patients, dramatically increase patient morale and, it is believed, speed up recovery rates. Dogs are now being trained for many more specific tasks, beyond Guide Dogs for the Blind.  Hearing Dogs for the Deaf (HDD) was founded in the UK in 1982, and at present has to rely on dogs obtained from rescue centres or the general public because they lack funds to start their own breeding programmes.  Hopefully it won't be long before they can start. Interestingly the HDD has found that the breed of dog tends not to affect its ability to be trained or subsequent performance, although they may find that some breeds are better when they can research a little further. So far, well over a hundred dogs have been successfullly trained and placed with deaf owners and, due to demand, HDD is now expanding to train about forty dogs per year.

A whole range of assistance dogs for the disabled is now being trained all round the world to help physically disabled people live more independent lives. The dogs perform physical tasks from fetching newspapers to opening doors, operating light switches, and raising the alarm in case of emergency, to acting as a steadier for owners with balance difficulties and, equally important, providing affection, companionship, confidence and security. At a Human/Companion Animal Bond meeting in Vienna in 1983, I was amazed to see a Black Labrador pulling a highly specialized wheelchair and responding to over forty commands from his severely disabled owner. It certainly made me realize how much the poor lady's life had been improved by the dog as she had flown all the way from America to attend the meeting and discusss pet facilitated therapy and pet assistance with others. That would have been impossible without her dog to help her once she arrived.

If we list the positive and negative factors associated with dog ownership, we find that we benefit from: improved social stimulation, companionship, relaxation, leisure activity, better preventive health care, friendship and protection, emotional attachment and security, regular routines necessarily based around the dog's requirements, positive challenge and responsibility, better understanding and sympathy, a rewarding sense of achievement in the appearance and nature of our dogs and associated prestige. But whether, as you read this, you are sitting with your dog on your lap, or he is sitting at the gate protecting you or showing off how well cared for and beautiful he is, you will know that the drawbacks of owning him rarely outweigh the benefits. Those drawbacks may spell restricted freedom, loss of free time, financial and emotional expenditure, a reduction in home hygiene, neighbours complaining about barking, or problems within the family if the dog dislikes or bites one member, or perhaps only obeys one, or dislikes family friends. We also worry about the fate of the dog if we die or become ill.

The first four drawbacks and the last are usually considered before we take on a dog, the rest except the last are all unpleasant consequences to having behaviour problems in the dog. Most of us live with those problems and perhaps treat them as they arise or when we are forced to. Most owners remain fiercely protective of their dog, no matter what problems he may be causing them, their neighbours or other third parties. Even with problems, if only temporary ones such as a puppy piddling on the floor a few times on the way to becoming house-trained, most of us feel benefit from the presence of the wolf in our den, and love him most of the time anyway. More than this, we are starting to *need* to care for something in our modern and increasingly emotionally vacuous society. We need a pet to activate us into taking formal exercise and meeting our own kind. The dog is often the perfect receiver for the release of our caring emotions and helps us keep contact with nature, our own kind and our own ancestry, simply through the joy of owning and observing a human bonded wolf at our side.

The vast majority of our pet dogs live out their lives in attractive style which couldn't have been designed better to suit their every whim. A few highly prized pedigree dogs, those at risk near busy roads and increasing numbers in our cities are denied the opportunity to express their complete behavioural repertoire and only get to explore the same old yard or garden, or local sparse area of green on a lead. While this may seem a pity in that the owners never see the natural explorer in their dog, the animal rarely seems bothered. Provided a dog of a carefully chosen breed, perhaps one the smaller 'lap dogs' such as a Lhasa Apso, is taken on as a puppy and never allowed to experience a more free-ranging life, it can often adapt well to a more restricted and managed life, taking all trips to the great outdoors securely attached to a lead. Hence the popularity of this breed, the Miniature and Toy Poodle, the Yorkshire Terrier and so on in the city. A case of 'what you've never had, you don't miss' applies to most, although it would be unthinkable to try to treat a dog like that if it was used to patrolling a range of outdoor environments or allowed to run freely as part of its daily exercise. Frustrations would understandably soon develop and alternative and perhaps unwanted behaviours such as pacing, excessive barking, over-reactivity towards apparently innocuous events, such as birds landing in the garden when over-vigorous territorial defence reactions may arise.

At last, the mention of some possibility that our dogs' behaviour may sometimes be less than perfect! My dear friend Kay White, a well-known and respected journalist for many veterinary and canine journals and a keeper and former breeder of Boxers, has recently had the courage to present the problem side of keeping dogs to audiences who may otherwise not wish to face some of the realities. In a paper given to the annual congress of the British Veterinary Association in

London, she said,'Maybe we have oversold on the dogs-are-good-for-you theory. No one ever gives the other side of the coin . . . dogs cause a rapid and dangerous rise in blood pressure . . . for instance when you walk out into the garden and find all your newly planted petunias dug up and wilting on the grass . . . well, you used to have grass . . . the puppy tugging a toilet roll about is adorable, except when it is your toilet roll. And unruly dogs can be a danger to heart patients and can cause a definite cut-off of relations between neighbours and even members of the family . . . let's tell it like it happens and cease glorifying dogs as breed-book writers have done for far too long. Dogs require the utmost tolerance and patience until they are adult.' Now there's frank and honest talking from an undisputed champion of dogs!

And, of course, as we all know, many dogs require even more of that tolerance and patience as adults and specific attention to overcome their problems. For the dog now expected to be happy and well adjusted with a confined lifestyle after having had wider experiences and expectations, the solution to ensuing problems of city life may be obvious − either take the risk and start to give your dog back its old-established opportunities for free-running by first training its recall, or rehome it to someone with more facilities and time so that it can start to enjoy life again.

Treatment for other problems with less obvious causes may prove difficult. For the dog that soils indoors, growls at you or your visitors, guards its food or trembles uncontrollably when an aircraft passes overhead, the quick solution of rejection by rehoming or asking the vet to end it all, may be the only prospect after you've tried all the best advice of friends, breeders, trainers and the vet.

But most of us are far too involved in that protective friendly relationship for such callous expediency with a creature that, at its worst, is well behaved for most of the time, and one on whom we have come to depend for more than just companionship. Small wonder that most owners of dogs with behaviour problems simply put up with them. Owners often blame themselves for their dog's behaviour problems and feel that their dog is simply responding to lack of love or the right type of home environment. They may feel that they are inadequate owners, rather than let the blame fall on the 'innocent victim'. Certainly, most would rather live with their dog's problems than face that ultimate solution and get another dog. As a result the emotional compromise of loving a 'rotter' who continually or, perhaps only occasionally but seriously, abuses all that love and care, can place enormous strain on owners and their families and ultimately far outweigh the joys of owning the dog in the first place. Owners of house-soiling, hyperactive or aggressive dogs invariably reduce their human social contacts coming into their homes because they are embarrassed. They do not wish to be seen as unclean or unwelcoming or as having no control over their dog. The dependence on the dog for company may rise still further and any desire to dispose of him falls. The circle becomes vicious and owners become more and more frustrated, until eventually family relationships may start to suffer and they are forced into taking some sort of action.

But just what constitutes a problem is highly variable. For some a single mistake on the carpet when their dog is 'caught short' is sufficiently damaging to their enjoyment of him to cause rejection. Others put up with far worse problems without turning a hair. The definition of a problem is a highly personal matter.

A behaviour problem is often only acknowledged when the pains of coping with a dog start to exceed the joy it brings. If a dog owner finds any aspect of its behaviour or their relationship problematic, it ill behoves anyone to tell them that they are worrying unnecessarily.

But if the dog simply isn't responding to the owner's efforts to resolve the problem, seeking further help involves no little degree of 'coming out' and, if nothing else, admitting to others in the world that they are sufficiently attached to their dog to have suffered thus far in putting up with his problems. Owners usually turn to friends or relations who also have dogs, to their dog's breeder or a local dog fanatic. The majority of problems are resolved by such help or, if not, at the next port of call – the vet's. However, there is a minority of problems which are either so rare as not to have been experienced before by these people, or which are so complicated that there is no obvious, easy or straightforward solution.

Then there are other persistent problems, including those of aggression towards other dogs in the house or towards the owners, or separation anxieties where the dog cannot be left at home alone, which either don't respond to such treatment or only temporarily and eventually still demand more in-depth attention. Relationship problems occur too where the dog does not respond to the owner's desires or expectations perhaps because of nervousness on the part of the dog or the wrong approach from the owner.

Tackling these types of problems, be they of difficult canine behaviour or relationship incongruities or, as is often the case, a combination of both, takes time – time to look at all the factors that may be influencing the dog's behaviour, from the structure of its home environment to its relations with each member of the family and its friends or rivals along the street. Time to look particularly closely at the dog's development and early upbringing in the true psychologist's style of going back to childhood, as so many problems have their roots in the dog's puppyhood; and time to examine its general character and disposition aside from the problem itself.

No two dogs are exactly alike, no two owners and no two problems, and so a very broad approach is required to identify likely causes of each problem, and to tackle the development of an individual treatment plan with each owner. It takes time, a good background in canine and general animal behaviour and, most of all, a caring approach in dealing with a very important and sensitive aspect of people's lives. Lastly, you need to be able to motivate owners to tackle the problem when they may be nearing the end of their tether, as well as the dog's!

It sounds like a blueprint for a consultant in canine behaviour with just a touch of human psychology and counselling skills, and it is! Do dogs need shrinks? Usually not and neither do most of their owners. If dogs were so prone to causing or being problems, they wouldn't be such a popular pet. What they do need sometimes is a canine behaviourist with the time and patience to understand why and when a dog is doing what it's doing, and how to modify it within the framework of the dog's relationship with its owners and their expectations, its lifestyle, and its home territory. The relationship we have with our dogs can often need adjusting, and owners of problem dogs are invariably in need of a little advice on how to restructure their relationship with their dog to establish the prospect of alleviating certain types of problem behaviour. The dog's behaviour may need only a little fine-tuning for owner and dog to appreciate life and each other to the full once again, or sometimes, even, for the first time.

As in so many other areas, we increasingly look for expert help from a detached professional viewpoint to help us iron out the difficulties when our own efforts fail to resolve those problems. The days of punishing or rejecting a dog for the crime of having a behaviour problem are over because help is now available. Given the right approach, those problems are usually resolvable. If the strength of relationship between man and dog wasn't sufficient even ten years ago to warrant a consultant in canine behaviour, it certainly is now.

# The Association of Pet Behaviour Counsellors

*'I am not fond of the word 'pychologist'. There is no such thing as the word 'psychologist', Let us say that one can improve the biography of the person'*                                      Jean-Paul Sartre

I am proud to say that I helped form the Association of Pet Behaviour Counsellors (APBC) in early 1989 as a result of getting to know others who were offering similar services as myself in the treatment of canine behaviour problems in other parts of the country. When we met we found that we all got on famously as friends but, more importantly, that we were all working to the same standards of practice and believed in similar non-forceful, scientifically based methods of treatment for our patients. As a result the APBC now comprises many practices and a demand for the members' services for the treatment of problem pets has increased greatly from veterinary surgeons and their clients. The member practices with various associates now have over forty regular clinic venues in Britain. Most of those clinics are held at veterinary establishments, including UK veterinary schools, with some also at animal charity centres.

APBC members come from a variety of backgrounds including veterinary medicine, clinical psychology, biology, and many years of specialist task dog training, but the most important features of our services are the experience, time and understanding that we can devote to each case. Time is a key factor in short supply in most veterinary surgeries, so while many problems seen by the APBC's members are straightforward and could be dealt with by veterinary surgeons, more and more busy practitioners are happy to refer cases for treatment. All of us work exclusively on referral from veterinary surgeons and cases seen include canine aggression, nervousness, house-soiling, livestock chasing, excessive barking, problems in the car, etc. In my practice, I also see cat problems including house-soiling, indoor spraying, aggression, nervousness and self-mutilation. The aim of treatment is always to benefit both the animal and the relationship with the owner to their improved mutual enjoyment, not simply to teach the animal new responses or in the case of dogs, to perform new tasks, as this is more in the realm of dog training (about which I am personally little able to advise, though other members of the APBC are regarded as leading experts in this area as well). Most of our cases, with the exception of severe aggression problems in dogs, are seen once only with subsequent client contact maintained by telephone. Fees are covered in part or in full by many pet insurance policies.

Further information about the services of individual members and the APBC is available from the Hon Secretary, APBC, 257 Royal College Street, London NW1 9LU.

I work exclusively alongside veterinary practitioners at their premises, with the exceptions of home visits for owners of pets with certain types of problem, such as over-zealous territorial reactions in dogs, or for owners who find it difficult to reach my usual referral centre. Clinical diagnosis and treatment of any likely medical causes of behaviour problems by the referring veterinary surgeon is essential before I consider applying behaviour modification techniques. I would hate to be seen by a human psychologist for being short-tempered, grumpy and lethargic when confined to bed with flu, when I am normally none of those things . . . (well, only occasionally !) and the same applies to dogs.

Some cases, such as those of dogs self-mutilating , are best seen by a combination of vet and behaviourist and preferably in a veterinary hospital or veterinary school environment, as the behaviour may arise from influences in both 'camps' and treatment involve a combined approach.

Ordinarily, I see cases in private with the owners and their dogs (or cats) for approximately one to two hours. During each consultation I record details about the nature of the problem, and the dog's and owner's lifestyle. Having discussed the problem and perhaps demonstrated some handling techniques for the owners to adopt with their dogs, I then try to work out a programme of treatment for the owners to carry out at home. After the consultation I forward a written report to them and a copy is sent to the referring veterinary surgeon, together with any accompanying suggestions for drug treatment, such as the prescription of sedative or hormone treatments that occasionally I may feel would assist treatment. The owners stay in contact with me by phone and we reassess treatment after two to three weeks. Only rarely will I need to see a case twice.

I count myself as very lucky because not only do I get to work with one of my favourite animals professionally, but I also get to meet the nicest people. Pet owners are more sociable than non-pet owners, and whatever their pet's problems, dog owners especially usually prove pleasant, practical and interesting. They often have a splendid sense of humour, and this is reflected in the following chapters where we will be looking broadly in turn at the types of problem that I treat and referring to past cases, typical and atypical, with a few unique cases included 'on loan' from my APBC colleagues, especially in the final chapter! Only the names have been changed to preserve client confidentiality and to protect the innocent!

# PROBLEMS PROBLEMS

# 5
# Nervousness, Anxiety and Phobias

*'When you suffer an attack of the nerves, you're being attacked by the nervous system. What chance has a man got against a system?'*
Russell Hoban

*Dear Mr Neville*

*I have two male dogs not related, three-year-old Arthur and four-and-a-half-year-old Brutus. Brutus is an extrovert, totally confident and very affectionate with everybody, including other dogs. Arthur is timid and jumpy, runs and hides from every sudden noise or unfamiliar person and seems to creep around in fear. When we go out, Arthur never goes far and runs back to hide behind my legs at the slightest challenge. He's really only at ease sitting by my feet, or if he can get there, on my lap. Should I worry? Is there anything I can do to make him enjoy life more?*

*Yours sincerely*

*Heather Ryman*

The dog, like every other animal, is born with the capacity to respond to challenge and protect itself from the life-threatening dangers of attack by predators and environmental risks, such as fire. The responses to such challenges are easily distinguishable from the dog's normal (most often expressed) behaviour patterns. The startle reaction is genetically programmed and, from the age of about eight weeks onwards, puppies are seen to flatten their bodies or erect their hair and flatten their ears when alarmed by a sudden unfamiliar happening. During the early weeks of life the puppy will depend on Mum for protection immediately after being startled, if she hasn't already intervened.

Gradually the puppy gets used to commonly encountered noises or environmental happenings through frequent exposure (before about eight weeks old when marked fear or escape responses develop) especially if challenges are never reinforced by being followed by anything harmful or painful, without ever losing the capacity for an initial startle response. In the average upbringing each puppy is challenged by a huge number of environmental changes and social encounters, first with its litter mates and mother, and later with other dogs in its group. So long as it occasionally comes across challenges it has learnt to deal with, it will remain able to cope with them. The more experience it gains, the better it will be able to cope with similar, but novel, challenges. Equally, when a startle reaction has been justified, occasional exposure will maintain the young dog's response dealing with the challenge. Repetition of exposure, maternal teaching, observation of how his litter mates react and the development of more exploratory behaviour, which propel the puppy into more new environments, help him learn to deal with novelty. Heather's Brutus is one such competent, confident dog which has gone through the canine school of life as a puppy and then as an older dog and, suitably manipulated by us, has learned to cope with just about everything that is likely to happen to him and has become the ideal pet. Thankfully, most dogs are like Brutus.

Others never learn which challenges are actually dangerous. Nervous youngsters may avoid any challenge by remaining in a dark corner, behind a solid protecting barrier such as a sofa, or run away at the slightest change and never learn to cope.

## Physical signs of nervousness

Animals adopt one or more of four major defence strategies to protect themselves and survive when faced with threats and challenges;

withdrawal (running away), immobility, deflection of the threat/ appeasement, and defensive aggression. The policy adopted depends on the scale of the threat, the competence and state of mind of the dog and his previous success at dealing with other and perhaps similar challenges in the past. The anxious dog is easily identified because he acts and responds in much the same way as we do when we are nervous, worried or threatened.

We can identify a suddenly alarmed dog by his slightly arched back and erect hair, especially along the hackles, which are involuntary reactions designed to slow the advance of the threat and 'buy' a little time while the dog decides which major policy to adopt. If withdrawal is selected, the nervous or worried dog may adopt a crouching gait, low carriage of the ears and a tail held down or between the legs as he retreats, all of which may also be adopted without attempts to escape as part of his efforts to appease another dog or human and so deflect their threat. If he withdraws, the dog may make a bolt for safety if he has time and space but otherwise moves slowly and timidly away from the problem to hide under a table or in a safe corner. He may whine or whimper as he goes, as a further threat-deflecting behaviour to an animate threat.

Once he is as secure as possible, the dog may then face the world, hunched and trying not to draw attention to himself, pupils dilated in response to adrenaline, a hormone released at such times to prepare his muscles for running away or for fighting the challenge if it proves necessary. His heart is beating faster and he may even shake and, in severe cases, may urinate involuntarily, though this is perhaps more common in nervous bitches than male dogs.

Alternatively, he may adopt immobility as a method of avoiding challenge. He may 'freeze' on being threatened or, having found a secure bolt hole, lie still, hoping for the challenge to disappear. A few pet dogs even bury their head, ostrich-like, under chairs or bedcovers when alarmed. But whichever reaction the dog chooses, he is often clearly distressed, especially if the threat doesn't evaporate in response to his efforts to reduce it. It is also distressing for the sympathetic owner to watch their dog being upset, particularly if he reacts in this way to harmless, everyday events and never gets to grips with life.

While such responses may be encountered in any adult dog in the face of new challenges or those not experienced before about 16 weeks of age, most will have been 'stress immunized' through their experiences with similar events when young and become experienced enough to work a way out of most of life's challenges quickly as adults.

Others may not and, while the signs of their distress may be clear, it is often difficult to comfort the dog at such times without drawing attention to him, which he may see as adding to the threat and thus contributing further to his anxiety. He may never learn that our efforts are designed to comfort him. If we push too hard, or corner him, he may even snap with a display of defensive aggression as a last line of defence when his attempts to hide or appease the threat have failed and there is nowhere to run. The threshold of his fearful reactions falls ever lower and his general state of reactivity and nervousness increases as a result. One such dog is Arthur, the opposite in the competence ratings to Brutus and clearly not enjoying life to the full.

## Insecurity

Puppies brought up by inexperienced or incompetent mothers are likely to be less competent themselves at dealing with change and challenge as they will often have learned to behave similarly by observation, even if they are not descended from a particularly nervous strain or from a reactive breed. As we have already seen in Chapter 3, those puppies relatively unexposed to challenge, especially during the critical periods of socialization, are also likely to be nervous or jumpy through never having learned to cope with a range of common, but harmless, events. Their survival in the wild would not usually be so good.

There is enormous individual variation in each puppy's reactions, even among individuals in a litter apparently exposed to the same events from birth. While puppies up to the age of about eight weeks are designed to habituate to new sights, sounds and smells faster than adults could later, a smaller or inherently less robust individual (especially any runt of the litter) may then back away from its litter mates as they advance to investigate a new toy because it has learned that it may get painfully bowled over in the crowd. This negative reinforcement of investigative behaviour means that the puppy will avoid this risk by waiting until last, and perhaps be reluctant to investigate anything much unless offered definite, safe, positive rewards for doing so.

Faced with the same toy later, the other puppies will already have learned to overcome any reluctance to investigate and leap straight into play, or ignore it. By contrast, the inexperienced puppy may show an initial startle reaction to the toy or, worse, never get to experience it at all.

Perhaps Arthur is the adult result of the reluctant and incompetent puppy. Such general nervousness is sometimes termed unhabituated anxiety, or generalized fearfulness. The dog simply received an inadequate range of experiences as a puppy to enable it to cope with the flow of challenges as an adult. Controlled exposure techniques can be designed to allow Arthur to be exposed to what we and Brutus would regard as commonplace and non-threatening events in the home and even outdoors.

Most dogs are constantly learning and unlearning conditioned fear responses; it's just that dogs like Arthur need to be helped and have their fearful reactions extinguished by pairing what is frightening for them with something positive. In short we can help provide fresh opportunity for Arthur to learn to cope.

In such cases it is rare to produce a totally competent, 'normal' dog, as certain things can only be learned in puppyhood. For example, puppies brought up with kittens, or even adult cats, rarely show nervous reactions when in adulthood cats approach them to play. By contrast, the adult dog which has no experience of cats is either likely to chase them, which we will deal with later in the book, or retreat submissively. Most older dogs can learn to live with a cat late in life, but will only get as far as tolerating the cat and rarely will any social interaction or play develop.

When treating any nervous animal, progress can only proceed as far as its present capacity to learn allows. If the fear has been learned, rather than arising from an inherited disposition or lack of early exposure, the greater the chances of unlearning it.

Improvements can be made with dogs like Arthur by providing them with a new den (a wire mesh indoor kennel is ideal), which is placed in the main activity room of the house. Normal family life goes on as usual around the dog, which is protected from physical danger by the pen. Most importantly, the dog is also prevented from running away and avoiding the challenges of changes in personnel, movement, noises from the television or movement of furniture going on around it. It has to face up to them and start to interpret what is happening. The dog is in a warm, safe womb from which it can take in and get used to those things which previously induced a fearful, avoiding reaction.

# Sedatives for dogs?

Severe cases of generalized nervousness can be helped with sedative treatment. Yes, dogs with certain types of problem can be given Valium, as can their long-suffering owners! In treating most nervous conditions it is important that the sedative is gradually withdrawn as the dog's ability to deal with 'life' improves with controlled exposure so that its new competence is not dependent on the drug. In short, the drug is a 'vehicle' so that the dog can learn without being overwhelmed by the scale of its initial fear. In some cases a low maintenance dose of sedative may be required long term, or even permanently, for the dog to be more confident. Fortunately, the majority of even severe cases need only a short course to accompany the exposure side of treatment.

While I am not an expert in alternative medicine, certain types of homoeopathic or herbal treatment have also been reported to serve as effective alternatives to sedatives and in certain cases are increasingly prescribed by some veterinary surgeons. But, as with conventional veterinary medicine, it is vital that advice be sought only from a properly accountable practitioner who is a member of the British Association of Homoeopathic Veterinary Surgeons.

It is true that many dogs with general nervous conditions will worsen if left untreated. The majority of such cases referred to me have concerned dogs aged two years and more. They are often described by their distressed owners as having been shy or withdrawn from the day they arrived and that their tolerance of the owner's lifestyle and home goings-on has steadily worsened. Almost any noise or quick movement is enough to make them run to a bolt-hole, or to their owners for protection, or stand and quiver in fear and stay that way long after the 'problem' has passed. Other typical signs include increasingly secretive withdrawn behaviour by the dog, which comes to avoid all change, and takes an ever increasing time to come out into the open areas of the house when the owner returns after being away. The dog seeks dark, quiet corners for shelter and spends long periods there, only willing to come forward to meet guests or go out into the garden with much encouragement.

More rarely, the nervous dog may cling to its owner constantly for security and show marked and generalized nervous reactions when parted. Over-dependence is particularly difficult to treat for the owner as well as the dog because it involves a loosening of the bond between them. Only then can the dog be encouraged to be more independent and begin to face those fears. By being the sweetest-natured and most rewarding dog when with its owner, it has learned 'incompetence' and, however otherwise pleasing, the dog should be treated for the sake of its own emotional state when away from its owner.

# Loss of confidence

*Dear Mr Neville*

*I wonder if you could help with my dog. George is now nervous of visitors and always runs away when anyone calls. He used to be very tolerant and even friendly with some and he's still okay with me and my husband, but I feel so sorry for him being afraid to stay in his own home. As soon as the door bell rings, he's off and won't return until after they've gone. Is there anything I can do to help?*

*Yours hopefully*

*Joyce Newbold*

George is a prime example of the dog which learned to cope with the arrival of strange people into the heart of his territory but then steadily lost the ability. I see a few such cases. The converse to this problem is the frequently observed pastime of confident dogs which leap up as soon as visitors arrive and proceed to welcome them effusively until finally dragged off protesting by their owners. The poor victim is naturally unwilling to offend their host by turfing the dog off and instead shifts, dances or sniffs uncomfortably while the dog, delighted with his new pack mate, dominates proceedings.

George's nervousness with visitors may not only be because of lack of suitable experience with enough different people when young. It could also be due to a single unfortunate experience with a particularly noisy or unkind guest who hit or frightened him, teaching him to avoid all risk of repetition by running away early. Such single traumatic incidents lie behind the development of many specific phobias in dogs and people. Nervousness of any type can perhaps be

64

described as more general or less specific than a genuine phobia, but the principles of treatment are based on desensitization, with controlled exposure to the stimulus in a diluted manner that does not invoke the fearful or phobic response in the patient. The stimulus intensity is steadily increased and the patient habituates to it as a learning process.

The dog is sometimes a natural avoider of potential conflict as a survival mechanism and has highly developed senses to enable it to detect danger and respond quickly with flight if necessary. That it does not wait to investigate an apparently dangerous, yet actually harmless, stimulus such as a car backfiring has helped to ensure the dog's survival as a creature that may not be able to rely on its normally protecting pack to look after it if caught napping. In adversity it may be a case of every dog for himself and the devil take the hindmost! The difficulty in treating some cases of nervousness lies in determining what is 'normal' and which dogs are actually 'nervous', and whose quality of life is affected as a result. More so than with cats, we can use our own impressions to judge how or to what degree a dog ought to be able to cope, because his demands and expectations of life are largely similar to our own.

Clearly George is not enjoying the potential benefits of meeting Joyce's friends. While running away may be a perfectly normal reaction designed to ensure the dog's survival, there is no reason for George to feel threatened in this circumstance. The more guests the owner has, the less she sees of George, and the less he regards home as a secure base. The end result is a worsening relationship with the dog which may, at all other times, be thoroughly rewarding, or a change in the family's social life because they stop inviting friends around for fear of upsetting the dog. Either way there is a problem to be resolved and, in most cases, this is perfectly possible.

Treatment is, however, rarely simple and does not involve simply hanging on to a panicking dog by the collar while trying to press him into the arms of even the most understanding, dog-loving guest (in fact they are usually the worst ones to expose him to). Throwing in at the deep end doesn't always teach you to swim – it can cause drowning! In cases such as George's, such action would be guaranteed to enhance his fear of visitors by adding the prospect of restriction by his owner to his apprehension, quite apart from any pain experienced from the owner's frantic efforts to keep a tight hold. Fortunately most owners only try this approach once and call me while their injuries are still fresh! Such dogs usually calm down quite quickly once at a safe distance (the flight distance) and, keeping a beady eye on where the next challenge may come from, get ready to run when they hear footsteps approaching the door, not even waiting for the bell to ring!

Treating George may involve the same sort of controlled exposure techniques as when treating Arthur in the early stages, but more targeted at overcoming the specific problem of accepting visitors. The first aim of treatment is to block George's attempts to escape. His success in doing so, although protecting him from the danger he perceives, also precludes any possibility of him learning to cope on his own. Instead George is denied the opportunity to avoid visitors by either being restrained on a leash or, more rarely and only in the more severe cases, by being kept in an indoor pen for short periods when his owner is to receive guests. Before they arrive this is placed in the area where guests are invited to relax, usually the living room. The more willing volunteers, the better, although George should first receive 'guests' that he knows, such as members of the family. They ring the doorbell instead of using the key. George's first reaction, if he hasn't discerned whose footsteps are approaching, may be the usual one of alarm, and an attempt to escape is prevented by the pen or restraint on the lead. Then the 'guest' enters and George, seeing that it is only Joyce or her husband, quickly calms down. Repetition should cause George to start to associate the conditioning stimulus of the doorbell with non-threatening arrivals.

Later, less well-tolerated guests can be asked to perform the same routine, entering George's room with an accepted member of the family and doing nothing more than sitting down at some distance from him. It is essential that George grows used to their presence in gradual stages. Now his cage serves to protect him from the challenge he has avoided for so long, and he should settle quickly.

Slow progress at this stage can often be speeded up by quelling the dog's over-reactions with a little sedative treatment such as Valium on prescription from the veterinary surgeon. However, it is essential that the dog's tolerance does not become dependent on drugs, and a tapered dose is usually prescribed. The tolerance of guests may be totally drug-dependent for a few days but, as he is exposed to more visitors, withdrawal of the drug ensures that his tolerance is increasingly learned and decreasingly drug-dependent. On or off drugs, with frequent exposure to as many different people as possible under the right conditions, George should perceive their arrival and occupancy of the core of his territory as being neutral. More importantly, they are able to remain inside his flight distance.

The next stage of treatment is a little more invasive. If previously in a pen, George is brought out and restrained on a lead to a secure fixture such as a table or chair leg. Now guests are asked to sit progressively closer to George to habituate him further to their presence. This stage can only proceed as fast as George can tolerate and guests should not attempt to touch him or even talk to him until he seems confident about their presence.

Then we introduce the prospect of forcing the issue a little. First we must ask George's owners to be far less available to him in the normal course of their life with him. This is so that while George continues to receive food, walks and play, other forms of contact are available much less and occur at the owner's initiation and less so at George's. George's owners are also encouraged to offer less direct physical contact to him overall and to ensure that he spends less time in their immediate presence. He must be prevented from following his owners around the house and given a warm, safe place to rest away from the family. In this way the bonds between dog and owners are redefined a little so that George is less dependent on them for emotional support while all the benefits of living in their group are available under their control.

While George may initially be a little confused by this change in policy, especially at no longer being able to follow his owners around and sit near or nestle to them when they are stationary, subsequently it should help to direct his demand for play and contact onto others who offer it later during the course of treatment. In short, by being less available themselves for a few days at least, the owners will be discouraging George from becoming over-dependent and forcing him to be more open and spread his loyalties.

The next stage, though it perhaps sounds a little unfair, is that George should be starved for up to twelve hours so that he is hungry when pressed into sharing space with his next visitor. The visitor, sitting close by George rather than bending down over him, which would alarm him, gently proffers a small titbit or tasty portion of a favourite food, perhaps dropping it close by him if he won't actually take it from the hand. George's positive appetite-stimulated reaction to the food is designed to equal or be in excess of the intensity of his nervous reaction and so help him to overcome it. The tastier the titbit, the greater should be the reaction. A tip on how to produce a morsel irresistible to every dog was given me by Neil Ewart of the GDBA. He suggests that one should bathe liver in garlic paste and then bake it until hard in the oven, offering small irresistible pieces. Many dogs will also come forward perfectly well for ordinary biscuits, but preferably from your biscuit barrel and not their own!

Again, this stage of treatment can be assisted by certain drugs from the vet which increase the dog's appetite and, therefore, his incentive to come forward to guests. The drug of choice, a progestin, which is used more generally as a contraceptive for cats and dogs, also has a calming effect and so is often used from the early stages of treatment in severe cases. Food may cement relations far quicker than gentle voices, though the visitor and owner should encourage proceedings by talking gently to the dog while offering food. Thereafter the dog should be fed frequent short meals for the length of the visitor's stay (or patience) and as many guests as possible, as well as the family, should take part in the process. This steadily spreads the dog's confidence and helps him view all guests as potential providers of food and, later, affection.

An alternative to reinforcement using food rewards has been particularly studied and developed by fellow APBC member, John Rogerson. He regards toys as substitutes for various aspects of fulfilment of a dog's hunting instincts. Being one of the most vital natural inherited behaviour patterns, this should provide the second highest motivation, after that to eat, with which to manipulate the dog's behaviour. The hunting replacement aspects of toys, namely chase (as shown by many dogs' responses to moving balls) and kill (squeaky toy or hide chew) means that many dogs have a natural desire to possess toys. This is particularly helpful with some nervous dogs, such as many of the German Shepherd Dogs I have treated, and the 'aloof of all that bribery' of many of the mouth-work gun dog breeds such as Retrievers and Munsterlanders like Bandit, who do not perceive reward in food titbits.

For them, having a mouth full of something firm, but not too hard, is the be-all of life and they will gleefully grasp a favourite proffered toy, both as a comfort and as a trophy when excited, even when nervously so. Owners of nervous dogs can often successfully orientate them to demand possession of one particular toy for two to three weeks before tackling controlled introductions to visitors.

The first stage is to collect all the dog's current toys and put them away, out of his sight and reach. Then the dog is offered one particular toy prior to all the good things of life, such as being fed, having his lead put on and being fussed by the family. Accepting the toy is the precondition for further contact and becomes a conditioned stimulus for a range of always rewarding after-effects. After a while the dog becomes excited and friendly simply when the toy is produced, and so will be in an aroused and more positive frame of mind to be introduced to visitors. Once this conditioning has been achieved the toy should be kept by the front door to help recondition the dog about it being the place of invasion by visitors. The dog should always have to follow the owner to receive the toy before being led back to another room for feeding, having his lead put on, etc, and receive the toy there whenever a member of the family arrives home. This incorporates grasping and possession of the toy as part of the ritual of greeting. Once the toy is firmly incorporated into all dog/family contact, it can be used to smooth the path of introduction with visitors.

The final stage of treatment is simply to restrain George on a lead and collar when guests arrive, and to have them offer food or the toy kept by the front door as before. It will often help to restrain the dog using a headcollar, of which there are many types worldwide, as these afford quicker, better and more directable control of the dog from the head, rather than trying to keep him in position with restraint around the neck via an ordinary collar. Worse still, would be to use a check (or more accurately in terms of action, a choke) chain. Headcollars such as the Promise, Walkeasy or Walkee allow the dog to open his mouth fully when relaxed, so he may still accept food or his toy happily. Used for centuries to control horses and farm animals and for large dogs as far back as the 1930s, headcollars have revolutionized normal physical control of pulling and facilitated better treatment of many common canine behaviour problems. For the nervous dog, a headcollar gives the owner the power to block attempts at avoidance kindly, without contributing to the dog's anxiety by strangling him. Indeed, there is little doubt that the dog will associate the sensation of pain or tension around the neck when trying to flee as coming from the visitor, not as a consequence to his own movement or the owner's attempts to control his escape. Instead Arthur's head can be held gently in place to enable him to rationalize the presence of the visitor. There is also an additional advantage to using headcollars in such situations, in that many dogs are calmed simply by wearing them. Pressure around the nose seems to have a reassuring influence on many dogs, perhaps partially because every slight movement by the owner's hand on the other end of the lead conveys a message to the head of the dog, and so alters its sensory intake. Presumably, the dog thinks it can then rely on the owner to lead the introduction on its behalf.

So the owner, who can now control the dog without a struggle, takes him towards the door once the bell has been rung to meet, initially, a single known and already accepted visitor. This should be done slowly so that George doesn't panic as he did before he started to learn that visitors could be nice. The advance should be slowed or halted if George starts to look alarmed or struggles. At the door, the owners should give the dog its food reward or toy before opening it to greet the visitor. The dog should continue to relax, or better, remain excited at the prospect of further food or games with its toy, such as tug of war. These enhancements may come from the visitor. Once he is inside the house, the owner should stroke the dog and continue to react with him – hence the importance of inviting people who won't be offended that they are not the centre of attention! Gradually the guests can join in stroking the dog as well. The process is complete when the owner stops and the dog is only being stroked by the guest.

Leading George away from his owner may not be possible for guests for some time yet, if at all, because this is an enclosing action denying escape and thus involving George's total confidence. He would only be acting in the same way as a large number of dogs if he were to restrict this social contact to his family.

During all contact guests' hands should approach initially very slowly from directly in front of George so that he can see and accept the advancing hand. It should be offered very gently indeed, bearing in mind that if the dog has come from an uncertain background, it may associate hands with punishment, not friendship. Occasionally it may be wiser and better accepted if the hand is offered from the side unseen and simply joins in the stroking being performed by the owner.

It may even help to approach George at the same level rather than intimidating him unnecessarily by bending over him. While the prospect of crawling along the floor to approach him may seem like carrying things to extremes, placing George on a table and having visitors approach face to face may be less threatening. Of course, all volunteers must be safe and if there is any prospect at all of George snapping defensively, then he should be muzzled when he receives guests for some time. Approaching face to face mimics some of the greeting behaviour of dogs and, as our face shape is not too dissimilar from that of many dogs with regard to forward-facing eyes, may be more readily tolerated than a big mitt landing on the top of his head.

Obviously all volunteers should avoid making loud noises or sudden movements as they approach him to prevent startling him and should avoid staring at him: this could be seen as a challenging gesture similar to the staring dominance or territorial struggles observed between competitive dogs. The non-territorial George would always run to avoid that type of confrontation with a visitor, so they should look below his eye-level or to one side as they approach him, perhaps making supplicating licking noises so as to be seen as submissive and non-challenging.

The next step is to follow a similar greeting pattern with less familiar guests and then finally with everyone who calls. Hopefully the dog's improving confidence will soon mean that the lead and collar can be done away with, unless, as sometimes happens, the dog has now become so enthused with the prospect of someone calling to feed and play with him, that he needs to be restrained to stop him bowling everyone over.

Progress with such cases where there has been a loss of an earlier learned acceptance rather than a failure ever to have learned, is normally steady and, once improved, the dog will rarely regress again provided it is regularly exposed to pleasant visitors. Essentially the methods of treatment are very similar to those with many other behaviour problems. The opportunity for success of unwanted behaviour or response is denied physically, the physiological reaction of fear or panic is muted by using drugs if necessary, and the animal is kept faced up to the stimuli which had caused it to be nervous in a slow, controlled manner. Then its correct or relaxed responses are positively reinforced. Gradually the patient learns to accept, cope with and tolerate the stimulus and, ultimately, even come to enjoy it. The key to success is to reduce all variables so that everything is controlled and all possible reactions from the dog are predicted, and to proceed in short frequent doses of exposure at a pace he can take without inducing panic. When not being exposed to visitors, the dog should be allowed free range as before but should be placed in its pen or on a lead periodically without being confronted by visitors so that he doesn't come to perceive this as an unpleasant restriction. Ideally he should be fed under the same conditions at normal meal times to maintain the idea of the restriction meaning a variety of things, some of which are good.

It usually works! However, children, loud, bad-tempered or drunken guests or disabled visitors may still be alarming to George because of their unpredictable movements or less rational behaviour. Given that controlled exposure techniques may be difficult to organize, he should perhaps be protected from such unusual invasion by being put out or into another room before they arrive. This will preclude any possibility of regression to his old fearful ways due to trauma unless, of course, drunkenness is more the norm than sobriety, as was once the case of a nervous cat I saw that had been rescued from a pub in Scotland. This cat, named Pernod, was very suspicious of people who were quiet and walked straight, but had no difficulty at all in coping with loud staggering drunks! All a question of early exposure, no doubt.

# Incompetence with other dogs

*Dear Mr Neville*

*Our female German Shepherd Dog, Bluey, is two years old and a first-rate dog with me and my family. She is an excellent guard and takes any amount of being pulled about by the kids without so much as a murmur. While she enjoys a walk, she never wanders far from us and is terrified by other dogs. Even a Yorkshire Terrier can frighten the life out of her just by walking up to sniff and say hello. She whimpers and hurtles away to the nearest open space or darts back behind us to avoid all dogs, even the friendly ones. We got her from a breeder at about six months of age and though she was nervous of dogs to start with we thought she would get used to them through going to the park every day if anything but she has got worse.*

*Yours sincerely*

*Amanda and James Butler*

This is an extremely common problem and something of an ironic one in that Bluey is perfectly able to interact normally with her human pack, and even accepts the right of the young ones in it to do with her as they will. With her own kind, she is a social incompetent and simply avoids all contact with any other dog by running away.

Sadly, dogs like Bluey keep appearing at my clinics and most are pedigrees rather than crossbreeds or mongrels. Bluey represents what happens to a dog that is not subjected to the experiences of meeting, playing, play-fighting and generally learning the social graces that enable dogs to live as a social group and interact with others outside it without violence and risk of injury. Dogs which are kept in boring, unstimulating kennels, or even in the houses of breeders who are unaware of the importance of providing facilities for full socio-behavioural development, will invariably turn out like Bluey. Kept on until six months old in an environment that prevents socialization with unfamiliar dogs, Bluey is suffering from what is known by some behaviourists as 'kennelosis'.

Interestingly, while such dogs may be totally incompetent with unfamiliar people and be generally nervous as well, there are also many like Bluey which are reasonably well adjusted with people and excellent as pets. They may have no problems at all in socializing and accepting other dogs in the household, and will often depend on them for security to the same intensity as they did with their mother and litter mates. Typically these dogs are the last to leave the breeding home, either by chance, in that all the others were chosen first, or because Bluey's original purchasers changed their mind and it was too late for the breeder to locate another buyer, or, as is sadly sometimes the case, the breeder 'ran the dog on' because it was felt to have potential in the show ring as a nice-looking puppy, but then grew up without the necessary requirements.

Probably even the most financially orientated breeders handle their puppies and show them off to house guests, so the puppies meet people in that critical second socialization period. But they don't have the experience on which to draw when faced with approaches from other dogs. I always liken it to being sent to school for the first time at the age of twelve and being expected to learn French when you haven't been taught to read and write in English yet. Astoundingly, and a credit to the learning capacity of the dog, many, if not most, are able to overcome this early deficiency and learn very quickly, sometimes through a few painful mistakes, how to communicate with other dogs and even to play with them. Still others are brought up correctly and then suffer the trauma of being attacked by a strange dog and thereafter avoid all others. Bitches are often the focus of rather different and more assertive attentions from male dogs as they approach their first season at about six to twelve months, and being frightened by it, they too can become nervous of all other dogs, male or female, as a result. But, whatever the cause, clearly a dog which does not know how to react with its own kind is not a 'normal' dog and though it may be successfully protecting itself from unwanted challenge and conflict with its avoidance tactics, it is also missing out on a lot of fun with other dogs.

Sad to say, dogs such as Bluey are unlikely ever to become the most sociable ones in the park, nor to initiate much of the social contact with other dogs, but they can usually be made tolerant and less afraid of others, especially if they have the basic experience of canine social communication of having been introduced to and living with another dog at home. As with so many other forms of nervousness and incompetence, controlled exposure to other dogs will help Bluey, though just occasionally dogs like her may improve by being swamped with huge numbers of dogs left to run free and investigate her. However, I feel this tactic could seriously compound the problem and perhaps make the dog defensively aggressive in its urge to protect itself. I favour a much more controlled approach to introductions.

As ever, good preparation is the key to successful treatment. Bluey must be as relaxed as possible prior to being introduced to other dogs. She should be given a good off-lead run and play with her owners and any familiar dogs from home in a quiet field safely away from the prospect of meeting any strange dogs. Then, when the owners have recovered from the run, Bluey should be kitted out with a headcollar, which she has previously been accustomed to wearing, and, attached to an extendable lead, walked more formally in a familiar recreation ground or park where she will be more confident. Selecting smaller and friendly dogs under the control of their owners but not necessarily on the lead (this restraint sometimes turns even the most pleasant biddable lap dog into a raging bull), the owner should head straight towards them, speaking encouragingly and reassuringly all the way. If Bluey tries to take avoiding action, the tightening action of the lead will in turn tighten the headcollar and enable her owner to take control kindly and quickly. Bluey should be made to look at the owner to establish eye contact and help with calming her down. Once settled, they should proceed to follow the other dog again, perhaps maintaining a discreet distance that enables Bluey to keep the dog in her sights. Slowly this distance can be shortened, with calming interventions as required. An important feature with many dogs is that the owner keeps talking during the whole process. If the other dog advances on Bluey to say hello in a genial manner, Bluey should be encouraged to accept it and not removed from the scene if she panics. Instead she should be calmed as before, and then put back into a fresh position of meeting the other dog. In this way, the success of her learned avoidance behaviour now meets with failure and she must decide what to do as an alternative. If she panics, the owner is there to reassure, but only for as long as it takes to settle her and begin again. Slowly and with frequent short opportunities to meet other dogs in an increasing variety of places, Bluey should become more tolerant of investigation by other dogs, though of course it all depends on the availability and co-operation of other owners and their dogs. Aggressive, uncontrolled or over-excitable dogs should be avoided if at all possible, and Bluey protected from them as one would any pet in the event of unpleasant encounters.

During the greeting, where the other dog will want to sniff Bluey around the face and rear end, and usually be giving off some very obvious body and tail language, the owner should be verbally encouraging, but otherwise neutral. As Bluey looks more confident, her owner should try to distance herself by releasing the brake on the extendable lead and, without jerking on Bluey's collar, slowly feed out enough line leave Bluey more unprotected in 'no man's land', so forcing her gently to continue to think for herself with regard to the other dog. Steadily most dogs like Bluey improve and even form close friendly relations with a few select local dogs that they encounter regularly. With time and effort, she should become tolerant of all but over-friendly or aggressive dogs, which may still frighten her, and be able to head towards and pass any other dog at any time anywhere. Thankfully, I think the message has got through to responsible breeders about the obvious ways of avoiding this type of problem; alas, the ignorant and unscrupulous remain.

## Anxiety

*Dear Mr Neville*

*My little mongrel bitch, Sukie, seems to look utterly devastated whenever life goes against her. I have never struck her, nor even had cause to raise my voice at her, yet one would think I beat her daily with a large stick from the look on her face sometimes. She seems especially distressed when asking to be let out into the garden to go to the toilet, but she knows that I'll always let her out if she asks by waiting by the door. How can I tell her that there is no need to worry so much about everything?*

*Yours sincerely*

*Violet Robinson*

Anxiety can be described as a state of mental conflict because of a desire to behave in a certain way, but a lack of opportunity to do so. It is expressed in all nervous cases when the dog is confronted with something it doesn't like yet can't escape from. But, as with people, anxiety can occur at times in otherwise well-balanced individuals.

The dog that is desperate to relieve itself but cannot gain access to the outdoors will quickly become anxious and probably engage in one or more of several types of alternative behaviour. The first may be to whine, bark or wag a tail at the owner and 'ask' to go outside but, if the owner is asleep or otherwise unavailable, the dog will become progressively more anxious and usually more excited. In outward-going, sociable, extrovert dogs the increased state of arousal will take the form of barking, panting, pacing or running up and down in a stereotypic or repeated cycle of movement, digging and scratching at the door. In generally quieter and more withdrawn characters, reaction to anxiety may be more likely to be self-directed and more introverted behaviour, perhaps even to the point of tail chasing or licking and chewing at their own feet, which can lead to physical injury. Either way, the behaviour can definitely be described as neurotic.

When finally the door is opened, and the dog rushes out to relieve himself, the anxiety is also relieved because the state of mental conflict is withdrawn. If the door is not opened and the dog is forced to urinate indoors, the action itself will relieve the conflict by removing the need to go. Under such circumstances, relief is certainly written all over the dog's face, even if we may be momentarily upset that he is peeing all over the floor. He'll deal with the conflict of his normally loving owner's anger after he's enjoyed the relief!

Anxiety can arise for all kinds of reasons in our dogs, often because we fail to offer outlet for a dog's full natural behavioural repertoire, for example by keeping a guard dog chained up all day with no opportunity to explore or investigate changes around him properly, or because we fail to communicate effectively just what it is we want of the dog. If we lose our patience and the dog doesn't understand what the command was, then he'll become anxious . . . just like Manuel in *Fawlty Towers* when Basil Fawlty spells out very slowly or shouts to reinforce the instructions in English to a waiter who barely understands anything but Spanish! Anxiety means '*Que?*' in Spanish waiters and 'bark, pace, tremble' in dogs.

To some extent, dogs which can be highly excited or lapse into very nervous and withdrawn behaviour when anxious are either born or

76

created through lack of the right experiences from four to eighteen weeks. It is not always possible to reform them. A calm consistent relationship with all members of the household is essential and a quick meeting to decide on all members using the same words of instruction for the dog, and agreement to stick to regular routines will provide a secure bedrock on which to get the best out of such dogs and teach them to cope with specific challenges. Avoiding punishment is essential if the dog is not to be put more into a state of emotional conflict when already excited or afraid. The use of positive reinforcers of food rewards, gentle words and touch from the owners will always be most reassuring and calm the dog down. In some circumstances, however, he may simply have to be removed from the anxiety-promoting situation or environment as quickly as possible before he can be calmed. Living with an anxiety-ridden dog can require quite a lot of protective management!

# Separation anxiety

*Dear Mr Neville*

*I am at my wit's end. Every time my husband and I go out, our dog, Pluto, who we rescued out of the kindness of our hearts from the local animal rescue centre, tears our house to pieces. So far he's almost totally destroyed the kitchen, torn up all the cushions and the valances on the three-piece suite and pulled countless vases and ornaments off the shelves. We've told him off every time and my husband has even smacked him hard, but it makes no difference. Soon we'll have no house left for him to wreck. How on earth do we stop him from doing this? When we're with him he's a fabulous dog and we'd hate to send him back to the shelter.*

*Yours sincerely*

*Rose Bramley*

This is one of the most common behaviour problems in dogs, accounting for about 15 per cent of all the canine cases referred to me. The range of types of dog from my casebook shows a similar spread to those found by other APBC members and other therapists in other countries. While most cases concern first crosses or mongrels, there are also many Labradors, Retrievers, German Shepherd Dogs and, particular to my caseload for some reason, Boxers. Aside from Boxers, the general numbers are probably only reflecting the popularity of those breeds in the UK and not indicative of any breed trends. Labradors, of course, do have something of a reputation for being destructive but this is often apparently part of their exploratory phases of development rather than a sign of separation anxiety. Others have reported that dogs most likely to suffer from separation anxiety are those like Pluto, obtained from animal rescue agencies, but this is probably the reason why their previous owners sent them there in the first place. With other behaviour problems such as aggression, a higher proportion of dogs rejected will be euthanased rather than put up for adoption with someone else.

Separation anxiety produces various behavioural responses in dogs as a consequence of their inability to cope on their own. Most owners have to leave their dog at home alone from time to time, some even for many hours every day while they go out to work to earn the money to pay for the dog food. Most new puppy owners expect a few problems when they first leave their puppy alone in the house and accept that he may be worried and whine a little or chew a shoe or two. After a couple of sad experiences, most puppies learn to cope with solitude and, although few are ever overjoyed at the departure of their owners from the house without them, simply settle down to rest in their basket or to chew a favourite toy to occupy themselves.

For puppies which are never left alone at all in the first months, or even years, in their new home, the prospect of greater and prolonged anxiety when left alone is highly likely. These unfortunate dogs simply haven't got the experiences to draw on to help them cope with their feelings of vulnerability and, as they are confined in the home, they are unable to relieve the symptoms by searching for their owners. The dog is naturally a social pack animal which relies on individual protection from safety in numbers. There isn't much instinctive inherited ability to help them cope with solitude. Interestingly, the response of an African Hunting Dog accidentally or deliberately isolated from his pack by man is to whine and cry to maintain a vocal link with the others and inform them of his distress. He may then become highly active in trying to rejoin them, or show hyperactive distressed pacing and circling if prevented from doing so.

So we are observing age-old reactions in dogs that can't cope without us. While it may be hard for the owners not to attribute the dog's damaging, messy or nuisance behaviour to a 'spite' reaction at having been left alone, it is essential that they realize that separation anxiety is a true involuntary incompetence on the part of suffering dogs like Pluto. It's even harder when you come home from a night on the town in your glad rags and have to clear up a mess around the house. It's infuriating, if not impossible, to control your temper if, as with one memorable case I saw in London, the owner returned from a five-minute trip to the local newsagent and discovered that his dog, a nine-month-old Boxer, had shredded an oriental rug worth over £8000!

The most common sign of a dog suffering from separation anxiety is indeed destructiveness of household property through often frenetic displacement activities, such as chewing and digging. Also commonly encountered are excessive and prolonged barking, howling and whining, panic symptoms such as pacing, hyperactivity and excessive salivation, usually at the base of the door the owner departed through, or the dog's usual access door to the outside. A particularly unpleasant sign is loss of toilet control, numbers one and two . . . often in vast, runny volume . . . everywhere. Bruno, the playful Yellow Labrador belonging to the landlords of my local pub, the Compasses Inn, nearly burned down their (and my) beautiful fourteenth century thatched hostelry when he chewed a box of matches while left upstairs alone one evening after opening time. As he chewed, the matches sparked, caught fire and set light to the carpet. Fortunately the blaze was discovered by Lyn and Andy, the landlords, and was put out before it could spread. With a little free (well, you know, in return for a few pints of beer) treatment, Bruno can now accept being left alone during opening hours without the risk of such dire consequences. He is otherwise a typical outward-going bouncy Labrador. Other more introverted characters may show self-mutilating behaviour, such as chewing at the tail or paws, in response to the anxiety of being isolated, but these are rare cases.

Treatment is usually successful, though severe cases can take some time. First it is essential that there are no relapses during the period of treatment and that Pluto either isn't left in a position where he could become anxious enough to engage in such costly displacement activity, or is physically prevented from doing so. This can be achieved by taking the dog everywhere in the car, by leaving him with a dog sitter, friends, in a kennel or, short term, by leaving him in his own safe, secure indoor kennel.

While an indoor kennel may sound like imprisonment, in fact the dog is being given his own safe den, the equivalent of a nice safe hole in the ground. The bars protect him as well as restrict his access to the valuables in the house and, if carefully accustomed to using it, many dogs voluntarily learn to pop inside whenever they want to rest, sleep or are feeling under the weather or worried. The pen is not simply a place to shut the dog away and forget the problem, it is very much a tool of treatment. A dog can be accustomed to the confinement of his den initially by placing his old bedding inside and leaving free access to go in and out while the family is at home. He can be encouraged to enter by throwing in titbits or favourite toys to retrieve and by being fed progressively further inside. The dog should be encouraged to sleep inside the pen by first tiring him with lots of exercise and play, then being fed on return and encouraged to lie down on the comfortable bed inside. Once he is drowsy or asleep, the door can be shut on the dog for the first time and then always at night too.

Sometimes this is all a dog needs to be able to relax and not reach the peak of distress that leads to destructiveness or other symptoms of separation anxiety but, usually, it enables the owners at least to relax and return home knowing that no damage has been done. This in itself can affect the dog's reactions when left as, if the owners are foul-tempered and punishing towards the dog on return to a wrecked house, the relationship is eroded and the dog will feel even more vulnerable about life in general. Additionally, being left at home may come to be associated with subsequent unpleasantness from the owner and lead to increased anxiety at every separation and increased damage. It is essential for owners not to blame the dog for such destructiveness, as it is simply a sign of inability to cope. If anything, the dog loves the owners too much and most certainly isn't getting back at them for leaving him alone.

Restructuring the family's relationship with Pluto is the key feature of treatment. If Pluto cannot cope without his owners then he must be helped to do so. This is achieved by looking at the way he is able to react with them when they are together. Establishing a better-defined relationship and one on which the dog is less likely to over-depend is achieved by reducing the amount of time he is allowed to spend in the direct company of his owners, sometimes by up to 50 per cent, if he is used to following them everywhere at home and sleeping in the same room. If the dog is used to sleeping in the bedroom, his bed should be moved progressively nearer to the door and then finally out onto the landing, or preferably downstairs and more towards the 'edge' of the home territory where a lower-ranking member of the dog group would normally be grateful for shelter. However, this process may be extremely difficult and may take some time to achieve even partially with over-attached dogs used to the unearned benefits of sleeping alongside, on, or even in the top dog's bed.

It is also important for the owners to proceed with restructuring the relationship, never allowing the dog to initiate any successful contact with them for two to three weeks, and even longer if required. All good things of life, including short periods of physical affection, grooming and play continue to be available at up to the same level as previously, but only ever at the owner's initiation and not the dog's. Virtually every dog suffering from this condition that I have seen has had a track record of being able to be with the owner whenever it chooses. In some memorable cases this has even included following the owner into the bathroom or scratching at the door if shut. In one astounding case of a Yorkshire Terrier, it even included being present on its doting lady owner's wedding night!

Dogs are often able to turn their owners on and off like taps, demanding attention and affection with a variety of behaviours both highly appealing and of high nuisance value. The begging dog with a wagging tail and big dark staring eyes is hard to resist patting, no matter how many times he does it in a day. The dog that barks and becomes an excited furry bundle if his demands for contact are ignored for a second, also gets attention, if only to shut him up! Either way, the dog learns to keep the attention on himself and, worse, may come to depend on the owner totally for all emotional security and reassurance in the face of the most minor distractions. Compound this with a dog's early or post-rescue experiences of an owner always being at home 'on tap' and one can soon realize why severe over-attachment and anxiety problems may arise when the dog is left at home alone.

Before being left at home alone, the dog should ideally be given a good walk to tire him out and fed a good proportion of his daily ration immediately on return. This should induce drowsiness which the owners can encourage by putting the dog in his pen or bed in a nice, quiet, warm, draught-proof place. For the next ten to fifteen minutes the dog should be ignored totally while the owners themselves prepare to leave. Hopefully the dog will fall asleep, but if not, the owners should ignore all attempts by the dog to intercept them or demand attention.

While it is tempting to go to the dog to say goodbye and beg him not to do any damage and to stay calm while Mum and Dad are out, don't! Ignore him and just walk out of the door. Prolonged goodbyes simply heighten the dog's attachment at the moment of contact and then send him crashing into panic even further when you shut the door and leave. His anxiety is likely to be at its peak at the moment of departure, indeed, as with the £8000 carpet demolition expert, most damage is done in the few moments after the owners have left the house.

There are exceptions, of course. Some almost seem to wind themselves up, charging around the house searching for departed owners and only entering the hyper-excited panic phase when they realize that they are truly alone. Others are destructive in bursts, perhaps tiring themselves with such intense displacement behaviour, sleeping it off for a while and then beginning again on waking and finding themselves still isolated. Others are normally just about able to cope with solitude but can become primed by extraneous events, such as someone ringing the door bell. The dog gets excited in defending his territory and then, worried that he is unsupported, begins the work of the destruction expert.

When the dog is settled after the walk, it may also help to leave 'security bridges' and comforts such as radio playing, or better still, a recording of a normal noisy family Saturday morning, a favourite toy or chew and, depending on the individual, leaving the lights on, dimmed or off. Some are more relaxed if allowed free range around the house, but this is usually too risky in the initial stages! Leaving smelly unwashed clothes in the dog's den or basket can also provide comforting scent reminders of his absent pack and keep him calmer. Many dogs with separation anxiety benefit enormously from having another animal as company. A cat or, in one extraordinary case I saw, a parrot may help the dog feel less isolated. Another dog will usually help even more, though careful selection of a solid character, used to being left alone, is required, otherwise he too may learn how to be anxious when left and double the scale of destruction.

When it comes to recognizing the signs of its owner's impending departure, the over-attached dog is an expert. It can be helpful to try to 'deprogramme' him as to the cues we offer. The sound of the back door being locked, windows shut and the collection of the car keys are all signs of impending gloom for the dog, and Pluto and his ilk get progressively more anxious with each cue. Avoiding those things by thinking ahead, or doing them out of the normal sequence will serve to confuse the dog a little and help dissociate stimulus and response.

Further confusion can be instilled by doing all the usual things, including putting on your overcoat and then not actually leaving, or only leaving for a short period, turning round on the doorstep and coming back inside. The neighbours may think that it is you who needs the psychologist, but it all helps to keep the dog guessing and just below the panic threshold for a little longer. Hopefully, with frequent practice and variable lengths of dummy departures, which gradually increase, the dog steadily comes to see the owners' departures as less of a contrast with their presence. This is helped in that the owners are only available to the dog at their calling when they are home. Sometimes a short and decreasing dose of Valium or progestins can help as a vehicle for treatment and, sadly, there are a few for whom a sufficient dose is necessary at every separation to keep them calm, despite the owner's best efforts. Others simply continue to be taken everywhere with the owners, and many of these can be left happily and without risk in that perfect small protecting bubble, the car. However, care is needed as some will also cause great damage to the car as well in their anxiety, though for many dogs, if the car is going to be a problem it is more likely to be so when it is moving.

## In-car nervousness

*Dear Mr Neville*

*Robbie, my normally confident Westie, is terrified of the car. I have to force him to get in and, when there, he whines, dribbles and paces up and down. This continues throughout the journey and he remains distressed for quite some time after we reach our destination. My vet has given me tranquillizers for Robbie which are useful for long journeys, but dope him too much and too long for our normal short trips. Can Robbie be made to tolerate the car better, or would it just be kinder to leave him at home ?*

*Yours sincerely*

*Paula Hunt*

Isn't it strange how there is such wide variation in the way dogs view cars?  Some can't wait to jump in and are in their element watching the world go by out of the window, others become highly possessive and bark ferociously at anyone who dares walk within twenty yards of 'their' car while others, like Robbie, have a fear and loathing of the infernal things. Much comes down to individual likes and dislikes and early experience, of course. There is a greater chance of dogs reacting like Robbie if they do not experience the movement, noise and confinement of car travel until they are older.

Some previously happy travellers also, understandably, become nervous about being in the car after being involved in a road accident but, whatever the reason for their distress, the principle of treatment is the same.  Indeed, it is the same approach as adopted when tackling all nervous problems and phobias – that of systematic desensitization.

In such a distressed state Robbie is clearly not in a position to learn to tolerate the car, so simply insisting that he is taken out as frequently as possible will not reduce his reaction through habituation. Instead Robbie must be introduced gradually to the car in stages, or systematically.  If particularly sensitive, Robbie can first just be walked by the car, with his owner simply encouraging him to go progressively nearer for the prospect of reward of praise, toys or titbits. Attempts to run away can also be blocked using a headcollar and lead as outlined for George earlier. The car doors are opened and the games should continue first around the car and then through and in it.  A ball can be thrown in for Robbie to chase and retrieve, food titbits and even his main meals, can be fed in the stationary car in the driveway or garage.  In this way the inside of the car simply becomes seen as an extension of the den/activity area of the house.

One very large and very beautiful Irish Wolfhound I saw for this problem some time ago had refused to enter the brand new and beautifully furbished caravanette  his owner had bought to accommodate the Wolfhound because he had grown too big for the old estate car, which the dog had happily leapt into at any time.  Faced with £20,000 of wasted money, we tried every trick to get the dog accustomed to being in the van with all the doors open – to no avail. He wouldn't eat in there, even if starved for twelve hours, neither would he follow the family, nor chase his favourite toys, nor be physically dragged in wearing a headcollar. When an Irish Wolfhound says 'no' then he can sit down and mean it.  Finally we threw in a raggedy old toy that the dog had had as a pup, but which he hadn't played with since – it had been under all his blankets in his basket in the kitchen. The dog leapt in to retrieve his toy, then sat down on the bed the owner had carefully prepared in the caravanette and buried it under the blanket there. For ever more the dog was happy to get in and travel anywhere, and the local Toyota garage didn't have to take back a vehicle of dubious resale value specially kitted out for an Irish Wolfhound.

So, whatever favourite things are required, Paula's aim is to get Robbie voluntarily to enter the car. Once this is happily achieved he may be left there, restrained for safety if necessary, with the doors now shut but the windows open. Then she can simply sit in the car with him, talking to him gently to keep him calm. Then she should get into the driver's seat and, with doors open, start the car. At this stage it will help if the dog is distracted with food or toys or maybe even tied in, if this doesn't alarm him. Frequent short practice sessions with the doors open again, engine running and operating the indicators, windscreen wipers, radio and other noisy features of driving in turn will all help Robbie grow used to them. Only once he is relaxed should the important aspects begin – closing the door to confine him and then driving the car forward. This should be done as slowly, gently and quietly as possible with gentle words of reassurance and distracting stimuli of food and toys. Initially the car should go forward just a few yards and then stop. Robbie should immediately be released and heaped with praise and love for putting up with it. In this way the journey is seen as a precursor to something positive for him.

Gradually the length of drive can be increased to a short journey, perhaps up and down Paula's road, ending with the joy of returning home. The critical feature of treatment of all such problems is never to proceed too fast. If the dog starts to become distressed, Paula will have been going too fast and must drop back to the previous stage of treatment and then continue more slowly.

Some dogs will respond very quickly to this staged approach to treatment, others, especially those with a long history of nervous behaviour in the car, may take months of slow practice. Few will ever be enthusiastic travellers, but most can learn to tolerate short journeys at least without over-reacting or becoming too distressed. Tranquillizers may still be required to keep Robbie calm for unusually long car journeys.

# Nervousness at dog shows

*'Nobody is on my side, nobody takes part with me: I am cruelly used, nobody feels for my poor nerves'* (Mrs Bennet)          Jane Austen

*Dear Mr Neville*

*The breeder of my Dobermann, Black Rinse Shinyback of Thetford the Ninth (Blackie for short) says that he has such a beautiful appearance and conformation that he should do extremely well at shows. As a puppy he certainly won a lot of prizes and soon qualified to enter Crufts. We all had hopes that he would go on and perhaps win his 'Best of Breed' award there, and even dreamed of winning the 'Best in Show'. However, once Blackie reached about ten months old he suddenly became very nervous in the show ring and started to back away from the judges. As a result, he stopped winning. Every judge has said that if he'd been more confident he would have walked away with the first prize. We've carried on showing him hoping he'd overcome his problems but, if anything, he's got worse in recent weeks. Is there anything we might do to help him win again?*

*Yours sincerely*

*Anne and Joshua Baxter*

I should start by saying that I have never shown a dog in my life, nor would I, no matter how good it looked physically or how well it conformed to its breed standards. I'm afraid my dogs will only ever be judged on how good they are as companions and pets and therefore I have no personal experiences on which to draw when treating cases such as Blackie. One's immediate reaction is to feel sorry for the poor dog and to suggest he be retired straight away from his show career which, after all, means little to him anyway – even if all the rosettes mean the world to his owner and breeder. That said, however, such problems can often be successfully treated adopting the systematic desensitizing approach.

My first advice for dogs like Blackie is that they should be withdrawn from all shows for the coming three to six months, as the show procedure and associated environment has already become too much for them to accept, let alone win at. This also gives the owner/handler a chance to establish a more dependable relationship with the dog, rather than contributing to the dog's nervousness through their own tension or excitement at the show. During this time the owners can handle the dog in the manner of a show judge (ask one what they're looking for, not me) in between preparing the dog's meals and putting the bowl down at meal times. This can be extended to occur at other times, to be followed always by something that the dog enjoys, such as food, play or walks, and carried out by all immediate members of the family. Again, short frequent periods work best and the dog should never be handled so long as to make it worried.

Then familiar friends and house guests can be asked to do the same thing to widen the dog's acceptance beyond its immediate pack. A mock show ring can be built in the garden and the routines practised further there with any other confident dogs of Blackie's household. Later, friends with dogs which Blackie likes can also be invited for a mock dog show. If this goes well, friends within the show fraternity can be asked to do likewise at their homes. Only when Blackie is accepting all this should the prospect of being shown properly again be considered, but if he won't accept it all in this form, it is time to hang up his show lead for his own benefit and start again with another dog, if the owners particularly want to carry on competing.

Assuming Blackie has done well thus far, he can be entered for a local multi-breed and mongrel combined, village fete-type fun show to see how well he performs in an unfamiliar show ring, but one where everyone, especially the Baxter family, is as relaxed as possible and in which taking part, not winning, is the aim of the day. If he competes happily, then he can be entered for more similar shows and then, some weeks later, for a small 'proper' show. Here, he should be entered and benched at the area, but not taken into the ring, so that he acclimatizes again to the whole procedure of the dog show. If this goes well, and only after he starts to enjoy the day out, he can be entered for the show properly, with the owners having done their best to ascertain that the judge is of gentle disposition and, preferably, one that Blackie has met before as a puppy and to whom he has not shown any nervous reaction. It may also be that Blackie will be more confident if handled in the ring by someone other than the Baxters, especially if they tend to get very excited or worried by the whole affair. Indeed, there are now professional and semi-professional handlers who, for a fee, will show your dog for you.

The suggested treatment for ring- or judge-shy dogs is all based on common sens, of course, and there are many in the show world who could usefully enlarge on this approach with various 'tricks of the trade' acquired over the years. There are ringcraft classes specifically for accustoming dogs to the procedures of being judged and these are highly recommended for all young dogs as early as possible if their owners plan a show career for them.

It's only fair to point out that I probably only see half a dozen such cases a year and more personal, experienced help is available from show enthusiasts. However, the owners of a couple of dogs referred to me who put in the necessary amount of effort in applying the treatment did get back into winning ways with this approach. I also remember one who tried to do it all, but without taking the first step of withdrawing from all shows for a few months. As with all fears, there is precious little prospect of desensitizing a dog to its fear if it continues to be exposed to it in undiluted form during treatment. But while the successfully treated cases have owners who still send me show reports highlighting the fame of their now confident and winning dogs, the one has never really forgiven me for not making her dog into a Cruft's champion.

All I can wish for in this case is that the dog finds a new owner who cares more about the dog than their own glory in the sometimes 'win at all costs' dog show world. Showing dogs should surely be fun for dog and owner, as well as competitive. Indeed it would seem to me, as an observer, that the dogs which do win at shows are those which seem to enjoy the day out and all the attention of being shown and judged. Their confidence shows and they attract the judge's eye as a result, so why try to compete with a depressed dog that just happens to look good?

# Phobias

Phobias are perhaps best described as extreme forms of fear which produce marked behavioural responses in the sufferer. These responses are not beneficial towards resolving the fear, may not be particularly directed at it, and may even lead to behaviour which puts the animal at more risk than the phobia-invoking stimulus itself. More likely, however, is that the dog's first exposure to a certain stimulus was traumatic and/or caused a marked physiological response via the autonomic or reflex nervous system. Such learning or association is often a case of Pavlovian-type classical conditioning to a single, intense and, perhaps, painful sudden stimulus. The dog reacts with an adrenaline surge producing a rapid increase in heart rate priming it for running away. The same level of reaction occurs at subsequent exposure to the same stimulus. This happens even if the stimulus becomes familiar and the dog does not physically suffer as a result of it. The fear response may occur with exposure to innocuous conditions that just happened to be there at the time of the first traumatic exposure. This is best demonstrated by the common human phobia about going to the dentist. Simply the smell of the dentist's clinic or the sound of the drill are enough to induce the same level of phobic response as the treatment itself. Despite frequent visits to the dentist, the scale of the reaction never falls and the person continues to suffer from the phobia.

I and my colleagues in the APBC have treated a whole range of bizarre phobias in the dog. I have treated a huge 140 pound dog with an irreconcilable fear of red telephone boxes; another was a big tough individual of a guarding breed which had a complete fear of light bulbs. This chap would cower and shrink away from table lamps when they were switched on and then run under the sideboard trembling, yet would happily disembowel anyone who thought they could walk through the gate at the bottom of his garden.

Other dogs have developed phobias about walls in their own houses, water (not always the typical hydrophobic sign of rabies), and even birds. More common phobias include those of passing traffic and of loud or unusual noises such as household machinery, especially that 'prince of darkness', the vacuum cleaner. Thunder, rain, windy or stormy weather in general also worry some dogs. They can best be exemplified by attention to one of the most common canine phobias, gunshot phobia.

# Gunshot and other sound phobias

*Dear Mr Neville*

*My Labrador, Clint, is afraid of all loud noises, but especially of gunshot. This is particularly problematic as I got him to be trained to the gun, but at his very first training session, he*

*bolted in fear and ran as far away as possible. He has contin-*
*ued to do this ever since, and is reacting even to the sound of*
*gunshot miles away and barely audible to me. He is also*
*equally afraid of cars backfiring and there is little one can do*
*to console him when he is so afraid. The result is that he is kept*
*on a lead for all his walks rather than my risking losing him*
*when he panics. Although I have given up with the idea of*
*working him as a gun dog, can he be treated and helped to cope*
*with sudden bangs?*

*Yours sincerely*

*Nick Waterhouse*

The main problem with treating gunshot or thunder phobia is that those events are, by their very nature, sudden, often unpredictable and dramatic. Of course, it must come as a real disappointment to owners such as Nick to have a sound-phobic gun dog, but many owners discover that their dog is gunshot phobic when out on a walk in the countryside. Suddenly there is the sound of a shotgun, sometimes only just audible in the distance and the dog has panicked and bolted.

Most dogs will look to their owners for protection and support at such times but, interestingly, some will run to the next nearest available person for support and ignore their owner entirely. Once sensitized, the poor dog continues to react to the same degree to all sounds of gunfire and/or thunder, cars back-firing and pigeon-scaring gas-bangers in rural areas. With thunder-phobic dogs, during the long period of changing atmospheric pressure, which the dog recognizes as preceding the event, it becomes progressively more agitated and nervous as the storm approaches. The full reaction may even set in some time before the first clap of thunder.

Treatment is often quite difficult to organize. While the principles of phobic desensitization are the right ones, it is hard to create the full scenario of an impending thunder storm or the suddenness of gunfire in a diluted form. Even a distant bang can be sufficient to tip the balance, and once already in a phobic panic, the dog can only be comforted and not reassured for the next time.

To help the dog habituate to various loud sudden sounds in the reassuring confines of its own home I suggest to owners of dogs like Clint that they purchase a sound-effects tape or CD from a company that keeps catalogues of the most amazing noises. One can purchase recordings of virtually any sound on earth, from someone getting out of a jacuzzi to the hum of voices at an ice skating rink from Digiffects of 5 Newburgh Street, London W1.

The idea is to play these recordings at low level, and sometimes variable tone, at home while the dog can successfully be distracted by play and contact with the owner, toys, food or titbits. Once the dog has started eating, the hi-fi is switched on at a low level and, assuming the dog continues to eat, the level is gradually increased at every mealtime. If the dog does habituate, the recordings can then be played at other times as background noise to normal family goings on, then via a portable tape or CD player outdoors in the garden and then on walks away from home. The constant aim of the treatment is for the dog to learn to associate the frightening sound with something rewarding from the owner, such as affection or food, but without the owner contributing to the dog's anxiety by being over-protective so that it avoids learning to cope.

Preconditioning the offering of the titbit or affection by insisting that the dogs sits prior to receiving it will also help keep him returning to the owner when worried, concentrating, we hope, on the prospect of the reward for being calm. Later, gunshot phobic dogs can be driven closer to a genuine shoot and rewarded conditionally for being tolerant, though thunder is a little harder to drive to! Most dogs improve with effort, though it is probably true to say that few become totally bomb-proof and may still be inclined to panic outdoors on occasion. It is important that, even after good progress has been achieved, the dog continues to be exposed to the stimulus that used to induce the phobic response so that the new learned patterns of coping are not extinguished.

Drugs have been commonly employed in the treatment of canine phobics but, as most inhibit learning, they have only ever achieved limited results. However, veterinary surgeon and member of the APBC Robin Walker, from Worcester, has recently been achieving some remarkable results using a combination approach of two of the drugs that have been commonly recommended by vets and behaviourists in the past.

Interestingly the dosage of both drugs has been much lower than that employed when they are used individually and there is no discernible sedative effect or inhibition of learning. The treatment has produced remarkable results in some generalized phobics, and even in many long-standing and sad cases where the dog has become phobo-phobic – the fear of fear itself. All APBC members now call

91

Robin immediately when treating serious canine phobias and very nervous dogs and, as a result, the success rate for treating these difficult cases has risen wonderfully.

It is important, as Robin Walker underlines, during the treatment of any phobia with or without drugs, to take the dog to as wide a variety of novel places as he can cope with to keep sharp his abilities to deal with any new or worrying situation of a more general nature. For thunder- or rain sound-phobic dogs it may also help to establish a secure den for them in a corner, under a table or using an indoor kennel. This should be used as a regular bed and as a place for the dog to retire to in the day or be put in to lie quietly as the storm approaches. This den is often far more reassuring to the dog than the efforts of the owner in trying to reassure him, especially as such efforts may also 'reward' his nervousness and sometimes encourage a 'display' of incompetence rather than a genuine phobic reaction.

Bonfire night in the UK, or firework celebrations elsewhere, are terrifying for many dogs, and there probably isn't much point in trying to desensitize them beforehand to such unusual occasional events. A large meal, a calm dark room, perhaps with the radio playing and a reassuring owner are the best treatment for this. The vet can provide tranquillizers specially for the event if necessary, but even here, Robin Walker's drug 'cocktail' has been making bonfire night no more than a harmless passing occurrence for many dogs with a long history of terror around fireworks.

Whether one treats or subdues the firework phobic dog depends on the individual dog's reactions, his age and the degree of concern of the owner. Guns, on the other hand, are fired all year round and all too often in the countryside in the name of sport, so attempting to treat the gunshot phobic dog with the appropriate drugs if necessary and by desensitizing him to the sound is always worthwhile.

# Agoraphobia

*Dear Mr Neville*

*My dog Blot is agoraphobic. For the past four or five months he's hardly been out at all, and really only to the garden when nature calls. I've tried dragging him on a lead but he just panics as we get near the front door and runs straight back inside. If I shut him out he screams by the door until I let him in again. Should I insist he goes out?*

*Yours sincerely*

*Francis Harrisson*

Fortunately agoraphobia, or fear of open spaces (indoor and out), is quite rare in dogs. Unlike most phobias, the condition can arise from a lack of early exposure to the outdoors, or exposure delayed too long and not coinciding with the puppy's phases of development. Sadly, from the behavioural development point of view puppies cannot safely be allowed outdoors until their vaccination course is complete at about 14 weeks of age. Indeed, many responsible pedigree dog breeders won't sell puppies until all their vaccinations have been administered. Ideally, puppies should be exposed to the outdoors as soon as they are weaned for maximum competence to develop at coping with the brave new world but, clearly, I would never recommend putting the puppy's health or life at risk to achieve this. Instead responsible breeders ensure that their puppies are exposed to as wide a variety of novelty, handling and challenge indoors in safety so that they all grow up with as wide a range as possible of abilities to cope, which will include exploratory behaviour patterns to help them cope with the outdoors as and when they are allowed access. It therefore follows that my advice to prospective owners of a pedigree puppy is to seek out a breeder who is aware of the behavioural needs of dogs and not just raising money-making puppies in an unstimulating pen at the end of the garden or in a spare room at the end of the house where the puppies have no chance to react with the family.

For such victims of callous breeders incompetence outdoors, fear of people or other dogs, sudden happenings, or even agoraphobia, are common developments. It is perhaps surprising that so many puppies overcome such a lack of early stimulation to become well-adjusted dogs, but the problems of the few could so easily have been avoided.

However, many of the phobias I treat arise because of a loss of confidence caused by a single traumatic incident, the most usual cause behind the onset of most phobias. The most common trauma in the development of agoraphobia is a fight with a rival just outside the dog's own house, either in its garden or out on the street where it used to be completely safe.

The risk of encountering the rival may be present every time Blot goes out and his reluctance to do so thus increases steadily. He may lose the ability to cope outdoors with even mild changes such as the noise of leaves rustling or the sound of a car and non-threatening or even friendly approaches by other dogs even if the other dog is not on the scene. Typically, the severity of the dog's reaction is pronounced with all exposures, even on apparently calm days when no other dog can be seen.

Blot's agoraphobia may be due to other causes such as major disturbance of access points to home during the building of an extension or garage, a near miss with a fast car or a sudden frightening noise that he associated with the outdoors. The consequences in all cases are usually quite marked and get progressively worse. The dog is clearly distressed if forced outdoors and a long, long way from enjoying its earlier outdoor lifestyle.

Treatment for dogs like Blot is similar to that for other forms of nervousness and involves controlled exposure, perhaps using a large secure pen in which he can safely spend some portion of his day outdoors. Such treatment is usually best delayed until the cause of the problem is removed. This may mean waiting until building works are complete or even coming to an arrangement with the owner of the despotic rival about better control of his dog and which dog goes out at which times to avoid further conflict. Once achieved Blot can be put safely outdoors in the garden initially to relearn that it is as safe as before the trauma and that every noise on the wind is not necessarily threatening. Francis should accompany him on the first few occasions and then walk around the garden with Blot on a lead and perhaps in a headcollar, if it comforts him, so that he acts as a security bridge for the dog. It helps to divide the dog's meals into frequent short rations and move his feeding area to the pen and later, just outside the back door, to use appetite again as a distraction when the dog feels vulnerable.

The prognosis for treatment of dogs such as Blot is often very good, depending on the control that can be achieved over the cause of the initial problem, because we are re-establishing old behaviour patterns rather than trying to teach them to the dog for the first time. Again, drugs can be most helpful under Robin Walker's treatment plan.

# Wife (and husband) phobia

*Dear Mr Neville*

*Our Labrador, Jake, adores me, my children and even our rabbit, but hates my wife. The poor woman has tried for months to get the dog to like her but to no avail. As soon as she enters the room Jake cowers behind me or the sofa, or even runs away to another room if he can. Sheila has never laid a finger on him and only ever wanted to stroke him and be friends. Is there a way to get them together? Jake is just over a year old and was neutered about six months ago, but this made no difference to his dislike of my wife. It's really becoming a problem now because my wife gets upset that I devote extra attention to Jake to make up for what he can't get from her. Please help before we come to blows!*

*Yours truly*

*David Hayward*

Dislike of wives is rarely, if ever, described as a phobia, but many dogs have favourite members of the household and perhaps are less happy with others. It is quite rare for the dislike to become so pronounced, but the treatment procedures are similar to those where we are simply trying to improve the bond between owner and dog. Some dogs do bond very closely to one maternal figure but are usually tolerant of other members of the family without doting on them in the same way. For a dog to reject one individual while remaining friendly with every creature in the house, including noisy kids and tasty prey items such as rabbits, is unusual and a real blow for the often innocent victim. As in this case, the wife has tried extremely hard to overcome the dog's dislike for her by trying to be ultra-calm and affectionate. Sadly the efforts seem to have failed and now other relationships in the family have begun to suffer because of the competition for affection from the dog and then between the accepted family members and the person rejected. It may seem strange to begin to quarrel over a dog but being rejected by any member of a social group is bound to hurt. If it happens to be a dog that you love dearly, treat very much as one of the family and spend much time and money on, then it is hard not to take the hurt personally or resent the success of others who perhaps expend less emotional effort in being nice to him.

Usually, dogs are more likely to be nervous of the man of the house rather than any other member because of less predictable moods and often louder, shorter tempers, as well as the deeper more growl-like voice. In some cases, the man is obviously short tempered and prone to crashing around and shouting when upset. But whether it is the husband or wife who has the short fuse, this is likely to upset the dog which will be unable to feel confident in their presence even when they are relaxed and as pleasant as can be.

First we must consider the early experiences of the dog and investigate who took the major role in feeding, being affectionate and playing with him, in order to understand whether the bonding process was a little unequally shared. Certainly for some wives there is no obvious reason why their dog should dislike them. It may be that they simply aren't at home often or that the family noise and excitement levels rise too frighteningly when Mum is with the kids. Sometimes the husband's arrival home sparks off much sudden family movement with Mum and kids rushing to greet Dad home from work which the dog finds startling so learns to keep out of his way.

Treatment of wife-or husband-phobic dogs has to be a family affair and often this necessary corporate approach immediately restores the strained human relations to their former strength. The common aim of helping the still-loved dog draws the family together, given the right explanations, although the advice is not always too pleasant for the innocent parties to carry out. The loved husband or wife and other closely appreciated family members are advised to be far less available to the dog and to reject his demands for attention for a few weeks. Meals are divided up again into short feeds available exclusively from the unloved family member, who is also the treat-provider and the one who should walk the dog. Games are begun by the friends in the dog's pack but taken over by the 'unloved' who is allowed the armchair closest to the fire or radiator so as to be more attractive for the dog to sit next to. If hot tempered, the 'unloved' is requested to be more in control of his or her emotions and advised how to present a more consistent appearance of calm and friendship to the dog.

The relationship usually builds quicker if the 'unloved' gives up trying to pursue the unwilling dog and waits for the dog to need him, while providing a few incentives. And big chaps especially are advised to get down to floor level to mimic those canine greeting behaviours again rather than leaning down from on high which can be frightening for the unsure dog. Progress may be quite slow in some cases but astoundingly quick in others, and for no apparent reason.

The most rewarding letter I ever received after treating a husband-phobic cat explained briefly that the cat was much improved but that, best of all, the husband was a totally reformed character who had given up all signs of macho, short-tempered or dominating behaviour in the home for fear of undoing the progress and upsetting the cat!

Nervous or phobic, insecure or lacking in confidence, the dog often makes a good patient for the dog shrink because of its intelligence, adaptive learning ability and highly developed survival instincts. The most difficult cases are those containing elements of learned helplessness where the dog rushes to its owner for support in the face of very minor challenges and finds constant support from a well-meaning, but over-compassionate owner. A similar situation can understandably arise as a consequence of the extra contact and care we must offer when looking after an elderly or sick dog. But because owners are usually compassionate about these aspects of problem dog behaviour they are more than willing to invest the necessary time and management practice to carry out treatment suggestions to help the nervous, incompetent, anxious or phobic dog. Usually their efforts pay off to some degree at least and the dog's quality of life and their joys of owning him or her improve steadily.

# 6
# Aggression

*'When a dog bites a man that is not news, but when a man bites a dog, that is news'* Charles Dana (*New York Sun*)

There is an enormous range of behaviour which we all too easily lump under a single heading of 'aggression'. There are normal or expected expressions of aggression, abnormal expressions, those we want and encourage in dogs and those we don't. Perhaps we are too quick to label certain types of behaviour as aggressive because of the potentially dangerous consequences of attack. We act defensively to avoid any form of aggression being directed towards us and this can prevent us from distinguishing between different types of aggressive behaviour because the end result may be the same – being bitten.

When treating aggression problems in dogs, it would be extremely unwise for me to treat all cases similarly, even though the actual behavioural response of each dog may be much the same – the use of teeth. Each must be treated individually, looking closely at what triggers the response, its scale, duration and direction, for treatment to have any hope at all.

The general reaction of owners in the face of all types of aggression is to become aggressive in return and try to subdue it with greater force than being displayed, unless the animal is already beyond safe control, or is likely to inflict injury on them. In nearly all such cases, meeting aggression with excitement or aggression in return simply fuels a dog's aggression and has little or no reforming effect.

More often, and particularly with canine aggression, owners are

98

attacked or bitten when they needn't have been. While that may be their fault, the sad consequence is that the dog becomes aggressive more quickly when next challenged, or more readily diverts other forms of aggression onto its owner. The end result is an upward spiral of aggression with the relationship in tatters, owners bitten and dogs punished or even destroyed. Sadly, the worst cases seem to involve owners who have received wrong advice from so-called dog trainers whose only answer to disobedience or defensive growls from dogs, frightened by over-assertive training techniques, is to clobber the poor dog with an ever larger stick. However, most trainers worth their salt know that to punish frightened dogs, which growl in an effort to deter the perceived threat, is bound to frighten them more and, instead, use calming techniques.

But just what is aggression in behavioural terms? Aggression is carrying out an act of hostility or causing injury to a rival, or a prey item, or to a threatening challenge. Indeed the term 'aggression' is often used to describe only the first hostile act between two parties, though the victim may respond in like fashion and be described as defensive until he starts to win. But, without doubt, aggression is an integral part of every higher animal's behavioural repertoire and is expressed in a range of types and responses.

## Body and other language

Predatory aggression is vital for the survival of all wild hunters, as are other forms of aggressive reaction for defence when challenged. But aggression in a social or interactive context between two adult dogs, or owner and dog, is a different matter altogether. Indeed the repertoire of responses between two dogs involved in some dispute may concern not only obvious displays of aggression in actual fights, but also a number of fearful responses designed to ameliorate the aggression in the competitor. The interplay between the two rivals is usually very interesting to watch (providing actual fighting doesn't occur) because of the dramatic tension and the range of responses in both dogs. Body movements and postures, facial expressions and vocalization are all used to communicate one dog's proposals or emotional state to the other. The other will respond with equalizing reactions if standing firm, raise the stakes with more assertive gestures, or show retiring responses in deference to the other dog's assertive gestures. Such reactions are probably best described as agonistic rather than aggressive displays, as they are actually designed to prevent violence. The bluff of staring your opponent in the eye, strutting and then settling into a fixed tense position as if ready to strike, raising of hackles, lifting of the lips to expose the teeth and sideways presentation to make yourself look larger are all statements of intent designed to convince the opposition to withdraw and so avoid actual physical interaction.

Two rivals may vary the sequence and combination of their agonistic gestures and sounds until one edges away or starts to avoid eye contact and drop his head, body and tail in a show of submission or even rolls on his back, evacuates his anal glands, sheds hair or urinates involuntarily. The interplay between even fellow pack mates is often referred to as the fluctuation of dominance/submission interchanges, and are usually carried out then in safer ritualistic forms.

This complex communication behaviour of a social animal allows animal behaviourists to get close to ascribing motivation for emotions in dogs, a dangerous area, as emotions are not immediately quantifiable for the scientist, even if he can bore you for hours telling you about his own dog's feelings and moods. I am happy to say that, out-of-date biologist as I may be, I try not to allow science to limit my outlook. Of course dogs have emotions, moods and feelings. They are difficult to measure and classify because they are so extraordinarily complex, but they are there, even if not to the same depth as our emotions. We can get closest to analysis when something dramatic is going on, such as when two unfamiliar dogs meet and engage in a ritualistic greeting displays involving facial expression, body manoeuvres, and postures, vocalization, physical investigation and even involuntary responses – but there I go already, using the jargon language of the behaviourist.

I am a great admirer of one of the great thinkers in the field of canine behavioural therapy, my old friend, Dr Roger Abrantes. Roger is a gentle-natured Portuguese gentleman who speaks about eight languages fluently, but said he only learnt the rudiments of 'dogese' after years in practice in Denmark and writing a veritable heap of books; unfortunately for us, mostly in Danish. Always a maniac driver, he has now turned his hand to Formula 3 motor racing and no doubt those years of avoiding attack by his aggressive dog clients have kept his reactions sufficiently sharp for his new lifestyle! It was Roger who first took on the daunting task of systematically comparing emotional expression in man and dog. He decided that the interplay between fear and aggression did not adequately explain the interactions between two dogs, and nor, by extension in the human pack, between man and dog. Looking closely at facial expression and body postures, Roger drew up a new model incorporating the concept of fear and aggression into the social arena of dominance and sub-dominance in the dog pack or man-dog relationship. This is nicely described and illustrated in a paper he has produced (in English). He emphasises the normality of dominance/sub-dominance between the dog and his own kind or with man, and that such displays are essential to both parties in communicating mood, intent and social position.

When we say 'NO' to our dog, we shouldn't worry if he shows a sub-dominant reaction by looking away 'guiltily', dropping his tail and cowering a little and acknowledges our right to alter his actions. He is only benefitting himself by saying 'Okay, I'll do what you say and hope you'll stay around to offer me protection'. This is taught early on by his mother when she growls at him or pushes him away from the nipple if he sucked too long or too hard. The statement is there – 'back off ' – but without compromise of the mother's desire and intent to continue to protect the puppy. The puppy learns that minor rejections are not the end of the world and interplay between showing a subordinate reaction and taking the benefits of protection allow relations with pack mates to continue. At other times, it may be he who is the one raising the dominance stakes and dictating the course of the interaction with his pack mates.

If, as human dogs, we mimic the actions of a dog so that our pet perceives it as beneficial to acknowledge us in this way, then we have, as we usually do, a successful relationship. If on the other hand, we don't just say 'NO', but we also attack him as well with a kick, then he may show a continuously fearful response, at every encounter which would be unusual in relations between dogs. This brings us back to the pointlessness of physical punishment in reforming unwanted behaviour. The dog may submit totally and show very obvious signs of fear, but still want to stay around us in our group. What we have achieved is a breakdown in normal modes of communication that should be ordinarily be able to fluctuate in their level of dominance and sub-dominance without needing to reach such extremes. It's the same as how human beings know where they stand when they shake hands with the 'boss' and don't look him or her straight in the eye for too long, nor grasp his hand more firmly than he is grasping theirs. The boss doesn't need to thump us to get the desired acknowledgement of his authority. Just watching the constantly changing face and body movements of our dogs when reacting with us or other dogs teaches us so much about their emotions. But Roger Abrantes has also tried to define further the altering states between dominance and aggression by desentising dominance without aggression, sub-dominance and sub-dominance with fear, and describes some of the subtle head and ear movements, head carriage positions and facial expressions that go along with it all. This is difficult enough with one dog, though we are all good amateurs with our own pets. All Roger must do now, as he whizzes around Brands Hatch at 130 mph, is to draw up such alphabets for Bulldogs and Chihuahuas, Borzois and Old English Sheepdogs!

It is interesting that a very submissive or slowly retreating dog fits within Roger's range of 'normal' interplay between dogs and those displaying this combination of fear and sub-dominance are usually allowed to withdraw by the 'victor' without being attacked. Yet dogs which try to run away, a very submissive gesture practised by many losers in the animal kingdom, invariably stimulates the 'victor' to chase and attack to enforce the message. Or is it just that movement easily elicits more predatory chase-type aggression in dogs? No-one, not even Roger Abrantes, seems to know for sure.

Aggression in terms of actual fighting between dogs is rarer than we might imagine because even a very confident dominant individual puts him or herself at risk from a defending dog's teeth while attacking. It is safer for everyone to resolve disputes with albeit often complicated but subtle displays, hence the need for adequate communication in a social animal. It certainly makes me wonder how we are able to get along so well with dogs when we are only now beginning to be able to understand what they are saying to us, even if we can teach them to do all sorts of things with a few simple words and hand and body signals. Perhaps the answer lies in what many dog owners have always said, that their dog knows them better than their own family does!

## Classifying aggression

The classification of aggression problems in dogs can still be neatly divided into two distinct types – 'normal', or expected under certain conditions, and 'abnormal', or excessive reactions. Exactly what constitutes a problem behaviour is largely a matter of opinion for each owner but, with aggressive dogs, the opinion is more readily determined by the risk of injury to other dogs, or to the owners and other people, and their tolerance levels are often lower. Most cases do not concern normal or expected aggression, as most owners understand the need for aggression in certain circumstances and are aware of their dog's armoury and predatory status and avoid conflict at such times.

As with many aggression problems it is not always the physical violence which causes the upset for the owners. More often it is the sharp contrast with the dog's normally placid, friendly countenance that comes as such a shock. It is the inability to intervene with the usual friendly, affectionate overtures that causes owners to feel detached from their dog. The communication system between man and dog, or dog and dog has either not been properly developed or has simply not proved adequate to relay what one is thinking to the other and so prevent an aggressive interaction, which is therefore all that remains to make sure the message is driven firmly home.

We will start in our review of aggression problems with a look at the often problematic, if natural, form – that of predatory aggression, though modern scientifi opinion often distinguishes predatory hunting and killing from aggression in a social context.

## Predatory aggression

*Dear Mr Neville*

*Jock, my Cairn Terrier, is known locally as the 'killer'. He is a proficient hunter of rodents, birds, cats . . . in fact anything that he can find. The garden seems to be empty of wild things, but the local countryside is still under threat from Jock. He spends the whole time on our walks scouring the hedgerows and crops for things to chase and kill, and once he's discovered something, he will never return to me until he's caught and killed it or it's managed to get away. It's almost as if he goes deaf . . . is there anything I can do to stop or control Jock's murderous ways and make him into a more enjoyable dog to take out? Indoors he's quite playful and fun to have around.*

*Yours sincerely*

*Moira Williams*

It's really quite remarkable that despite the way in which the wolf has evolved over the last 2 million years, and what we have done to the dog in the process of domestication over the past 10,000 years or so, that such basic instincts should still be so pronounced in some dogs. In some we have deliberately selected for prowess at certain aspects of the predatory game – detection of prey in the brush by spaniels, speed of the chase by Greyhounds and the ferocity against sometimes fierce opposition and the snap-bite-and-kill of many terriers. In most, certainly in more recent times, we have tried to select for docility or perhaps other forms of aggressive behaviour such as guarding or even fighting. But even many otherwise very placid family pet dogs are just unable to resist the chase and kill. Given the opportunity of following the scent of prey or chasing the moving target, the wolf in our dogs makes a sudden resurgence and, as with Moira's Cairn Terrier, it may be very hard to stay in contact with them once the predatory chase has begun.

While we have generally selected and trained the hunter in many breeds of dog, our policy has been to reduce the level of predatory response in most breeds. However, there is little in the modern 'beauty' show rings to rival the sight of a dog at work, or showing how well he can perform in field trials. Most of us are privileged with our tempered-down version of the wolf, to enjoy the occasional sight of his low crouch stalk and sudden burst of speed in pursuit of some hapless squirrel in the park without having to suffer the inconvenience of constantly having to control a predator in full hunting frame of mind at all hours of the day.

The idea of being able to harness such a well-evolved, and then finely-tuned, controlled killer clearly appeals to us, though it isn't quite what Moira had in mind when choosing Jock. Then the unfettered predatory behaviour that lies dormant in our dogs can be extremely annoying. This is partly because we think that either it shouldn't be there at all, or that we definitely ought to be able to control it in our pet dogs.

Terriers, of course, were developed as ratters and diggers to go to earth after animals such as badgers, rabbits and foxes. Their tenacity and speed is famed, indeed in centuries past they were put in rings often sited outside pubs, or in temporary catch areas outside farm buildings when the rats and mice were flushed out. Bull Terriers are credited with the most proficient rat killing in these barbaric spectacles though, naturally, the rats were rarely afforded any public sympathy. Over a ten week period in 1862, a Bull Terrier called Jacko accounted for 1000 rats in 100 minutes, or one every six seconds. The rats were presented in batches of 100 at various rat killing public venues in England, and by the last 100, Jacko had sharpened up and accounted for them in five minutes and twenty-eight seconds, or one every 3.28 seconds. Jenny Lind, another Bull Terrier, killed 500 rats at a single 'sitting' of 90 minutes at a pub in Liverpool, or nearly one per second!

But while this bloodletting would be unacceptable on such a scale today, it does at least give us an idea of what can be achieved...and not by dogs looking for food. Such killing is the representation of the chase and kill aspects of hunting behaviour only, not of the very hungry dog desperately seeking food. Once a particular rat is dead, dogs may lose interest in it and, stimulated purely by the motivation to hunt, move on quickly to the next terrified target. Similar reactions are occasionally reported by farmers whose chicken house protection has been penetrated by a clever fox or, more rarely, by a stray dog. Attracted by the smell of prey, the fox has gone into the chicken house and killed every bird in a murderous carnage, yet will probably have only actually carried off one to eat. Not all foxes do this, but most farmers will not take the risk and will kill them as vermin if they can't or won't invest in adequate fox proofing for the hen house.

Away from our chicken houses the predatory aspects of wolves, foxes and other canids are now better understood as having a vital role in nature. Even in Australia, where the much persecuted Dingo has been reviled since the white man arrived, and especially since the famous case where a baby was alleged to have been taken and eaten by a Dingo from a tent pitched near Ayres Rock, public opinion is starting to shift.

That the ratter dogs of the last century enjoyed their work is probably beyond question, but if this type of orgy could be arranged relatively easily with certain breeds such as the Bull Terrier, I have personal experience of much the same behaviour in a couple of old beach-roaming mongrels in Mombasa. When staying with an old friend, Dick Sparrow, I used to walk along the silvery Indian Ocean beach in the moonlight. Dick, who is an outpost of the British Empire all on his own, lives right on the coral cliffs on the coast just up from the town, and has his own set of steps leading down to the shore. I take a walk there most evenings when I am staying in Dick's house . . . if only to avoid having to listen to the BBC World Service news on his crackly old radio! The last time, sadly some 8 years ago now, I was always joined by these two dogs, probably owned by one of Dick's near neighbours, but clearly used to the free life along the beach. They'd follow me for a couple of miles and back, but with every stride would be looking for little fiddler crabs that appear at night in vast numbers all along the beach. They'd single out a crab each and then chase it. The poor crab would either try to scuttle out to sea, or get back to its hole in the sand. Few made it, so quick were the dogs, but once the crab was either safe or despatched with a lightning quick crunching snap of the jaws, the dogs immediately moved on to their next victims. Fortunately, the crab population seemed able to withstand this nightly carnage as there were always just as many on the sands the next night. It was interesting that even though they were used to hunting alone, the dogs were prepared to follow me on those evenings, although I soon gave up with my humanitarian efforts to stop them killing the crabs. This was what they lived for, and maybe still do.

After these forays, I used to get back to Dick's house overlooking the calm sea and join him for a scotch or two, shared in the company of his old faithful and far less hunting obsessed Black Labrador, Bess. As the warm wind blew up to cool us from the sea I once asked Dick why he had never been home since 1955. 'There's no trams in London now,' I said, 'wouldn't you like to see how it's all changed?' Dick paused, took a sip of scotch and patted Bess, who, sensing the reflection of the moment, nuzzled up closely to him. 'What the bloody hell for?' he replied softly after a few moments. As we both patted Bess and got quietly drunk, nothing more was said.

The interesting feature of predatory aggression in dogs is that unlike other forms, there is no preliminary statement of intent from the dog by growling or snarling in threat. He simply switches quietly and quickly into hunting mode. Once the chase is on, spaniels especially may 'give voice' and yip or bark excitedly as they pursue their game but the moment of death, as the Terrier snaps or the wolf disembowels or strangles its victim with its jaws around its throat, is usually quiet. There is quite a lot of snarling once the prey is dead, although this is probably aimed at the rest of the pack telling them to back off. Terriers are sometimes more vocal and growl when shaking their victims to death but the whole event is usually noted for its quiet efficiency.

Trying to shape Jock's predatory behaviour may be rather difficult for Moira. Apart from the little-understood nature of such 'instinctive' and fundamental behaviours, there is not much that could be done now to convince Jock that there is something more interesting to do on a walk than go hunting. Had he been brought up around a variety of other animals such as cats, rabbits, sheep and even pet rats his desire to hunt them would probably not have developed, though of course plenty of dogs do know the difference between the cat they share their home with and next door's cat, with whom they share nothing! Taught early, Jock's hunting prowess could perhaps have been shaped and controlled to his owners' demands in much the same way as spaniels or retrievers are trained to the gun, but this is achieved through maintaining contact with the more impressionable young dog while allowing him to fulfil his natural 'instincts'. Once the dog has developed his own hunting strategy and one which doesn't involve the owner it is hard to re-programme.

Some, of course, won't even follow the leader like the beach dogs in Mombasa, and disappear over the horizon in hot pursuit of any small and furry or large and feathered creatures that they manage to detect and put to flight. Calling, whistling, throwing a ball, screaming, begging and threatening all go un-noticed not through disobedience or spite, but because the dog's senses are locked on to the most important function of survival – pursuit and capture of food. Once that concentration is adjusted by its capture or the quarry makes an escape, the dog will often turn and look for its owner and return happily when called, oblivious of the anger he has caused. Punishment then will be totally confusing to him, indeed punishment even if he is caught with a rat in his mouth will not stop him chasing the next one, even if he can be frightened into dropping the one he has.

The crucial feature of predatory attack being simulated by the victim's movements was shown to be beyond doubt by an American study in the early 1980s. When two dogs suddenly appeared from nearby woods and ran towards a couple of 11 year old boys playing on some waste ground, they naturally tried to run away. One fell over and was totally ignored by the dogs, which continued to chase, bring down and savage the other boy until they were beaten off by a passer by. Scientists then subjected the dogs to some simple tests. In one, a cyclist went as fast as he could around the fence of the compound in which the dogs were housed. The dogs chased him, and once in full flight, the cyclist moved off out of their line of vision and a suitably protected runner ran directly in front of the dogs. Immediately and without investigation, they switched the full force of their chase onto the runner and once caught, their aggression, as had happened to the boy. However, such attacks account for a very small proportion of canine attacks on man (less than 1 per cent of cases treated by one American behaviour therapist and about the same for APBC members in the United Kingdom). Most predatory aggression problems are of pursuit of real prey as with Jock, or other moving, but often inanimate targets.

So, if Jock is to be reformed, Moira will first have to be consistent, and not, as many of us do, allow him to chase some things such as rabbits but not others such as cats or squirrels. It's all the same to Jock! Next a period of total and consistent control will be required, with Jock only walked on a lead for some time, perhaps an extendable one to allow a degree of freedom to be maintained. Then all attempts to chase anything he does discover will fail, and Moira can quickly regain control if he does set off in hot pursuit of something that attracts him. Frequently throughout the walk, Moira must call Jock to her, and with an attention-getting call rather than a painful jerk on the lead, insist that he comes. She should be encouraging in her tone and reward him effusively for coming to her. Titbits may help, as may being offered a favourite toy to hold for a few moments, though the importance of this will be dependent on Moira 'tuning' Jock in to wanting the toy at home prior to any contact with her for a few days as described earlier. Then it's a case of practice, with Moira walking Jock in as many places as possible and calling him to her frequently both for rewards and simply after a change of direction. Only once he has learned to respond to every call, even if he is already excited after discovering something, should Jock be allowed off lead to roam again. Treatment by such training is likely to be totally effective in only a few cases. Dogs like Jock may be recalled when just setting off in pursuit of a scent, but still be 'incommunicado' once the prey is in view and running. Other dogs may be controlled if pursuing a cat, or even starting to chase a rabbit which hasn't yet spotted them. But once a fast-moving or darting retreat has begun, as practised by every squirrel in every suburban park, the dog will still be very hard to stop using verbal intervention with even well-taught commands or the prospect of reward.

# Pre-conditioning avoidance reactions in dogs

Dog Training Discs are five small brass saucer-shaped discs which create a unique sound that is different to any other common everyday sound. Designed by my great friend and fellow APBC member John Fisher, it is no understatement to say that the methodology that John has pioneered with his Dog Training Discs is revolutionising dog training and canine behaviour therapy. John has taught me more about dogs than anyone else I know, but the development of the Dog Training Discs and the techniques that go with them has been his master stroke . . . and no, I'm not on commission!

Unlike other sound-creating objects like keys, pebbles in a can, or throwing chains, Dog Training Discs are designed to be picked up, carried and put down again without making a noise – so they can be used at exactly the right moment to interrupt unwanted canine behaviour without inadvertently causing reactions at any other time. First the dog is introduced to the sound away from any immediate problem behaviour, until an avoidance response has been achieved. This is usually performed by dropping a few favourite titbits on the floor and dropping or gently throwing the discs somewhere near, but not at, the dog as he stops to eat the food. After two or three such experiences, but often after only one, the dog becomes wary of approaching the food, and may look a little confused. At this point the owners reassure the dog and call him to them encouragingly. Thereafter the dog remains  wary of the food but also, and most importantly, continues to turn to the owner for support whenever the distinctive sound of the Discs is heard.

Once the dog has been 'tuned-in' to the sound, its scope can be broadened and used to interrupt any unwanted behaviour. The sound always stops the dog doing what it was originally going to do, and happily centres its attention onto the owner, who can then offer it a more rewarding alternative behaviour to perform. The dog soon learns that its own action creates an unusual reaction – the sound of the Discs - and so it steadily (and sometimes immediately) learns to avoid repeating that action in future.  More than this, the dog is programmed to turn to its owner for reassurance, an act that is constantly reinforced by the owners kindness of word and perhaps occasional food rewards. This approach is entirely different to being startled, or worse, punished by the owner. There, the reaction comes after the unwanted behaviour and is seen by the dog to be directly administered by the owner and, as it is usually not related to its actions, rarely reshapes the dog's motivations for the future.

Dogs do not habituate to the sound of the Discs, providing they first used to precondition their reactions and then introduced to reshape a particular problem behaviour.  Other aversion therapy methods based on sound such as the use of personal alarms or thrown cans filled with pebbles simple startle the dog, and  invariably cause him or her to associate the sound with the owner,  thus decreasing their bond and the dog's willingness to be directed.

Because the sound is consistent in tone, it can be used effectively by any member of the family once the dog is fully 'tuned-in'. Owners with more than one dog should introduce them to each individually, as some are more responsive than others, and because the success of the response depends on individual preconditioning. Hence the Discs are not recommended for use in a dog training club environment.

The techniques made possible by the use of Dog Training Discs can be used to overcome a variety of training and behaviour problems and will be referred to frequently and unashamedly henceforth in this book. As well as instructions for use and 'tuning-in', they are supplied with an alphabetical behaviour fault-finder and a separate training manual. To avoid confusion, it's always advisable to concentrate their use on the most urgent problem in the dog initially, progressing to other minor problems later, after the dog's response to them has become nicely established.

For the owner of a problem dog, the preconditioning of an avoidance reaction with improved owner dependence (see later in this chapter) can prove an invaluable way of re-shaping any unwanted aspects of the dog's behaviour and of avoiding potential confrontation. At any point where discipline is required or the dog is behaving inappropriately, the owner can interrupt without having to challenge or threaten the dog, or put himself at any risk of reprisal. The dog happily stops whatever it is doing and turns to the owner for its next move, which will be an acceptable and rewarding alternative.

The main criteria for success using preconditioned avoidance techniques are an accurate initial diagnosis of the problem behaviour, good conditioning of the dog's relationship with the owners and effective preconditioning of the avoidance reaction with the Dog Training Discs and judicious use thereof.

# Chasing of cars, joggers, cats, bicycles, skateboards, etc

*Dear Mr Neville*

*Cosmo, our Border Collie, chases everything that moves. No horses, joggers, skateboarders, cyclists or even cars are safe in our road. Naturally we try to keep him in, but we are very worried that he will get injured or killed if he escapes. We're worried too that he may injure a child as skateboarders are his favourite and he has already drawn blood on our own son's ankle after a mad chase. We've tried being nice to Cosmo, and hitting him, but nothing seems to stop him other than keeping him indoors. We don't have any sheep for him to herd in south east London and though we try to give him lots of play and ball chasing to use up his energies, we wondered if is there another way to treat him and make him safer in the community?*

*Yours sincerely*

*Simon and Georgina Willis*

Movement, and sometimes sound, are the key triggers to most predatory canine chase problem behaviour, and Border Collies seem particularly adept at identifying a whole range of suitable targets. Suitable for them, of course, because the quarry keeps moving quickly and usually speeds up to avoid being snapped at in the case of joggers or cyclists. It is easy to suggest that Border Collies may be better off being kept in more open spaces than London suburbia and given the job of herding sheep for which they have been selected over the years. But the fact is that most Border Collies, even in cities, don't chase everything that moves and most can live quite happily without such purposeful and directed activity. Such problems are also not limited to the breed, and anyone who has ever driven through Ireland will know that the national pastime for dogs is chasing cars. One brakes in panic at the first few, but thereafter keeps driving and lets the dog tire himself out and go home to wait for the next passing victim.

Punishment after the event, or even shortly after the chase has begun, is never effective in reforming such dogs as the motivation for the behaviour is far too deep rooted to be counter conditioned so late. And there was never a better example than an Irish working collie I met a couple of years ago while driving past a farm near Kilkenny. I stopped abruptly to avoid a collision. She was clearly experienced, having lost a leg in a previous encounter with an English tourist! Not that one would know she was 25 per cent down on legs from the speed at which she chased me. Indeed, so intent was she, that I could only presume she was even more determined having lost a leg to a car, to get her revenge on every other one that subsequently turned the bend past the farm .What she showed was that even the ultimate pain of being run over had not reformed her motivation to chase one bit, and so there is precious little chance that late or subsequent punishment of the dog can be used successfully to treat these problems.

However, aversion therapy is the most successful tactic to employ with the predatory chasing dog, no matter what it is that the dog prefers to chase. It's all a question of timing. For dogs such as Cosmo and Jock, if they don't reform with frequent controlled exposure and training, it is simply no use waiting for the problem to occur and trying to deal with it afterwards. Instead the dog must be deliberately put into the position of being challenged with the very stimulus that prompts the chase, but under controlled conditions. This will call for volunteers. A willing victim jogger, cyclist, car plus driver or skateboarder must be found and asked to jog, cycle, drive or skateboard deliberately just past the dog, coming from behind or from the side, rather than heading towards the dog from in front. With the exception of the car, which should travel noisily and at no more than about 10 miles per hour for safety, the victim should be at maximum speed as he passes the dog. (For treating traffic chasers, recreation grounds often afford better opportunity for safer, controlled exposure as the dog can be walked along the road protected by a fence between the grass of the park and the road itself). The dog is restrained and relaxed on a normal collar and long training lead, or extendable lead. The owner should also be as relaxed as possible while walking the dog gently along. As the 'prey' shoots past, everyone knows the dog will set off in chase, and the instant he sets off is when the owner reacts. The best tactic for Collies at least, and as a first effort with all such dogs, is to use the loud, startling piercing noise from a rape alarm as the dog sets off. The aim is for the dog to associate the frightening noise with the sudden arrival of the prey, be startled out of the chase and come to pair the stimulus of the moving target with unpleasant consequences (negative reinforcement of the noise), rather than the positive reinforcement of the 'joy of the chase'. Most dogs, however, respond far better by being pre-conditioned to the sound of 'Dog Training Discs' developed for treating this problem and for general training by fellow APBC member, John Fisher. If there is something that the dog has previously been mildly frightened by, such as the odd dog which is afraid of the squeak of some toys, then this can also usefully be employed as an aversion. With correct timing, most dogs will immediately pull up short on their chase. Many will be rather frightened, and it is at this point that the owner must be kind and comfort the dog, the vital second stage of the preconditioning stop engendered by the Dog Training Discs. The dog is quickly but calmly rewarded with titbits or grasping his favourite toy and  the calm relaxed behaviour becomes paired with the movement of the victim.

Once again, no punishment or heavy handed tactics are necessary. In fact it is vital that the owner continues to remain as calm as possible during the whole process to avoid fuelling the dog's excitement even further and, is seen as a 'port in the storm' for the frightened dog. The unpleasant noise is ideally issued by the owner or a close-by assistant as this enables it to be timed more accurately.  However, a few dogs, perhaps those with true killer instincts rather than an easily aroused chasing instinct, respond better to noise coming from the 'victim'.  For best results, these dogs need to be allowed  almost close enough to bite before the aversion is employed.

Many chasers, especially the often very sound-sensitive Collies and first Collie crossbreeds reform totally after just one or two such controlled exposures using the Dog Training Discs to moving targets, and many quickly and simply learn to run to their owners for reassurance as soon as any of the old favoured victims appear, so great is the association of them with the new unpleasant consequences. Once again, occasional practice in a variety of environments and novel situations will ensure that the new association is retained by the dog and doesn't become extinguished through lack of exposure.

# Herding behaviour

*Dear Mr Neville*

*My Border Collie, Shep, is a great one for herding the family around. He does this in the garden with the kids and indoors too from time to time. While I realize he's only treating them like the sheep he was bred to work with, I've become a little worried because Shep has now started to snap at the kids' ankles if they are won't move in the direction he wants them to. He doesn't snap at my ankles or my wife's but the kids have a couple of scratches and are a little frightened of playing with him. How can we stop Shep doing this without upsetting him?*

*Yours sincerely*

*Barry Gorman*

Collies, as we have seen, are often stimulated by movement, but they can also bring a couple of interesting specific behaviour patterns to us. One is the famous 'Collie eye', that powerful tense stare used to fix sheep and hold them in a set position. When Collies are kept as pets, this can often be transferred onto the cat and help keep the dog amused for hours! Cats, being much more intelligent and versed in the art of self-defence than sheep, tend to ignore such psychological tactics, though if they run away, are always likely to be chased by the ever-eager dog. More rarely, Collies may give the 'eye' to other dogs in the home and, especially out on walks, to other dogs, who may then fall victim to the full repertoire of the sheepdog's herding skills of crouch, stalk, dart, crouch, stare, chase, herd and snap! I used to hike frequently in the Lake District in north west England and often encountered a couple of working sheepdogs whose joy it was, when 'off duty' to chase and herd we hikers, snapping at our ankles and trying to corral us into the corner of the dry stone walls. Fortunately we all wore heavy hiking boots and gaiters, so their ankle snapping had no effect. They would give up chasing us after a while to go back down the hill and wait for the next party to pass.

Another city-bound Collie I once treated used to escape from time to time and pop along to the local school to round up and herd the children in to a corner of the playground. I have also even seen one Collie in London who, deprived of any suitable amount of activity and exercise, would carry out the same routines with the furniture in the fifth floor flat, clearly imagining them to be be moving and darting about the flat to head them off from different vantage points. Being a 'natural', and because his lifestyle was so obviously unsuitable for him, I suggested he was rehomed to a farmer friend of mine, where he now lives a totally contented life helping to work the cattle rather than sheep or furniture.

Barry's problem with Shep is clearly one of misplaced 'natural' activity that is going a little far. Shep doesn't snap at the heels of the adults of the family perhaps because their status is better defined as being high up in the family hierarchy and so beyond challenge, but probably also because they do not charge about so excitedly as children. Fortunately the problem with the kids should resolve well with exactly the same aversion or preconditioning treatment prescribed for the chasers in the preceding section. First Shep is preconditioned with the Dog Training Discs. Then he should be restrained on a long lead by Barry or his wife and the kids asked to run past. While the dog is calm, he is rewarded with praise and titbits, and even his crouch and stare may be tolerated, but if he sets off in chase to herd the kids, the Discs used to distract him. Once again, he should be rewarded for stopping and turning to his owners. Additionally it will help if the kids can participate in training Shep, especially in teaching a response to the 'down' command, as this could then be used at any time Shep gets over-excited when playing with them. This, and other measures described later in this chapter will also help define them as being of higher rank in the family in the same way as their parents and so not approachable in this manner by the bottom-of-the-heap dog Shep!

# Sheep chasing

*Dear Mr Neville*

*Sabre, our two-year-old German Shepherd Dog, is a sheep chaser. We only discovered this on a recent holiday in Wales. We let him off the lead as we normally do in the park at home but, instead of sniffing around and generally keeping fairly close to us, he lifted his head, caught the scent of the sheep and ran off out of the field. We chased him calling him to come back, but he ignored us and leapt the gate into the next field full of sheep, where he chased them around and around. Fortunately he didn't actually catch any and eventually Dad managed to jump on him and put him back on the lead. We told him off thoroughly but if we'd let him off the lead again, we're sure he would have gone looking for more sheep to chase. We know that farmers will shoot dogs seen chasing their sheep, but can this behaviour be treated as we would love to still be able to take Sabre on holiday with us to Wales in future if he can be safe? Otherwise, we'll have to leave him in kennels and our holiday wouldn't be so much fun.*

*Yours sincerely*

*Joanna and Emma Carson*

Sheep chasing is one of the most publicized and heinous 'crimes' of the pet dog. Some dogs will actually kill sheep by throttling them, others go on orgies of ripping and disemboweling. In a few short minutes, a single large dog or, worse, a temporary group of dogs formed into a hunting pack, can cause devastation we would scarce believe of our pets when curled up by the fireside.

Farmers are naturally very concerned about the scale of the carnage which amounted to over 10,000 head of livestock being savaged in 1989 and insurance claims exceeding £1 million. Small wonder many farmers will happily, and justifiably, shoot any dog found off a lead among the sheep, sometimes even if the owner is present. While there are trigger-happy farmers, there is little doubt that they have just cause to be so reactive. Even if the dog is only a chaser and not a killer, the sheep can be so frightened as to suffer cardiac arrest, drop from exhaustion if pursued relentlessly and, perhaps commonest of all, abort their lambs if harried by dogs when pregnant. So a dog loose in a field of sheep can spell disaster and farmers may shoot first and ask questions later. Similarly, horse riders are often the victims of the chasing dog, with accompanying risk to rider, horse and anyone in the way of the rearing or bolting horse.

Typically, in sheep country the problems are not caused by local pets. Their owners tend to be well aware of the risks and get their dogs used to the presence and movement of sheep early on. Those which don't habituate are usually kept tied up permanently or disposed of quickly to avoid problems with the neighbouring farmers. Sheep-worrying problems are more usually caused by dogs which, like the Carsons' Sabre, only encounter sheep when beyond the puppy stage or occasionally on the family holiday away from the city. Already stimulated by the exciting new array of smells around him and the change of scenery, the dog soon gets the whiff of sheep, and on rushing up to investigate one, is delighted to find that it runs like hell. One bobbing bottom may be enough to excite the dog into a predatory chase, but the arousal is even greater if, as sheep tend to do, lots of panicking bobbing bottoms all join together and veer across the field. Faced with so many moving targets, the dog may go on a snapping ripping orgy like the fox in the hen house, stopping only when too exhausted to chase further.

For dogs fortunate enough to be recaptured, the prospect of treatment may not be paramount in the minds of their shocked and exhausted owners. Responsibly they may decide that the dog will never again be taken to where there are sheep, or never let off the lead again if he is. For others keen to enjoy their annual holiday with their dog or those who live close to sheep, treatment of the dog may be a question of life or death for both the dog and the sheep. The permission of the farmer is clearly a prerequisite for treatment using controlled exposure techniques, and this permission may not be forthcoming at certain times of year, such as when the sheep are pregnant or have lambs at foot. But there is no other way to treat the problem other than by taking the dog to meet sheep, being safely prepared for his reaction and knowing what to do as he reacts.

Some dogs can be successfully treated using exactly the same techniques as for jogger, car and cycle chasers, though it usually helps to be even more relaxed with the dog wandering quite some distance at will from the owner, though firmly attached by a long training lead. If the owners are in any doubt as to the speed of their reactions, or the dog is particularly powerful, they should seek assistance and ensure that the dog is muzzled during the treatment, so that if he does break free, he at least won't be able to bite the sheep. Ideally, however, the dog should be relaxed and walked under as near normal conditions as possible. A relaxed calm approach, heading directly towards the sheep is essential, but sharp wits are needed to react as soon as the dog makes a lunge towards them. The noise or other aversion should be employed immediately, and the owner should position himself between the dog and sheep as quickly as possible to break the dog's eye contact with them and encourage him to focus attention on his reassuring owner. As soon as the dog is calm the owner should repeat the process, trying all the time to keep the dog calm as they approach ever closer to the sheep. Gradually the dog should accept the proximity of the sheep with a progressively muted reaction, until finally being able to be walked among them without reacting.

Obviously, the more used to dogs the sheep are, the less likely they are to panic at the sight of the dog and so not magnify his interest just as the owner is trying to keep him calm. However, the old farmer's trick of taking this a step further and putting the dog in a small pen with a tough aggressive ram to beat him up for a while is unlikely to give lasting results, if any, for the average dog. Doubtless, such terror tactics have worked with some dogs. And a stoic, tough cat can often help reform the ardent cat-chasing dog with a swipe of a pawful of sharp nose-rippers and those dogs which are so impressionable would probably have got the message much more quickly and kindly with a little controlled exposure. But the sight of all those moving bottoms across an open field will still be a huge irresistible stimulus to chase, even for treated dogs. For most pet dogs, the opportunity to meet sheep and be reminded of their schooling just cannot occur frequently

117

enough to achieve lasting extinction of their chasing, killing and hunting behaviour.

Another tactic of the farmer is to tie a rotting old dead lamb around the dog's collar for a few days unpleasant experience that it deters the dog from having anything to do with sheep ever again. To the scavenging side of the dog, it must simply be frustrating being unable to eat the rotting carcass! Like most old wives' tales, the method probably has had an occasional success, perhaps coincidentally, but it has no foundation in learning theory for dogs and is unlikely to do much to reform the sheep chaser other than slow him down a bit with the weight of the carcass.

Timing is the crucial aspect in treatment of the sheep chaser, or cat chaser, for that matter. Where more severe tactics are employed, it's still the timing rather than the strength of the intervention that determines the success of treatment. We know that severe and painful consequences to a given behaviour pattern in the dog can remove it or modify it, it's just that there are few circumstances that warrant truly painful intervention from us – most problems can be treated much more gently. At risk of being boring by referring to that fount of all reference for canine behaviour problems, my own inimitable Bandit failed totally to respond to the usual anti-sheep chasing treatment, even as a highly trainable and quite eager-to-please young dog. He was treated successfully by pure chance while being walked in beautiful Glencoe in Scotland. Once I had surveyed the scene and failed to spot the only sheep for about ten miles, Bandit was duly allowed off the lead to have a good run and flush up a few birds. Having known there was a sheep not far away since we'd got out of the car, Bandit set off in hot pursuit and drove the poor creature some yards before, on encountering a fast stream, it turned sharp left and ran straight in front of me. I guessed that somewhere not far behind would be my beloved dog and so stuck out a hopeful leg as he passed. With a foul of sufficiently disgraceful proportions to earn a red card on the soccer pitch, Bandit was sent sprawling headlong into the freezing torrent. I ran downstream to where I could catch him and hauled him out to receive the grateful thanks for pleasures received by owners of all wet dogs – a good shaking over! But Bandit saw his sudden misfortune not as an intervention from me, deserving of a growl or a bite in response, but as the secret weapon of the sheep he'd been chasing. He's never chased one again, and now looks slightly worried as he walks through a field of them off-lead and tucked behind me for protection. That was quite a holiday for poor Bandit. I saw genuine fear in his eyes for the first and only time as I dragged him up an ice wall on Ben Nevis in the mist a few days later. But he made it up, and ran down, and got the last word by only taking a day to rest up after his 5000 ft climb. I took three and had to suffer from the hyperactivity of a very fit but largely unexercised dog for the two extra days!

With the dog that has failed to respond to the mildly startling tactics of sound or water, and for which a freezing torrent in Scotland in late autumn cannot be arranged, something more severe may be required, and justified to prevent suffering of the sheep and even death of the sheep and dog itself. Only under such circumstances of animal welfare could the use of electric shock-collars be justified and, even then, it is questionable whether such tactics are ethical in the case of Sabre. Given the lack of opportunity for Sabre to meet sheep for most of the year and compound any learning, it may be wiser simply to kennel him during the family holiday or keep him strictly on the lead in hill country. But for dogs likely to encounter sheep more frequently, the electric shock-collar may just about be justified. Sadly these horrific implements are used in the United States and in many countries of Europe, as tools of the trade for dog training, both in basic obedience and more specific task training. Every time the dog makes a 'mistake' it receives a shock and so learns what not to do, presumably only leaving those things it should do as free to continue without pain. David Wilkins MRCVS, Chief Veterinary Officer of the RSPCA in the United Kingdom, is rightly concerned about the use of such equipment. If used for basic training instead of usually effective gentler methods, electric shock-collars could cause substantial and unnecessary suffering to a dog sufficient to render the trainer or owner liable to prosecution under the British 1911 Protection of Animals Act. The RSPCA would therefore certainly consider bringing prosecutions against anyone using shock-collars for basic obedience, or any other form of training, given sufficient evidence to support the case. However, David agrees that, used correctly under the supervision of a veterinary surgeon, and by extension of referral, a qualified animal behaviourist, such equipment may be used ethically to treat sheep chasing in dogs in cases where the dog has failed to respond to milder forms of treatment and where permanent confinement or euthanasia of the dog are seen as the only safe alternatives.

The treatment, which I have carried out reluctantly, but successfully, on a small number of dogs involves the same basic approach as when using milder aversions. First the dog is accustomed to wearing a 'dummy' collar for a few days and kept well away from any sheep. The collar is then replaced with the real thing, a collar to which a rechargable box containing a receiver and shock imparting circuitry is attached. The shock is delivered between two electrodes which nestle against the dog's neck, and the intensity of the shock can be varied by altering the resistance across the electrodes. The collar must be quite tight on the dog to ensure adequate contact, and the electrodes are usually dampened a little to ensure that the current flows. It all sounds a bit barbaric, and it is. The shock is set off by the operator of the hand held radio sender unit, and will function from 200 metres and more away if required, so enabling the operator to be well away from the scene in case the dog starts to associate the presence of any one individual with the shock. Ideally, the owner has control of the dog on the lead and the behaviourist, perhaps lurking out of sight in the bushes, has control of the sender unit.

The instant the dog sets off in chase, he hears a tone emitted from a small speaker on the collar, followed immediately by a shock. The minimum shock is employed to achieve the desired effect, which is that the dog yelps in pained surprise and stops the chase. Immediately the dog is called or gently pulled towards the owner to be comforted. As soon as the dog is calm, he is led towards the sheep again and the process repeated, though after one or two such exposures with the shock adjusted to the right strength, simply the sound that precedes the shock is sufficient to cause the dog to stop chasing the sheep. Steadily the dog is allowed more freedom among the sheep, but only let off-lead with a muzzle on for absolute safety and when he has failed to react to the sheep at all on several exposures. Ideally, as he associates the shock with the presence of the sheep, the dog should look worried on approach, and perhaps even be trying to run away from them before he is allowed off the lead in the same field.

Such is the distressing nature of the shock that virtually every dog treated with the shock-collar can be expected to respond successfully, though for some, the preceding tone isn't sufficiently associated with the impending shock to be really useful. For others, the attack is successfully blocked with every shock but the motivation to chase sheep is unaffected by the experience. This usually applies to the breeds such as Bull Terriers which were previously bred for fighting or baiting and for whom pain often serves only to excite or is not felt as much by dogs without such thick and protected necks. They, perhaps, are best kept away from sheep altogether or must wear the collar on every walk near sheep. Others, like Bandit before his dunking, learned that when wearing the collar, the sheep could shock him, but when not, they were strangely disarmed and he could chase at will without painful repercussions. For his ilk, the wearing of the dummy collar on all walks acts as sufficient reinforcement, though most dogs aren't quite so perceptive and do as we wish, quickly associating the sheep with the likelihood of receiving a shock if they advance on them. For the conditioning to persist, frequent exposure is required – this may not be practical, as the treatment would have to be repeated before going on holiday every year to be effective.

To cite one case where this treatment was both justified and effective, I remember treating a large black Newfoundland called Cook prior to him going to Australia with his owners to live in the heart of sheep station country. Cook was not only a sheep chaser, he had actually recently managed to kill one, and he quickly demonstrated his intentions when we first exposed him to sheep during our meeting. Despite his bulk, he was astoundingly quick and initially failed to respond to the shock, mainly because of lack of proper connection of the electrodes to his neck through his extremely thick coat. Thankfully the 'victim' sheep escaped and we hung on to Cook and then started again with improved success. His owners wrote to me some time later from Australia to say that Cook had successfully integrated into the community and that all was well as he hadn't chased a single sheep.

However justified this treatment may be in some circumstances, I am pleased to say that I have only had to use it on a few occasions as most sheep chasers I have seen have responded to much milder forms of intervention such as using Dog Training Discs. The only other circumstances where the use of the shock-collar can possibly be justified is as the ultimate aversion, when all else has failed, in the treatment of dogs which are extremely aggressive towards all other dogs, and after one has given up attempting to socialize them. The aim of treatment has become to inhibit the aggression, and render the dog safe around others, rather than to teach social manners. It usually works. There has also been one occasion where the shock-collar was successfully used a last resort to treat a tail-chasing and self-mutilating German Shepherd Dog after he had failed to respond to all other treatment and was starting to divert his aggression onto the owner if he tried to intervene. Again, the shock-collar was only employed as a last resort in these cases and because the only alternative was euthanasia of the patient.

In all such cases there has been obvious benefit to the dog and to third parties, canine, ovine or human, but hopefully our knowledge of such problems will advance rapidly and enable us to treat them without such last-gasp and painful tactics in future. That the shock collar is presently the last resort for treatment of predatory chasing problems does indicate the strength of the motivation to hunt lying dormant in some pet dogs, and one we should all bear in mind before disappearing to the hills for a weekend in the countryside normally populated only by sheep.

# Maternal aggression

*Dear Mr Neville*

*As soon as our Corgi, Queenie (what else?!) had her litter of six puppies she turned from being a typical Corgi, a bit hot tempered but basically a lot of fun, into a very hot tempered mother of no fun at all. Even we could not approach her puppies, and received a deep growl if we so much as went into the room to feed her. If we persisted she turned into a raging bull, leaping to her feet and really snarling at us from half out of her bed. She has improved a little as the puppies have got older, and we wondered whether she will return to normal when they're weaned or homed or whether having the puppies has turned her this way for good?*

*Yours sincerely*

*Jane and Donald Evans*

Aggressive defence of puppies is another form of aggression which is acceptable because we understand it, even though the scale of the previously friendly family bitch's reaction would be intolerable in a pet at any other time. The vast majority of bitches don't defend their puppies as vigorously as Queenie but when they do, it can be one of the most pronounced types of aggression we can ever see in our pets. Thankfully, the bitch is unlikely to leave the nest to launch an attack on any passer-by, but the half-in, half-out, threatening stance with young puppies trying desperately to hang onto nipples is typical. The Evans may have to let Queenie do all the work unassisted, give up stroking her for a couple of weeks and simply leave her food and water in the same room and her aggression will be contained around the nest. It would be unwise to turf Queenie out for a pee in the garden as this will obviously provoke her desire to defend her little genetic investments. Instead, the door should simply be left open from time to time and Queenie will dart out to stretch her legs, do the necessaries and, pace back in to her litter.

But, while this protective aggression may be acceptable, and the owners are safe if they don't insist on approaching the litter for some time, it does become a little more difficult to live with when there are no real puppies! Many bitches will collect toys or other small objects such as cushions or slippers from around the house and treat them as a pretend litter during phantom pregnancies and defend them just as vigorously as a real one against the confused family. Reproduction causes all sorts of new behaviour patterns to appear even in a bitch which has just produced her first litter. She is born with the neural pathways already in place to enable her to alter her behaviour to care for her puppies from birth to independence.

We have touched little on the effect of hormones on the behaviour of the dog thus far, but maternal defence of puppies or pretend ones is almost entirely due to hormonal influence. During pregnancy or, in any case, for two months after ovulation during her oestrous cycle, the hormone progesterone is produced by the bitch to help her body cope with the physiological changes involved with being pregnant and nursing her litter. Progesterone also has a calming influence on many of the areas controlling emotions in the brain, helping usually to reduce activity and generally calm her at this sensitive time. With the birth of the puppies, the level and therefore some of the influence of this hormone is lost, and the bitch may bounce back into becoming highly reactive and easily provoked into emotional expression, including marked protective reactions of her litter to relatively minor or previously tolerated challenges. Such reactions decline as the bitch's hormonal cycle stabilizes again, as the puppies grow up, and handling of puppies or retrieval of long given up slippers and cushions can later be achieved with a little gentle encouragement and assurance that the owners are not about to harm the little things! Until then, it's often a case of providing as secure and quiet a nesting area as possible for Queenie until she seems more relaxed, and quickly sneaking in to clean up and make sure the puppies are okay in those few short moments while she is outside.

With the effects of phantom pregnancy, bitches may not only collect and protect a litter of pretend puppies, they may even produce milk! The vet will often administer hormone treatment to stop the milk flow, and decrease the bitch's interest in the 'puppies'. It will usually help to remove the puppies shortly after the treatment and, if it is not intended to breed from her, to have the bitch spayed as soon as the vet advises and prevent these slightly bizarre fluctuations in behaviour due to cycles of reproductive hormones.

Interestingly, bitches such as Queenie may not respond similarly with every litter. They may be perfectly tolerant of the Evans being more closely involved with her next litter, perhaps having learned that they mean no harm, and could even be beneficial in caring for the puppies in the same way as 'aunties' can help share the load in the dog pack for the hard pressed mother. Then there are other bitches which, far from being over protective, make very poor mothers and neglect or abandon their puppies entirely, forcing us to take on the role of surrogate mother. Here we are propping up incompetence in dogs, for in the wild such poor mothers would never reproduce successfully enough to pass on their incompetence to the next generation. Perhaps the loss of vehement defence of puppies by most bitches also represents a watering down of maternal qualities in the domestic dog and we should be glad to see it persist in the occasional bitch such as Queenie.

## Protective aggression – resources

*Dear Mr Neville*

*Zoot, our Black Labrador X German Shepherd Dog, seems to regard his bed as the Bank of England. He growls and snaps fiercely at us and no-one is allowed within ten feet when he is lying in it, nor to come between him and his bed if he has a mind to go and lie in it! He also steals things from the floor, such as tissues, or handbags off the back of chairs and takes them to his bed to guard. There's simply no getting these things back until Zoot has gone outside or wandered off to another part of the house, which may be hours later. Can we make him less possessive? Telling him off only makes him more angry so we tend to give him a very wide berth indeed when he's in these moods.*

*Yours sincerely*

*John and Betty McCormick*

Many things in life are worth defending, particularly survival resources such as a safe den and food and edible lucky discoveries and, with some dogs, even water. Many dogs also defend possession of toys or other trophies such as tissues and articles belonging to the owners. Much of this trophying behaviour is closely tied to the dominance status of the dog in the family, which will be looked at later in this chapter. Food guarding is often related to the dog's social position as well, but will be covered in greater depth in Chapter 8 on food related problems.

Aggression shown by dogs when guarding their bed is almost as forgivable as puppy-guarding by their mothers. We can sympathize with the desire to defend such a valuable and much used resource and most owners with dogs such as Zoot manage the problem by putting their dog's bed somewhere out of the way of family goings-on and simply leave well alone when the bed is occupied.

With bitches, the desire to guard the bed may be even more pronounced just after a season as the bed may then be seen not just as a resting area, but also as the place where the puppies must be raised and protected. However, in fairness, dogs are just as likely to guard their beds as bitches, in my experience.

Many owners make a rod for their own backs with regard to bed-guarding. Instead of the dog being offered a bed as his den, a place to relax when tired or feeling a little under the weather, it is used as a sin-bin. Every time the dog needs to be reprimanded, he is punished by being sent to bed. Worse than this is that having obeyed the owner, or even having slunk off there on his own after some misdemeanour, the owner follows up and delivers a slap on the backside or a good telling off. What had been a safe haven has then become a place of 'dog's last stand'.

With nowhere else to run and hide and confronted with a serious challenge, dogs like Zoot may have initially growled in self-defence, been walloped again and then had to come out fighting a little way as a last ditch effort for self-preservation. Forever after the bed is no longer a safe haven unless it is defended, and rather than wait for a real challenge, the dog may simply growl at the approach of every passer-by. Look at the dog or move deliberately towards him and a full scale reaction can result, designed to make everyone step back very sharply. With a big dog like Zoot, it works well and he'll easily preserve the sanctity of his den that way.

Treatment may be as simple as removing the dog's bed entirely (when he's not in it of course!) so that he has no resource to guard. He

125

must simply learn to rest and sleep in more open, communal and, therefore, shared areas. Alternatively, the dog's bed can be taken up in the morning and only put down for him last thing at night just prior to shutting the door and saying goodnight. In the morning the dog is likely to leave his bed to say hello, be let out into the garden, or given his breakfast, all of which are usually sufficient distractions to enable removal of the bed without conflict. Unfortunately, some dogs then simply learn to rest in corners and defend them, or are likely to growl whenever resting and so present more of a problem than if they were only to be found in one place when 'taking it easy'. Again these dogs usually require a close look at their general rank and lifestyle for treatment to be effective, rather than dealing with the problem only as it occurs.

Whether withdrawing or limiting access to the bed is effective or not, it is essential, as with all problems of canine aggression, that force or counter-challenge is not employed in treatment. This simply makes matters worse as the dog, already perceiving itself as backed into a valued corner will fight as one might expect, like a cornered rat. However much access is allowed to the bed, the dog must be allowed to rest there undisturbed. The bed must never be used as a place of punishment and, if in the course of other discipline, the dog shoots off to his bed for safety, he mustn't be physically pursued there. He's got the message of the owner's displeasure by retreating, there's no need to compound his submission with a show of further violence.

Instead, the dog should be rewarded for tolerating gradually the closer proximity of people passing and approaching. So, owners should adopt a light friendly attitude, crouch down a little to avoid being seen as large looming challenge and avoid staring at the dog or, even making eye contact with him. Speaking gently to him and only advancing slowly should help reduce the scale of the threat that Zoot perceives in the approach of people. Offering or gently throwing small, tasty and quickly consumable titbits will also help convince him, but larger offerings should be avoided as, if not consumed, they may simply add to his resources to guard. For the same reasons, toys should not be offered as placating gestures. Slowly this approach may diminish the dog's need to guard his bed, but owners should also establish their right to occupy the dog's bed by standing or sitting in it from time to time in front of the dog, while rewarding his acceptance with kind words and titbits. Owners are usually not at risk with this policy as possession is nine-tenths of the battle and, providing there isn't a competitive race to get to the bed, the dog won't challenge the owner in his bed any more than the owner should the dog if the positions are reversed.

Also, the dog should be rewarded for coming off his bed when called. This may have to begin with the owner calling him from the garden and rewarding him with play or a walk. Soon, the dog would respond to being called from the back door and then from an adjacent room to where his bed is. As long as the rewards are immediately received when the dog reaches the owner, he should continue to respond well and should soon tolerate being called off his bed at any time. Though he may still be possessive in his bed if guarding toys or other trophies, at least the ability to call him off has been established in a non-confrontational manner and can hopefully be used to advantage to defuse other situations when the dog may be more entrenched.

Once the dog is a little less sensitive about his bed and more approachable, and any associated dominance problems have been tackled, the problem of trophying can be attended to in greater safety. Objects such as toys and chews may be seen as valuable resources worth defending simply because other dogs or people desire them. Possession implies an increased status, just as we are often possessive about who drives the new car or who operates the remote control for the television, even if we aren't actually interested in what's showing on any of the channels! The desire to defend possession of the control is all the greater if we are in conflict with another member of the family and desperately want to watch a particular programme, and this is also true of possessive behaviour in dogs. The more the owners chase or challenge the dog in an effort to regain the object, the more valuable he perceives it to be and the more insistent he will become about retaining possession. So the first part of treatment is to discontinue any direct confrontation over any trophies, and especially if, like the tissues taken by Zoot, they aren't worth the conflict. If the dog has stolen or discovered your wallet and is busily dribbling on it, or has taken it to his bed to guard just when you need to dash to the wine shop two minutes before it closes, then quicker intervention may be required. In such cases, the dog should be distracted by ringing the doorbell or rattling his food bowl or titbit can in another room. Hopefully these stimuli will be sufficient to make him dart out and forget his trophy. Once shut into another room, the owner can safely return to collect his wallet and make that all important trip. However, though this wins the battle, it does little to alter the war, as the dog may still be motivated to take and guard such things in future.

A general policy of disinterest at the time the dog takes things may make him perceive less advantage in possessing trophies. Ignoring the rumblings from his bed as you pass, aware that your left slipper is nestled between his paws and hidden from view, rather than rising to the 'challenge' will also help, but really the dog needs to be offered some of his favourite trophies under more controlled conditions where the owner can establish an advantage or retain possession. This is best done initially on more neutral ground, perhaps in the garden, where the importance of 'indoor' trophies is reduced and the dog cannot escape, prize in mouth, to a safe defendable area such as his bed or under the furniture. The dog should be restrained on a lead and collar and encouraged in a very light encouraging manner, to sit. Then a relatively large trophy, such as a slipper, should be offered for the dog to take in his mouth . . . but, having got this far, the owner should retain possession and not actually let go of the other end of the trophy. Instead, the dog should be encouraged to let go and relinquish its share of possession, though the owner must be careful not to become involved in any competitive tug-of-war games over the trophy. If the dog won't let go, it should be gently distracted by being walked on, with the owner still hanging on to the end, or distracted with something that will make the dog bark and so let go, like an assistant ringing the door bell. Better still is to offer the dog a better alternative to the object he has, such as a food titbit or possession of a more favoured toy which also involves him opening his mouth to relinquish possession of one object to regain the next. But whatever approach is used, the dog must be rewarded effusively and immediately upon letting go of the first object. Then it's a case of moving indoors to the combat zone and frequently practising with a variety of objects, from those that the dog may rarely have shown interest in, right through to the favourite toy, handbag, tissue, or – the trophy of choice for so many because of the smell associations – dirty underwear belonging to the family.

Usually, once the conflict has been removed and dogs such as Zoot start to perceive greater reward of increased contact with the owner or food, progress is made rapidly and the dog is a much pleasanter house-mate to have around. Until the doorbell rings, that is!

# Protective Aggression – Territory

*'Let dogs delight to bark and bite, for God hath made them so'*
Isaac Watts

*Dear Mr Neville*

*Though he looks a little odd, Scooby, our Jack Russell X German Shepherd Dog (yes it can be done!) is a wonderful family pet, with one exception. As soon as he hears unfamiliar footsteps approaching our door, or the doorbell rings or the postman or bin men arrive, he becomes a total maniac. True, we've never been burgled, but his reactions are now becoming costly and even dangerous. If we don't keep him out of the way when the postman arrives he'll shred the mail and has already demolished one of those wire basket mail protectors. He barks continuously with a horrible high pitched and repetitive note and rushes about furiously, first half way up the stairs, then to the window and then back to the door in the hope of inflicting GBH on the unfortunate visitor. No amount of yelling will shut him up and, now, if we try to grasp his collar to hold him back, he's actually bitten us on two occasions. He will relax if the caller is a member of the family or someone well known to him but otherwise he would bite any visitor, I'm sure. Indeed, it's only down to luck that he hasn't already connected with a few callers. Now we have a notice on the door saying 'Please wait while we put the dog away'. Fortunately most people don't mind and can see the funny side, but even once they're safely in, we daren't let Scooby out from the utility room and can hear him yelling away the whole time our guests are with us. We know he's only trying to protect us but how on earth do we instil some discretion into him?*

*Yours sincerely*

*Joan and Brian Greenwood*

Probably the most common difficulty encountered by dog owners, though not always severe or frequent enough to warrant referral to a behaviourist, is the dog that takes its guarding role of the family home too seriously.  The dog's willingness to protect our den was probably one of the fundamental reasons why it became such a close companion for us and is, in our increasingly violent times, still much valued for this trait. We have even developed certain breeds such as the German Shepherd Dog or Dobermann specifically for this purpose and others have the propensity for guarding highly installed in their genes. And, of course, most of us value the extra feeling of security at home that our dogs can bring us, even if it comes as a free extra to his main function of providing companionship or specific work as a gun dog, for example.

Few of us have to teach the dog when to stop barking and let us take over the role of defence of home base as they naturally give way to the more dominant, advancing animal.  They quickly learn by watching us just who is non-threatening and to be allowed across the threshold into the den, who is non-threatening but not sufficiently well known or on important enough business to be let in, and who is attempting to enter against our will and deserving of a little repulsion. And when we are absent, most dogs will assume the authoritative role and defend our homes by barking at strange noises until they go away, or, in some cases, severely attacking those who ignore the warning. A few don't carry the threat through and seem to accept anyone once they are inside.  There are also numerous cartoons of the traitor dog pointing out the safe to the burglar but, by and large, dogs fulfil their self-appointed role very well indeed for us.

And for those dogs which do become a little over-excited when the postman or milkman arrives, it's really not too much of a hardship to usher the maniac temporarily into a room away from the front door while we conduct any necessary business.  Inconvenient and noisy perhaps, but also clearly letting any undesirable, who might just be 'casing the joint', know that there is a dog to get past if they want to get their hands on the family jewels. Often the over-territorial dog is a very affectionate pet towards his owners and the closeness of the relationship probably contributes to his desire to defend the home. But for many dogs the daily arrival of the postman and milkman becomes almost a predictable game.  Many start to get agitated well in advance and pace up and down in anticipation of the huge assault on the door. After all, every time the postman calls, the dog threatens him with blue murder and the postman usually goes away quickly in response thus reinforcing the dog's actions. The dog isn't to know that he's just done his job of delivering the mail and has no further need to hang around!  Some dogs do redirect their aggression onto the mail as it is pushed through the door and, with absolutely no selection, tear bills and cheques to pieces in a few frenzied seconds. A few shredded letters are usually all we need to put up a stout collection basket behind the letter box, or an American style mail tube by the gate and so keep our post intact.

Sadly, if the dog is outside and has free access to the front entrance, it may be the postman who gets shredded. Indeed, while dogs are the traditional number one enemy of the postman, it is no laughing matter when over 6000 attacks are reported annually. Corgis are singled out (sorry ma'am, but I bet you don't have to get your own post!) as a particular menace by Eddie McTigue, Bradford Branch Secretary to the Union of Communication Workers in the UK. 'The bloody things'll take a chunk out of your ankle,' he says, and it's often quoted that the smaller breeds, especially terriers, are more feared than some of the larger, more traditional guarding breeds by burglars – albeit that those asked were failed burglars doing time in prison! Many owners of such highly territorial dogs fail to take proper precautions and keep their dog safely inside or away from the front access to their house and, as a result, find that their local postman declines to deliver their mail, and rightly so. More than a few clients have contacted me only after their mail stops arriving and on going to their local post office to complain, find it neatly piled up awaiting collection, marked 'Dog at Large' by the postman.

Clearly there is duty on us all to keep our dogs under control around our homes, yet here lies the difficulty – you don't keep a dog and bark yourself. The dog locked in the utility room as soon as the door bell rings serves no protective function whatsoever to protect his owner against the assailant on the doorstep. The hyper-excited dog, rushing madly around barking, may be as likely to bite the restraining hand of his owner as he is the attacker, is worse still.

Then there are the often extremely nasty problems of dogs who threaten or even attack and bite our friends when we have welcomed them into the home, or who pin them to walls or keep them sat in armchairs with highly threatening displays if we leave the room for a moment and hand the responsibility of protection of the den back to the dog for a while. Other nasty cases I have treated have concerned dogs which haven't recognized all members of the family as having rights of access to their own home and have aggressively tried to deter these members of their own 'pack' from entering their own house. So, on the one hand, we want and perhaps need our dogs to be territorial and to deter threats against our property while, at the same time, we expect them not to be over zealous about it, to recognize who is acceptable and who isn't, and to let us take over instantly once they have raised the alarm. Such demands are bound to be unrealistic for many dogs, and many more will require specific attention and training by us if we are to bring their territorial aggression under our safe control.

The most important feature of treating the over-protective dog is to remain calm at all times during treatment. This may seem a little difficult if one is dealing with a wildly rushing dog with an excited set of teeth flashing in all directions like Scooby's, but the point for Joan and Brian to remember is that if they try to shout the dog down into being quiet, he will simply think that they are barking along with him and that they are equally as intent on dispelling the invader as he is. The result is that next time the door bell rings, he will perceive even greater challenge because of the disruption it causes to everyone, and so he will become even more excited. And if Joan or Brian were to smack Scooby in an effort to discipline him into being calmer, the de-stabilising effect would be even greater as the arrival of visitors would become associated with the owners' aggression towards him – all the more reason to bark louder and earlier to make the enemy back away as fast as possible. Grabbing Scooby once he is already highly aroused to gain physical control would be seen as a restriction on his efforts to defend the place, and without realizing just who he is biting, he may simply lash out defensively and to regain the mobility he needs to fulfil his intentions.

So just how should Joan and Brian treat this problem in their otherwise friendly and lovable family dog? The answer, as with all behaviour problems, is to think ahead rather than trying to deal with the problem as it arises. Once Scooby is excited, one can only ever hope to control him on that particular occasion, and there is little hope of restructuring his motivation to behave in better ways for the future as by the time Scooby's owners intervene, they are already too late. Scooby has already been successful in barking and starting to dash around and get excited before he was brought under control.

Treatment can however, be surprisingly successful and quick if the owners think ahead, invest a little in some appropriate equipment and arrange for a supply of calm volunteers to act as mock callers to the house.

First, to facilitate quick intervention when callers arrive, the dog is fitted with a medium-length trailing lead to wear permanently around the house for a while. Initially he may get a little caught up in it and look a little impaired in his movements, but dogs soon get used to the idea after a day or so. The lead can be grabbed and the dog brought under physical control far more safely if he is prone to showing when the owners need to intervene. Taking a chomp at his owner's hand may not be intentional, but it's just as painful as a deliberate bite! As well as keeping the owner's hand out of the line of fire, the lead means that Scooby can be restrained quickly from dashing up and down excitedly. This is important, as the dog's excitable activity is self-reinforcing. The more active he is, the more excitable he becomes and the more adrenaline is released, the more excited he becomest. If the dog gets particularly nasty when excited at the prospect of someone knocking on the door, then he should be fitted with a comfortable lightweight muzzle to wear around the house as well. This not only makes the dog safer, it also means that the owner can approach the excited dog far more confidently and bring matters under control much quicker.

As well as continuing to practise Scooby's basic training in 'sit', 'stay' and 'down', the Greenwoods should now invest a little time in training him to sit in a corner in the hallway or other convenient room close to the front door. Naturally this is best done when there are no visitors waiting at the door and, as ever, using kind reward-based techniques practised frequently, with all members of the family sharing the job. It is essential that when Scooby is given the command 'corner', that he goes there willingly and enthusiastically in anticipation of the pleasures of a tit-bit, favourite toy or praise, and not out of duty or more simply because he views the owners as being cross with him.

Once Scooby has got the idea, the Greenwoods should ask a series of volunteers, beginning with friends or relations well-known and liked by Scooby, to call at the house at pre-arranged times. The advantage of using friends is that they will not be upset if they are left standing on the doorstep for a while as the Greenwoods deal with Scooby and, once the door is opened, Scooby should relax quickly on recognizing them. Just prior to their arrival, the Greenwoods should keep Scooby close by them, but otherwise be as relaxed as possible. To prevent enhancing the already excessive desire to protect his family, the Greenwoods should also be rather off-hand towards their dog in the moments prior to his anticipated eruption.

As soon as Scooby hears the footsteps of the visitor, or the doorbell rings, he will, as ever, explode into a cacophony of barking and attempt to hurtle towards the door, or to his favourite vantage point. Ideally, the owners will be prepared enough to grab the lead before he gets there but, if not, they should quickly but calmly approach him and pick up the lead. They shouldn't become excited themselves, and no matter how great the temptation, they shouldn't yell 'shut up', or anything else for that matter. With some dogs, simply taking control with the lead is sufficient to calm them appreciably because they are used to the owner directing them outdoors and will happily then let them do so indoors as well ... however, few owners of over-protective dogs will be so lucky!

We know that shouting at the dog will either fall on deaf ears or only contribute to the dog's excitement, but sounding aloud, startling noise such as a rape alarm, or, once pre-conditioned to them, using John Fisher's Training Discs may be a sufficient distraction. A jet of water or spray of Down Dog (a harmless foul-tasting solution available from vets and most pet shops) directed at the mouth, may also act as a suitable distraction and temporarily halt the dog's excitement. This lull in the storm, no matter how short, must be seized immediately by the owner as an opportunity to communicate with the dog. With a friendly 'sit', or better still, 'corner', the dog's behaviour can usually be brought more under the control of the owner, who can also safely use the lead to reinforce the 'sit' command or to direct the dog to the corner. To reinforce the desired response, Scooby should be instantly rewarded as ever and gently stroked, providing this calms him and doesn't have the opposite effect of exciting him further.

An alternative to such tactics is to use the concept of the reward of possession of a favourite toy kept hung up by the front door. As before, all other toys should be put away, and play and social interaction between the dog and the family or known friends be made to focus around the single graspable, favourite toy. If all greeting behaviour between dog and family only occurs after the dog has taken hold of the toy, it helps condition him to expect positive interactions when the toy is produced. These may usefully redirect his territorial aggression into more friendly excitement and establish a line of communication with the dog even quicker than the Discs or spray of Down Dog. Where the dog is not particularly bothered about possessing the toy, if he can at least be conditioned to grab it, it will usefully occupy his teeth while the rest of the procedures are followed!

Only once a good degree of control is obtained should the Greenwoods turn their attention to their visitors ... and when these techniques are first tried, it may be very apparent why patient, pre-informed friends are asked to call! If Scooby is sufficiently trained and calm enough to remain in his corner or can be safely restrained there, so much the better, but this would be a rare and outstanding success! Ordinarily the dog can now be led to the door, pausing to repeat the intervention tactics and calming procedures if required. At the door, Scooby should again be encouraged to 'sit' when asked and only when calm should the door finally be opened. While he will probably switch from territorial defence excitement to friendly excitement at the sight of someone he knows, the routine of answering the door should be maintained. Scooby should be kept in the 'sit' position and informed that the visitor is acceptable by the Greenwoods telling him 'friend' or that everything is 'okay'.

However, the visitor should not be allowed to enter the house by passing the dog at the threshold. As every kennel owner knows, doorways and narrow passageways maximize a dog's defence reactions as they can more readily monopolize small areas with aggressive displays and so protect the main territory behind them. More than a few normally placid family pets become vicious snarlers at the kennel door and have to be fed through a small hole in it!

At home, it is wise to reduce the dog's confidence at the door either by asking the visitors to retreat into the wider and less defendable space of the front garden or out onto the street for formal introductions. Alternatively the dog can be led back into the house with the visitor following, but once outside, or in the hallway or other more open room, Scooby must again be calmed before being allowed to approach the visitor. It is essential that the visitor is also as calm as possible and avoids speaking to the dog, making sudden movements or staring at him. Quite often the worst people to use as mock visitors are those who are used to their own friendly dog at home or those who claim to be unafraid and well used to dogs, as they may tend to advance confidently on Scooby in a premature attempt to be friendly, which will only arouse him further just when we want him to stay calm.

If indoors, ideally everyone should sit down and try to carry on a normal conversation, with Scooby still restrained by the lead and encouraged to sit near the Greenwoods, though not too close if he has decided now to protect them rather than the house. As the crisis of the visitor's arrival declines, most dogs will calm down and can then be helped to make contact with the visitor. While it is tempting to skip this phase with someone well known and not under threat from Scooby, it is still vital that the guest starts to mention Scooby's name in a gentle manner and throws an occasional titbit gently towards him. If accepted, Scooby can gradually be allowed closer to him to collect more titbits by relaxing the lead. Once Scooby realizes that the

135

visitor is actually a source of something pleasant, the visitor can start to precondition the rewards by expecting Scooby to earn them by obeying a 'sit' command from him, backed up by the owner if necessary.

Scooby should only be allowed to investigate the visitor by sniffing under careful control regulated by the length of lead extended by the owner. If all goes well, Scooby can then be allowed to make physical contact, and under the same conditions, to be stroked by the guest. If this is being carried out in the garden or street, now is the time to go into the house, guest first and owner encouraging Scooby to be calm with every step. Only once everyone is happy indoors can the lead be let go for Scooby to move around more freely, though it should remain attached in case an accidental sudden movement by the visitor prompts a resurgence of protective excitement in the dog and quick intervention is necessary. If happy to do so, the visitor can take Scooby for a short walk in the garden or into the road, perhaps initially accompanied by the owner. All this is of course designed to help Scooby further perceive the arrival of visitors as the precursor to pleasurable events.

In most households, the arrival of callers and visitors is not very predictable, hence the importance of the trailing lead being attached to the dog's collar permanently for a while. With the unexpected knock at the door between arranged calls, the dog may beat you there and be as excited as ever, but you can soon pick up the lead and cut into the same treatment routine quickly. A note pinned to the door advising callers of a temporary delay in being attended to may help. This is preferable to the 'Beware of the Dog' notice, or one I laughed at while treating this type of problem in Spain of all places, which said, in English, 'Violators will be eaten'! Bad luck, I suppose, if the visitor didn't speak English! In England, at least, such notices may imply legally that the owner of a dog known to be sufficiently aggressive as to require informing the public accepts legal liability for any injury it may cause, even in defending it's own home. It seems to me to be one of those ridiculous legal anomalies that a burglar, having broken into your home and ransacked the place can sue for damages if your dog injures him in trying to protect his and your territory (if he survives)!

Highly territorial dogs will also usually benefit from being exercised in a wide variety of places and encouraged to socialize with as many dogs and people as possible, as this can help reduce the importance of the home a little. The dog then comes to see it more as a place of rest. Certainly dogs kept in small enclosures or which spend most of their life in an unchanging garden and home are far more likely to become hyper-excited at minor changes to routine, or irregular but otherwise familiar happenings. Hence dogs which are never taken away from their home patch may begin to over-react or become obsessive about relatively normal happenings such as a bird landing on the grass or the arrival of a visitor. A good dose of activity and interest away from home will help normalize their sensitivity and activity patterns.

But, with food, physical stroking and a walk in the offing, Scooby may just learn to wind down a lot quicker if his excitement at the arrival of visitors can be managed. Frequent practice is essential and needs to involve increasingly less familiar visitors. If Scooby has become particularly conditioned to the sound of the Greenwood's door bell, it may even help, in the first stages of treatment to change it or disconnect it for a while, though he will, of course, quickly become conditioned to any replacement.

The aim of treatment is to allow the dog a steadily less restricted lifestyle around the house, to respond to the owner's voice, or other distractions if necessary without the need to wear the trailing lead for evermore. However, until Scooby is absolutely predictable and controllable, great care should continue to be exercised with such dogs. If allowed to run freely around the garden or yard, or he has access to the front entrance, the dog should always be muzzled for the ultimate safety of visitors.

People in remote areas who receive few visitors may have to rely more heavily on the distraction techniques to control their dog's reactions, or perhaps employ more effective physical control measures. A head-collar attached to a trailing lead for those dogs who will accept it, affords better instant and safe control of the excitable or aggressive dog bound for the door or the visitor's leg, but if wearing it upsets the dog, then it may be counterproductive and so cannot always be recommended as a feature of treatment.

One would expect most dogs like Scooby to show an improvement in accepting visitors proportional to the effort invested by the owners. Controlling the dog at the more predictable arrival of the postman and milkman, or the noisy invasion of the refuse collectors, may be more difficult because the dog will often seem to be even more excited then than with other callers. Treatment of this more specific problem will usually involve gaining the cooperation of the postman or milkman so that he or she may help establish a friendly relationship with the dog. Without such cooperation, the problems are difficult to treat and may best be managed by keeping the dog well out of the way in the morning until the mail and milk have been delivered. But, as most postmen will be used to having at least some friendly dogs on their beat, they may just be able to spare a few moments to help. They should preferably meet the dog out in the street on neutral ground, where, unless the dog has already come to recognize his postman from his uniform or hat, he will be treated as just another passing person. With the dog on a lead and perhaps a head-collar, as before, the owner should stop to talk to the postman, and encourage the dog to sit. Again, his compliance should be calmly rewarded, and the postman should be encouraged to stroke him if the dog is tolerant of being touched by strangers away from home. As with visitors indoors, the postman can try asking the dog to sit and offer the reward of titbits backed up by the owner if neccessary. Then everyone should head calmly into the garden and towards the front door where the postman can hand over some mail to the owner while simultaneously dropping some treats for the dog to pick up.

If this all goes well, the dog should get to know the postman's voice and footsteps and come to look forward to the arrival of his new friend in the morning. And if the postman doesn't have time to say hello to the dog every morning, then he can keep the positive association going by dropping a few tit bits through the letter box (leave them out for him the night before) before pushing through the mail. Sometimes this works too well as the dog gets hyper-excited and barks just as loud because his friend has arrived, and then gets frustrated because he can't get to say hello . . . there's no pleasing some folk.

# Car guarding

*Dear Mr Neville*

*Our normal, placid little spaniel, Danny, is a perfect gentle-man unless he is in the car. He loves riding in the car, but woe betide anyone who walks within ten feet of it once it is parked, for they shall receive an almighty display of snarling and barking from inside! While we are pleased that Danny defends the car, and thankfully lets us in on our return, he is reluctant to get out of the car once we are home. He sits at the back and growls fiercely at us. Once I tried to grab his collar and pull him out, and he bit me, so now I leave the hatch up and let him come out when he's bored. Is there a quicker way to get him out of the car?*

*Yours sincerely*

*Clare Amberley*

Cars often do bring out the worst in some dogs. While some like Robbie as we saw in Chapter 5 are extremely fearful in the car, others relish the joy of travel. Most will defend the car against people unwise enough to try and break, in and a few, like Danny, become rather obsessive about guarding the car against everyone and everything in a manner quite in contrast with their normal disposition. Like many dogs in kennels, Danny sees the car as a suitably defendable small area with restricted access points. By monopolizing the area at those points with a very fierce display he keeps both himself safe and the car, his temporary den, free from challenge. Most are more relaxed when the car is moving, but a few also become highly excited at anything that is passed and need to be restrained for safe driving. Most car guarders relax and return to their normal selves as soon as their owners return, or as soon as the door or window is opened, but a few direct their efforts all the more through the open window as the weak point in the system deserving of extra defence. It certainly does keep all passers-by at bay but, clearly, one must be careful about ensuring those teeth can't connect while one is away shopping.

Some dogs feel so confident in the car that not only do they love to jump in and go for a ride, they want to stay in it even once they're back home. Danny simply won't come out because he prefers it where he is. He feels much more confident and, because he is in a nice protective corner, he can stand up and defend his desire to be there. To drag him out involves confrontation and he is simply in too defendable an area to be challenged without risk of injury. He is also probably too excited to recognize his owners or, perhaps, simply too defiant. Either way, confrontation is not the way to deal with an angry cornered dog. As before, he must be encouraged out for the prospect of reward, so if the Amberleys can arrange to step back a few paces from the open car hatch, call him gently and rattle the titbit can, he should come out. If not, a favourite toy may induce him or simply running off into the house very excitedly while calling him may encourage along. If he is still too entrenched, the Amberleys will have to attach a long line to Danny before setting off, and leave it just dangling a little outside the car when the hatch is shut. They can grab this safely before opening the hatch on return and gently pull him out while encouraging him with gentle words and the prospect of reward. Most will jump out willingly once they have been pulled a little out of the corner or slightly beyond the door line as they are then more vulnerable and more likely to obey. The reward should still be offered immediately for coming out and, with a little practise, Danny should soon be jumping out without needing to be pulled. It may also help to desensitize him by encouraging him to play games through the car, and being offered titbits or toys, alternating from being given just inside and then just outside on the ground to make him jump in and out more willingly. He should be attached to a fairly long lead for such games in the initial stages of treatment and until he is less sensitive about guarding the car.

# Fear aggression?

In the last chapter we saw that fearful reactions are a natural part of any animal's survival tactics and, alternating with aggressive displays and in relation to dominance status, are a key part of the communication system from one dog to another and between dog and man. At the 'bottom' of Dr Abrante's emotional scale of fearful expression by any dog, and especially likely in the very low ranking individual, is the expression of fear as an aggressive display when all else has failed, and the threat is too close to be tolerated. This too is a natural behaviour but can obviously be painful, and especially so if like the vet or groomer, one has to approach and ignore earlier warnings and is only trying to help!

*Dear Mr Neville*

*Our little dog Jodi is a rather fearful character and is forever snapping at other dogs who approach her in the park. We tend to avoid other dogs a lot now but unfortunately Jodi shows the same reactions at the vet's. As soon as we enter the surgery she tries to run back out. We stop her by keeping her on the lead and so she just sits there shaking with fear. We have to drag her into the surgery and lift her onto the table. Sometimes she snaps at us and she certainly snaps at the vet and his nurses if they try to approach her. We usually end up wrapping her in a towel and then tying her mouth up with tape just to make her safe enough for the vet to look at her. Can't she realize that the vet is only trying to help?*

*Yours sincerely*

*Edwina Carlton*

Defensive aggression is what used to be known as fear aggression until Dr Abrantes explained things more clearly (see The Behaviour of Dogs and Cats by the APBC, edited by John Fisher) and of the type shown by the dog keen on self-preservation. It is typically used in the wild by dogs which are under direct physical threat and is probably as likely in male dogs as females, though most of the cases I have seen have involved bitches, and those of a rather timid disposition generally. Dogs and other animals resort to aggressive displays and actual physical attack if they are unable to escape from something they see as a challenge or threatening to them. Initial growling and snapping may force the threat in the shape of another dog to back away and so reduce the tension and increase the comfort of the fearful dog. In many cases, the nervousness in bitches has been caused by the unfamiliar and more intense investigations shown by male dogs towards them as they approach their first season. Frightened, they snap at their suitors and soon teach themselves that such behaviour helps protect them from anything else they don't like. As a result they tend to avoid some of life's character-building rough and tumbles and so become generally nervous and over-quick to bring teeth into play. Most times the display is sufficient to ward off the threat, but occasionally it fails. Vets must do their duty, as must groomers and owners, sometimes, in having to bath the dog , remove thorns from their feetetc. Indeed pain-induced aggression is usually an intense form of self-preserving, defensive aggression by a dog that may be unable to run away because it is restricted and hurt by its injuries.

If the policy of loud and dramatic threat of aggressive display fails, real aggression may be all the dog is left with to defend itself. Bites are usually of the snap and release type, rather than the more predatory snap and tear, or grasp and crush. The idea of the bite is still to make that unwanted hand or dog back away. As with so many other forms of nervousness discussed in Chapter 5, defensive biters, of which there are many in the dog world, often develop their behaviour as a direct result of lack of socialization with other dogs, people and life in general at those critical early periods, though some breeds are notably more prone to suffer from it than others and some strains of certain breeds are more 'jumpy' than others. Most of my cases have concerned German Shepherd Dog bitches and castrated male Collies, but Poodles and Cocker Spaniels, with their often sensitive ears and paws, Yorkshire Terriers and others which have to be groomed frequently, are also fairly regular callers to my clinics.

Treatment, as one might expect, involves a gentle, controlled desensitizing approach to the perceived threats and is identical in most cases to the treatment of many other nervous conditions as outlined in Chapter 5. However, it simply may not be worth treating some cases because the treatment is too traumatic and the dog only presents the problem rarely, or in specific circumstances. A typical example would be Jodi with her reactions at the vet's. She will probably know where she is going two or three streets before she actually gets there, and that, or the smell of the waiting room may be all that is necessary to make her afraid and likely to bite in defence if approached or cornered. While the vet can do his best to get to know Jodi in the waiting room or outside and offer appeasements of titbits, come the time for the examination, she will still probably still lash out. Rather than put her through the trauma of being restrained in a towel and her mouth tied up, which will simply make her more frightened, it would be far more sensible either to take her along already muzzled to decrease the whole time of the consulation or ask the vet to provide a light tranquillizer to give to her before she goes. If possible the vet can also be asked to see Jodi in the peace of her own home and leave his white coat at the surgery to avoid any nasty associations. (I never wear a white or green 'lab' coat at my clinics – as a result my clients are less likely to be afraid of me, though of course all my clothes get covered in dog hair and slobber as a result!) A home visit is not always practical, usually more expensive, and Mrs Carlton will probably still have to muzzle Jodi and have her on a lead well beforethe vet arrives anyway. Dogs which bite defensively at the groomers are usually much better when their owners have left as they will not know where to run to even after a 'successful' bite and so tend to stand trembling but otherwise unmoved and take what is coming. Many even come to enjoy the experience and stop snapping at the groomers, yet still snap at their owners if they try to groom them themselves at home. Grooming salon staff are usually well used to dealing with the problem, and I always think it is best to let them groom the defensive-biters of this world, though muzzling the dog can help overcome any conditioned or initial fears in the dog.

Some dogs, afraid of being groomed or handled, protect themselves successfully for so long that their coat becomes dreadfully matted and dirty. This may often be the case with the long-haired active varieties such as Westies and Cocker Spaniels. Sometimes the only way to get the treatment started is to ask the vet to anaesthetize the dog and close crop his coat so that he can be handled and become accustomed to grooming afterwards when it will be less painful and less essential. By the time the coat has fully regrown, the dog ought to be more tolerant of regular grooming and usually will have learned to enjoy it.

# Learned aggression

*Dear Mr Neville*

*When my last dog, a perfectly sweet natured GSD called Baz, died a few months ago I was heartbroken. I thought I would give a new home to another unwanted GSD as so many people seemed to be getting rid of them because of all the publicity in the media about big dogs. I picked out Bruno at the local shelter because they said he'd been badly treated but he was basically like my old Baz, a big softy. And so he was for several weeks. He fitted in well with my family including my three young children and the cat, and despite his sometimes unnecessarily fearful reactions of people on the street, he was well behaved and not in the least aggressive towards people or other dogs. He soon learned to bark well when the doorbell rang, but would be quiet when told. Just as we thought everything was going perfectly, Bruno showed just how powerful he can be. We were playing in my brother-in-law's garden when John arrived through the back gate. Bruno looked at him, I said 'okay' and he went back down on to his front haunches ready for the next game. As a joke to frighten John, I simply said 'Kill him Bruno'. He must have been trained for attack by his previous owners, because that's exactly what he tried to do. With a frightening burst of speed he hurtled towards John, clearly intent on tearing him to pieces. Fortunately John reacted quickly and just managed to escape through the gate. Bruno leapt up and growled and barked ferociously at him until I was able to call him to me and calm him down. The strange thing was that later on, Bruno met John again and was perfectly friendly towards him as if nothing had ever happened. The crucial question is, of course, can Bruno be de-trained and made safe?*

*Yours sincerely*

*Jason Collins*

Many dogs are deliberately trained to respond aggressively to certain commands or situations. When done professionally, there is little doubt that properly controlled learned aggression in dogs can be very useful for helping the police apprehend villains or in security work by the armed forces for example. In World War II, a volunteer group called 'Dogs for Defense' selected and trained dogs for the K-9 corps of the American Army. Thirty-two breeds were recognized as acceptable initially, but nearer the end of the war in 1944 only the German and Belgian Shepherd Dog, Dobermann, Giant Schnauzer (all used by police forces or armies in Europe today) and the Collie were being trained. No mention was made of Rottweilers! We have usually deliberately selected certain larger breeds, usually the German Shepherd Dog, to fulfil this role because of their trainability and intelligence. But, as important as the need may be for some dogs to be taught how and when to show aggression, it is absolutely vital that the aggression can be turned off as quickly as it can be turned on. It is also vital that it is specifically directed at, say the villain's arm to restrain him rather than consisting of a savage and life-threatening attack at his neck or head. Such training is usually taught as an extension of holding and retrieval training by the police or armed forces in the United Kingdom but wherever it is done, it is essential that it is carried out only by those who have a genuine requirement for it and who are responsible enough to know how and when and by how much to employ it.

Sadly, owning a large guarding breed is not sufficient for some ordinary pet owners; they have to go a step further and attack train the brute as well. Such amateur training by owners, or even by many so-called specialist trainers, is usually based on unkind goading techniques and produces an aggressive response based on pain or fear of anticipated pain and a dog which just can't be considered safe as a pet. While remaining with the owner, such dogs may be safe-ish to a greater or lesser degree dependent on the quality of the training, self-control of the dog and the owner's desire to activate the aggression. If the dog is subsequently rehomed for some reason, new and well meaning owners like Jason may end up with a potential killer on their hands.

While colleagues with more experience in this area have successfully de-programmed some attack-trained dogs by re-pairing the attack commands with other activities, personally I would not attempt it, particularly where the dog is intended as a family pet and lives with young children. It is one of the few cases where I feel that while the dog is a sad victim of man's inadequacies, there can be no place for him as a companion, and that he should be kindly put to sleep by the veterinary surgeon. This does not usually apply to the properly trained police dogs that are retired after their active duty to live as pets with their handlers because the owner can continue to maintain the same relationship and responsible control of the dog. But the poorer the training, the more risky it is to keep the dog and the less likely it is that a new owner will be able to switch off the aggression whether deliberately or accidently activated.

*Dear Mr Neville*

*Rosco is our St Bernard and a very big dog he is too. Unfortunately, since he was attacked as a puppy by a nasty Belgian Shepherd Dog he has attacked every other dog on sight, and of course usually knocks them flat. Once this is achieved he stands over them and growls for a while but providing they don't fight back, he can then be called or dragged off quite safely. He is the best of friends with our other dog, Chip, a Kerry Blue and our neighbour's Japanese Akita, so he is not an obligatory aggressive dog. Can we teach him to be more gentle with other dogs in the park?*

*Yours sincerely*

*Simon Tilter*

There are of course, self-taught components to many forms of aggression. Success for a dog which is aggressive in defending his toys, bed or food or his kennel compounds his efforts when next challenged and. for certain dogs, the threshold at which they become aggressive falls when they are challenged or seeking to exert their will in other situations. A typical example of self-taught aggression is the case of Rosco, who is a bully dog. After being forced to use his teeth and weight to defend himself against attack by another dog, Rosco learnt that the best way to avoid being attacked again was to get in first with a very aggressive attack against all other dogs. This development could be said to have arisen as a form of defensive aggression) initially, but being a big chap, his attacks always succeeded, and were thus self-rewarding. The end result is that Rosco had become a self-taught bully, incapable of sociable contact with all but a few other dogs. In turn, he was probably the cause of many other dogs learning to defend themselves prematurely and unnecessarily with their own marked displays of defensive aggression.

Treatment is aimed at introducing Rosco to as many other dogs as possible under controlled conditions. His efforts to preclude social contact are engineered to fail, and he is encouraged into using other options, preferably those involving more normal methods of canine social communication. We want him to learn to decide which dogs are friendly and are worth getting to know, and which are not, walking away from them rather than trying to upend them into total submission.

Physical control is a key feature in treatment of such problems, especially with such a large example, and the head-collar is a vital tool for such cases. Nowhere is it more plain that the system of control used on horses, cattle, llamas and most other large domestic animals is highly applicable for the control of the large dog. So, once Rosco had been acclimatized to wearing his, the owners were able to set about deliberately introducing him to other dogs. Previously they had been adopting a wise policy of keeping him away from all other dogs. But, of course, while this had kept other dogs safe, it had done little to reform Rosco. Indeed, by turning dramatically to avoid other dogs as soon as they were spotted in the park, Rosco had probably had his reaction even deeper ingrained because he felt that even his 'mum and dad' were reacting defensively to the challenge of that other nasty dog! The simple act of heading straight towards them helped relax Rosco, even if Simon was enormously apprehensive inside.

Approaching other dogs on unfamiliar territory is inclined to produce a less confident reaction in dogs like Rosco because they don't know where to escape to if things go wrong for them. With a calm approach led by Simon, and with Rosco being reassured all the way with kind gentle words, he soon proved to be far more tolerant of other dogs than Simon could have believed. Typical of many bullies, as he approached his intended victim, Rosco became highly agitated, whimpering and trying to rear up. The head-collar facilitates very effective control, and once Rosco's attempts to break free had failed, he quickly calmed down but then tried to steam on ahead with all his weight. But, as with schooling a horse, the headcollar enabled us to turn Rosco's head and break his eye contact with the other dog. Simon was able to make him sit to command, relax him and then reintroduce him.

While some dogs have wisely vacated the scene by this time, or their owners rushed in to protect their pets, other dogs seem largely unaffected by the approach of a snorting St Bernard. Getting closer and closer, blocking every effort on Rosco's part to mount a charge and rewarding any calm breaks, he was gradually introduced to the other dog. And when finally they touched noses, Rosco actually liked what he found . . . a highly flirtatious young spaniel bitch. Allowed to sniff each other in more private areas, the two dogs soon engaged in more normal sociable behaviour, which we knew Rosco was perfectly capable of because of his acceptance of the Kerry Blue at home and the dog next door.

Thereafter it was case of frequent practise and plenty of opportunity to meet other dogs. We usually begin with less challenging and more rewarding smaller bitches, but very soon Rosco was able to meet all other dogs without trying to attack them. In short, his previous policy had failed repeatedly, and with controlled exposure to other dogs, he had learnt that his aggressive behaviour was unnecessary. Once in a position to do so, Rosco learned that other forms of social contact were more rewarding.

What this type of treatment doesn't affect at all, even with a smaller dog than Rosco, is their ability or willingness to defend themselves if they are attacked again by other dogs. It's just that they learn not to make the first move. Many cases of learned aggression in dogs are made worse by the patient only ever being walked and meeting other dogs when with his or her own dog 'pack' from home. With mates around to protect them and back them up if things go wrong, such dogs are bound to be more confident with their assaults, so treatment is always carried out initially with them on their own. They are only walked with any other dogs from home once they are improved and the owners are sure of the dog's reactions and their ability to control it verbally.

An important aspect of treatment with learned aggression such as Rosco's is to be able to distinguish it from other forms. As we shall see later in this chapter, the signs of learned aggression may be very similar to other forms of aggression but arise due to entirely different reasons.

# Aggression between dogs

*Dear Mr Neville*

*Our one-and-a half-year-old Collie X Weimaraner, Rambo, quite simply hates all other dogs. He tries to attack every dog in the park and, try as we might, we cannot stop him except by keeping him on the lead. He came from a rescue shelter, so we don't know about his previous life, but with us at home and with any person he meets outdoors, he is perfectly well behaved. You wouldn't think it was the same dog when he charges up to other dogs, large and small, and attacks them without so much as a 'hello'. Of course we've always pulled him off, though he has caused some nasty injuries to other dogs. In most fights, as we pulled him off, he seemed to be 'winning', no matter how big the opposition. Is there any way of teaching him some manners?*

*Yours sincerely*

*Elizabeth and Jonathon Fisher*

There is little quite so embarrassing for the average owner of an otherwise pleasant companion pet dog than to find that he or she is an attacker of other dogs and a luster after violence. The owners of such dogs are faced with a series of difficult prospects. First there is that dreadful first day where their dog attacks an often innocent, non-provocative other dog owned by someone else who uses the same park regularly to walk their pet. Once the aggressor has been separated from his victim, put on the lead, suitably dressed down by his owner, the apologies must follow quickly to placate the naturally irate owner of the victim. Usually they will hear the words 'Oh, I'm so sorry. I can't think what came over him. He's never done anything like that before!' (This seems like a good thing to say, and will be used in future to excuse the dog's aggressive behaviour in any future encounters.) Veterinary repair must then be arranged, with the owner of the aggressive dog hopefully feeling guilty enough to pay the bill.

Then follows a questioning period by the owner of the aggressive dog. Usually they put the incident down to bad luck, a clash of personalities between the two dogs or even unseen provocation on the part of the victim prior to the assault. But after a couple more incidents, owners of aggressive dogs start to become more wary. They may walk the dog in the same place, but keep him on a lead to keep him away from other dogs and under control at all times. They will often adopt a policy of avoiding other dogs, deliberately turning out of the path of any heading in their direction. If, as many do, their dog then becomes excited and barks aggressively at all other dogs, they may decide to walk him at a quieter time of day to avoid the risk. Fearful of their reputation locally, they may even join the '3 o'clock in the morning club' in the hope of being able to exercise their pet without risk of meeting any other dogs. It's ironic, of course, that if they do meet any, they too are likely to be members of the same club!

The end results are that the owner's lifestyle can be drastically altered, their enjoyment of walking the dog definitely becomes a worrying chore and they may start to experience problems in the local community about their dog's behaviour. No more can the owner of dogs like Rambo enjoy meeting fellow dog owners if he is intent on tearing what he sees as the opposition to pieces and it is often the pressure from other local dog owners and feeling of isolation that causes owners like the Fishers to seek help.

Many such problems arise as a direct consequence of the lack of early socialization with other dogs referred to earlier. Maintained too long in isolation, or not having had the opportunity to meet enough other dogs and learn social graces, dogs may become nervous when faced with their own kind later or, commonly, become over-excited and then aggressive. Typically, this type of dog is non-selective with its aggression. It attacks all dogs, large and small, male and female, running or still, home or away! Being trounced a couple of times by larger dogs or those locally which prove particularly capable in the art of self-defence may modify the dog's aggression a little but, by and large, dogs like Rambo are generalized despots.

149

Sadly, many do end up in rescue shelters, though thankfully are nowadays increasingly likely to be spotted through the character assessment programmes carried out by progressive welfare societies, before being let loose onto its next owner. Often, dog-aggressive individuals such as the Fishers' Rambo will be contrastingly extremely pleasant, obedient and playful with the family, their friends and anyone who stops to pat them in the street. This simply compounds the worry about just what to do with them. The safety-first policy that is sensibly adopted by many owners precludes embarrassment and keeps relations with the local dog-owning community reasonably safe, if rather distant. Unfortunately, being walked in the middle of the night, and perhaps only meeting other nasties, does nothing to reform the dog, and he or she will suffer from less general exercise as a result. With more pent up energy by being kept on a lead during exercise, and the physical restraint of being held back from the focus of their intended aggressive outbursts, dogs like Rambo are far more likely to become excited when they do see another dog. It's all rather a vicious circle of worry, inconvenience, dissatisfaction and tiredness contrasted by the relief and joy of owning a perfect dog at home.

Once again treatment will involve reversing the policies of the owners in preventing Rambo from meeting other dogs, and doing exactly what they fear most but under very controlled conditions – very similar to those employed in the treatment of Rosco earlier in this chapter. However, Rosco's aim was more to force his victims to submit than to preclude the possibility of them investigating him, while Rambo is clearly intent on greater levels of violence. And so, prior to any treatment, the safety of other dogs that Rambo is to meet must be ensured. A head-collar and extending lead is essential for the effective and quick control of Rambo when led towards and introduced to other dogs. Certainly until the owners are confident about the speed of their reactions, Rambo should be muzzled as well. He will look like a Kendo warrior for a while and his appearance may deter the owners of other dogs from allowing them to be investigated by this gladiator. But, hopefully, local understanding owners may be found for the initial stages of treatment to enable the Fishers to get used to handling Rambo when he is aggressively excited, and they may move quickly to working with Rambo as safely without his muzzle.

The level of Rambo's excitement will probably exceed that of Rosco when faced with another dog, and simple controlled approaches and mild intervention, control of eye contact and calming as required will usually not be sufficient to bring an aggressive Rambo under control to enable him to profit from the experience. The same calm approach should be adopted by the Fishers when walking Rambo, but they should begin by only targetting dogs least likely to arouse Rambo. Sometimes these will be large imposing dogs, or those who have dispelled him in the past, with the implication that defeat or the prospect of it may have had some reforming effect. Smaller dogs may arouse less passion, perhaps indicating that there are some elements of competitive aggression in Rambo's approach which don't require proving with 'easier' opposition. But, having decided to select those dogs presenting the minimum of 'challenge', and in an unfamiliar environment, Rambo may still require a greater level of distraction to bring him under control at the moment of first sight, or during introduction to others. Simply steering him away or blocking his charge is unlikely to wind him down much. Instead, at the moment of assault, the physical control and turning of the head afforded by tension through the lead on the headcollar should be accompanied by some form of distracting stimulus, such as the sound of a rape alarm, the clattering of John Fisher's Dog Training Discs or a jet of water aimed at Rambo. As with the aggressively excited territorial dog, these tactics usually give a 'window of opportunity' for the owner to regain control, make the dog sit, reward him and calm him down, before reintroducing him to the other dog . . . if he or she hasn't been frightened off by the whole palaver of being charged at by a fierce dog and its accompanying screeches and clatters! And if Rambo makes good progress with certain types of dog initially, he can then be led towards more exciting canine prospects later, until dogs in all their shapes, sizes and sexes can be accepted without undue excitement. With many dogs like Rambo it is simply a matter of continuing with this policy as often as possible in as many different places as possible as the speed of progress may simply be dependent on the number of dogs which can be found.

It will often help to take Rambo to a place where he will meet other dogs under more control than perhaps can be found in the local parks. A properly organized and sympathetic dog training class may be ideal for some, though the Rambos of this world can sometimes be too disruptive to the classes to be admitted without prior treatment. Others are nicely swamped by the presence of so many dogs and start to tolerate them much better close up and without switching into an aggressive frame of mind at the mere sight of another dog, perhaps through being unable to decide which one to attack first! With every dog under better control and hopefully responding reasonably to their owners' commands, the whole introduction process is much more manageable but obviously the whole prospect must be discussed first with the class organizers, as Rambo will need special treatment and not just thrown in withall the other dogs.

The traditional method of dealing with Rambos has often been to punish the dog at the moment of attack by yanking him hard on a choke chain, smacking and yelling at him. With some cases, any reformative effect achieved by this will have been due to the probably lucky appropriate timing of the intervention. The dog came to associate unpleasant consequences to his behaviour or the presence of the other dog in the same way as the distraction tactics of the rape alarm may counter-condition Rambo as well as enable the owner to make contact and reward temporary calm behaviour. In such cases it is less likely that the dog will be able to socialize correctly with other dogs; it will simply learn to avoid them when with his owner, rather than attack them. This may be all that can be hoped for in some cases, especially where the dog has a long history of this problem. With other cases, violent intervention may have helped by increasing the owner's dominance and right to control his 'pack' in all encounters. Increasing dominance is a much used and rather indefinable concept that has been employed far too readily in the past to treat a range of canine problems. There is no doubt that it can work well with a few cases, but with the majority, over-forceful intervention by yanking and yelling simply excites the aggressive dog all the more and makes the direction of his own aggression less focussed on to the other dog and more likely to turn on the owner. Yanking and yelling at the normal or generally more nervous character which happens to be aggressive only in the face of other dogs is likely to make matters worse as it decreases any bond between the owner and dog and only helps the dog to relate the presence of other dogs with pain and confusion in his relationship with his owner. The end result in most cases is that aggressive interventions only make maters worse, though with just a few, quite dramatic interventions with the headcollar and a sterner instruction to 'sit' do have a reformative effect that can then be built on. But there is never any justification for hitting or painfully yanking the dog-aggressive dog.

The concept of owner dominance will be looked at a little later in this chapter when the problems of canine aggression towards their owners will be examined, but increasing the owner's right to intervene and the dog's willingness to let him or her do so when the excitement stakes are raised can be helpful with treating dogs like Rambo. This is best developed by altering the general way the dog lives with its owner as we shall see later, and with frequent concerted efforts in obedience training based on reward, perhaps at a suitable training class or with an experienced trainer on a one to one basis. Most owners could manage perfectly well for themselves after a little basic instruction on how to handle their dog but, whoever is involved, violence should never be used, only kind understanding and patience in improving their control. An improved level of control, conditioned by verbal commands and the relaxed prospect of titbits and holding toys provided by the owner, increasingly in the company of other dogs, can then be usefully applied in more difficult circumstances.

The physical failure of Rambo's attacks on other dogs afforded by control with the headcollar are compounded by the fact that he ends up in a more vulnerable, side-on position relative to his intended victim. In short, the consequence of his assault is likely defeat if the other dog chooses to repsond. Without a head-collar, this defeat used to be compounded by making Rambo roll on his back and adopt a submissive postion relative to the other dog, but such a total display of submission is never necessary. Such an over-reaction would constitute a case of expecting Rambo to reverse his tactics too far, and probably frighten him and put the owner at risk of being bitten. What we are hoping to achieve with controlled introductions is to teach him that his aggressive policy fails and may leave him a little vulnerable if his victim decides to defend himself. We also want Rambo to learn that normal investigation by other dogs through sniffing and visual contact is not threatening, and can be tolerated without risk. Later, dogs which for some reason are not acceptable to Rambo can be dispelled with calmer normal social displays or vocal signals and there is no need to inflict grievous bodily harm unless grievously bodily attacked. As with Rosco we are not affecting Rambo's ability to defend himself if he himself is the unfortunate victim of another aggressive dog.

Hopefully, the Fishers will soon be cancelling their membership of the three o'clock in the morning club and getting themselves and Rambo back into a more normal routine where other dogs are simply a part of a regular general facet of outdoor life. It may take some weeks before they are all relaxed enough for Rambo to be allowed off-lead in the presence of other dogs, though of course it is vital throughout treatment that he will have been allowed to run free and play to release a little energy in a safe place. His first excursions off-lead again should only occur when he is reasonably obedience-trained, can approach other dogs, sniff and be sniffed and perhaps even show friendly inclinations towards some of them. And he should still be muzzled on the first few occasions as a safety measure to protect other dogs in case there are still a few who make him forget his new behaviour.

# Inter-male aggression

*Dear Mr Neville*

*My Black Labrador, Andy, is a real scrapper with all other male dogs. Irrespective of their size, he will catch a whiff of them and wade in to impress himself. He starts with a stare and stiff walk, and then tries to stand with his head over their withers, while growling and generally 'fizzing' away with threatening body language. His tail is often arched over his back initially but may fall a little, wiggling malevolently at the end while he stands growling. If the other dog submits by running away, Andy may chase half-heartedly but will come back when called in most cases. Sometimes he does pursue them to beat them up, however. If the dog rolls over, Andy usually comes when called, but occasionally will attack the other dog anyway. We have had several nasty incidents and both my wife and I, as well as owners of Andy's victims have been bitten while trying to break up fights. He seems more tolerant of castrated male dogs and is positively gentlemanly with all bitches. Those he really likes, he may follow for ages, refusing to come back to us when called. Is he an unreformable 'macho' lout?*

*Yours sincerely*

*Edmund Pringle*

This is a rather different type of dog to dog aggression than that of the learned displays of Rosco or the unsocialized responses of Rambo. Andy is indeed a macho lout, but while some aspects of his behaviour may be fuelled by the success of his fighting victories, his aggression is originally hormonally inspired. He is, after all, perfectly capable of socializing with bitches where his aims are more of courtship than trials of strength, and he can recognize submissive displays in some of his victims and these inhibit any further aggression in him. In other words, aggression is part of Andy's normal behavioural repertoire and expressed when meeting other males, especially those who also have all their 'equipment'. They too are more likely to show assertive male behaviour and be competitive with other males, even though their behaviour may rarely involve the use of physical aggression compared with Andy. They will also smell more challenging to Andy and, if resisting his attempts to dominate them, are more likely to feel the power of his teeth. This type of behaviour occurs largely as a result of the effects of the male hormone, testosterone, early on when the pup's brain is first masculinized before birth and later on at puberty when a dog's more adult social behaviour starts to develop in response to the production of his own testosterone.

Testosterone is produced by glands in the testicles, hence 'lop 'em off ' is the usual cry when dealing with this type of aggression. There is little doubt that castration of the specifically male-to-male aggressive dog will usually reduce his competitiveness quite markedly if carried out at the correct time, usually before about three years of age. Research has shown that castration has been found to reduce the problem of intermale aggression in 50-60 per cent of cases looking at dogs of all ages but, for best results, the surgery must be followed by application of controlled exposure techniques to help the dog learn to be sociable with other males. Their smell may still arouse him into being assertive despite his lack of testosterone, and one must build on his more malleable frame of mind after surgery if his old habits are to be reshaped.

Most dogs like Andy start to demonstrate their aggression towards other males, and a marked sexual interest in bitches, during adolescence, when testosterone production comes on stream to facilitate the development of the secondary sexual and behavioural characteristics. The behaviour is obviously a competitive one with Andy seeking to assert his high-ranking dominance status over all other males, except towards a few who show their submission quickly and unequivocally. Even then one suspects that if they have learned to do this to avoid conflict or are naturally showing submission to a more dominant dog, Andy may still attack them if they smell as if they too are high ranking. As Andy approaches social maturity, one would expect him to become worse and be intolerant of all males.

It is logical to associate this type of behaviour with Darwin's theories of 'survival of the fittest' as Andy, by adopting a highly competitive profile, will be more likely to keep the other males away from any bitches and be more likely to pass on his success to the next generation. His testosterone level, or response to it, is likely to be more pronounced and this will also inspire his desire to chase, court and mate with bitches, whether they are in season or not.

Most dogs will go through a period of challenging and being competitive with other males during adolescence as do most human male adolescents. It's a rotten time for everyone but usually the sharp or unacceptable ends of developing adult male behaviour and competitiveness become honed down through experience and their failure compared with more gentle, but nonetheless competitive display behaviours of other dogs. Certainly in a dog or wolf pack, the assertive young male will often be put firmly in his place by older experienced males and kept back from the bitches if he tries to challenge directly too soon. For him, upward mobility in the pack and success at breeding will be a slower process than for the average pet dog brought up more in a human pack. There many types of interaction, such as sexual behaviour, are not acceptable to the older packmates, not even in play form from a younger immature dog.

However, few, again typically well-behaved non-aggressive family pets do seem to get what they're after with displays of aggression when out meeting other dogs. The relative infrequency of contact with other dogs means that Andy will be likely to be even more excited when he does meet another male (or bitch for that matter), and the success of his assaults fuels the continuation of aggression. It is interesting that while large chaps like Black Labradors are more likely physically to 'win' their encounters with other males, smaller dogs which may lose more often when picking on bigger competition are not usually affected by defeat. A case, no doubt, of 'balls ruling brains' that is usually more notable in *Homo sapiens* than other species!

I well remember one Black Labrador who was a typical male dog-aggressive character. His owner followed the advice of a famous, and now sadly departed, dog trainer and inserted a finger into his dog's rear end when it was in mid-combat. To his delight his dog gave up the struggle, so he continuted to employ this policy as and when required. Unfortunately, one day his dog met the equal and opposing force of another large male dog-aggressive Black Labrador. Our man's dog duly stopped fighting when the finger went in, but the other dog kept coming at him, so a finger from the other hand was inserted into his rear end as well. Peace prevailed until the other dog's owner arrived on the scene and demanded an explanation. The first dog, which was owned by a very prominent London executive, was brought for treatment shortly afterwards and responded totally to castration.

But with the adolescent male dog who is starting to become aggressive with other males a little too consistently, it may not be necessary to castrate him surgically immediately. Instead, the vet can give him an anti-male hormone injection to peg back the effects of his hormonally induced behaviour for two to three weeks. This may just see him through a reactive developmental period where his testosterone output is unusually high. As the injection wears off, he may be less assertive as the levels re-establish at a lower and less fluctuating level. If his old ways return, the treatment can be repeated until the dog is generally more adult, both physically and socially. But, if his aggression keeps reappearing as the effects wear off, then the treatment will have shown that the behaviour is largely hormonally inspired and that castration is likely to give more permanent resolution of the problems. Castration alone, particularly with the older dog, is unlikely to be helpful without some controlled approach to resocialization with other males. This can be self-taught through normal exposure to other dogs by the younger male after castration or as a deliberate effort by the owner to maximize the reformative effects of the anti-hormone treatment. For those dogs which don't respond well enough to castration and resocialization alone, a further course of progestins (female hormones) from the vet has been shown to help another 15 per cent or so of cases and is well worth trying.

*Dear Mr Neville*

*We have two Springer Spaniels, brothers of two years of age called Spritzer and Merlin. At about 15 months they suddenly started to fight severely and have continued on and off ever since. There is no warning of their battles; they can be sitting in the same room quite peacably together, when suddenly all hell breaks loose. Both have been to the vet on several occasions for repairs, and though he felt that they would grow out of this, clearly they are not. Their fighting seems to be getting more frequent and more severe and though we try to treat them both equally, they just don't seem to like each other. The vet has recommended castrating Spritzer, as he seems to start most of the fights, but is this likely to help? Wouldn't we be better to castrate both of them or should we find one of them a new owner?*

*Yours sincerely*

*Sarah and Arthur Garing*

Andy from the previous letter was really demonstrating a specific and more outdoor form of generalized dominance aggression towards other dogs. Most problems of dominance aggression concern dogs which share a household and which are part of the same pack. I have seen so many cases of fighting brothers that my advice to prospective puppy purchasers is always to select a dog and a bitch if they must buy from the same litter (with due attention paid to interbreeding later) or, if they must have two males, to select from different breeds or certainly different litters of the same one.

Merlin and Spritzer are typical in that unrest began with a sudden flare up as far the Garings are concerned, though the competition between them had probably been going on for many weeks beforehand. Eventually possession of a favourite toy, access to food or proximity to the ultimate top dogs, the owners, may have triggered one to attack the other. Or perhaps the potential was always there, it just needed the testosterone levels to reach a certain threshold for the reaction to be fired. Either way, the Garings now have a situation which, on the face of it, may not be easy to resolve. Merlin and Spritzer are of roughly equal size and intent, being of the same breed and litter and will be rather unlikely to back down from each other having got this far without having established the necessary rank order between them to co-exist without such problems. Dogs are not democratic, no matter how much we usually more egalitarian people might wish them to be. Males especially, even in the home that provides everything in more than ample supply for both dogs, still need to establish a hierarchy. Though it may not always be a particularly obvious one, nor rely on even agonistic displays to be maintained, the structure must exist to enable them to resolve conflicts as and when they arise. A heirarchy fails to develop usually because of one or more of three reasons. Perhaps the dogs are too closely matched, as is likely with brother dogs or perhaps one is a particularly dominant and intolerant male and seeks to victimize the underdog to the point where he must fight to defend himself whenever challenged. In some cases, fights occur simply because we, as ultimate top dogs, in our desire to treat both dogs equally, unwittingly raise the status of the underdog to a level where the other male perceives him as threatening and needs to put him in his place. Sometimes the underdog obviously feels that with us behind him, he can challenge the top dog for his position and will start the fights whenever we enter the room, but whatever the reason, the aim of treatment of dogs such as Merlin and Spritzer is to establish a proper canine hierarchy between themselves. If that can be achieved, the chances are that fighting will cease or only occur at predictable times, such as when they are fed, which can be managed or controlled to prevent conflict.

With two brothers especially, because they will be so equally matched, it is unlikely that the problem will be resolved without castrating one of them. Certainly anti-male hormone treatment from the vet may be worth a try first but, in my experience, this will usually only give temporary relief and the fights return when its effects wear off. The critical question is which dog is to be the one for the vet's knife! So often the wrong decision is made and owners and vets alike plump for the apparent aggressor in the fights in the hope of calming him down by castration. Sadly, this is often the wrong choice and may make no difference at all to the problem as it may simply lower the status of the 'just dominant' male and help the 'just subordinate' one to take his chance to try and seize power. Alas the castrated dog will still have a history of at least equality, if not slight advantage in the conflict, and even without his testosterone, may continue to battle on. The dog of choice for castration is always the underdog in such cases, even if he is a non-provocative victim. If there is no apparent underdog to the owner, then we may be able to decide by seeing which dog stops to allow the other through a doorway first or gives way at the food bowl or see who will give up a toy to the other. If the dogs are still indistinguishable, then we may have to select one by guesswork and hope we have made the right choice, but in such cases the dogs are probably so evenly matched that it may not even matter which one is castrated, so long as one is.

Let us suppose that the Garing's top dog is Merlin and the now castrated underdog is Spritzer. By castrating the bottom dog, Spritzer's smell will be perceived by Merlin as far less of a challenge. Spritzer's testosterone levels will fall rapidly, but as he may still smell challenging for a while from the residual oils on his fur and urine on the fur around his penis, it is always worth bathing him as soon as the vet advises it is safe to do so after the surgery. If the dog is relatively young at castration, the problems between the dogs may be resolved without further attention, so the message for owners of pairs of warring males is to act quickly rather than delay. The older the dogs and the longer the history of conflict, the more their competitive tactics and foci for competition will be established, and the longer it will take for things to calm down. Afterwards, Merlin may still be very intolerant of Spritzer on sight and be motivated to react aggressively if he happens to sit near a favourite trophy, without even sniffing him or allowing him to back away submissively simply after being stared at. If this persists for any length of time, it may help to give the castrated dog a course of female hormones as before to further reduce the challenge presented by his smell to the other dog. This is a tactic that can also be used to help treat two castrated males which are fighting over rank, as can sometimes happen, though it occurs much more rarely.

With underdog Spritzer suitably re-perfumed by castration and/ or female hormones, the next step is for the Garings to enforce the rank order of Merlin and Spritzer from above. Like officers keeping order in the ranks, they must ensure that the uncastrated top dog receives all the privileges of his rank. Merlin must be fed first, greeted first, stroked and patted first, have his lead put on first before going out for walks and generally allowed to have a more open line of access to the owners than Spritzer. Their affection and contact for Spritzer is usually best reserved in the initial phases of treatment at least, to occur when Merlin is asleep or in a different room. Later, it may just be case of getting the order right, and Merlin won't object to Spritzer receiving attention from the owners providing it only occurs after his.

Any trophies that the dogs used to compete about should be removed and items likely to promote possessiveness, like bones, should not be offered to the dogs at all unless they are safely separated. Toys should also be withdrawn but can still be offered in play, preferably outdoors in the garden to each dog on his own or together, provided no aggressive competition then occurs between them. Home should generally become a better organized and calmer place where both dogs are kept as level tempered as possible. All excitement should be arranged to occur outdoors where fights are always less likely simply because the accompanying rewards of status, such as access to resting areas and proximity to the top dogs are less important away from the den or are not immediately available anyway.

It will generally help if the Garings can be more aloof from both dogs, using techniques to be described later in this chapter when dealing with dogs that challenge their owners for rank and status in the family pack. The aim with two fighting males is to make the protective benefits of proximity to the owners for affection and physical contact with them less available to either dog. If such contact is always initiated by the Garings, neither Merlin or Spritzer can secure a raise in status by getting close to them unless they are invited, and that can be controlled by the owners.

It is especially important that Spritzer, as the underdog, is not afforded the immediate protection of his owners and thus encouraged to by-pass having to earn it through outcompeting Merlin. This can often be rather difficult, as the underdog is often the more attractive and affectionate character. The Spritzers of this world are more often naturally submissive, obedient and 'loving' as pets and also learn how to get us to respond to them with big eyes and waggy tails. The higher-ranking canines of the world may be more independent, less 'loving' and more competitive and though Merlin may not seek the Garings' affection as often as Spritzer, he will nonetheless object if Spritzer can gain access to such an important resource. It may be very hard for the Garings to favour such an aloof character as Merlin and reject the friendly overtures of Spritzer when they are all together, but in the initial stages of treatment, this is exactly what they must do. Steadily the dogs relative positions when the whole family is together in the living room watching the television will then become less important. Merlin's status is reinforced, Spritzer learns that he cannot compete and a calmer atmosphere eventually prevails. Gradually, the Garings may be able to relax more and be less rigid in their application of these rank-enforcing ideas but, if by doing so, the antagonism or the fights return, they may decide that they would rather live with only one dog that they can spoil to death, and in such cases will usually decide to keep the the underdog as a more affectionate pet.

Fortunately, most owners of fighting pairs of male dogs do successfully overcome the problems using these tactics, though it is often the case that older the dogs are before treatment begins, the less well defined will be the social order later on. The underdog may still only just be prepared to accept that position and will seize any opportunity for a bloody coup that may arise in future, such as the advancing age or temporary illness of the top dog. With other cases, particularly those involving dogs where a more arbitrary decision was made regarding which one was for the 'unkindest cut of all', castration of the bottom dog may improve the situation but not resolve it sufficiently. In these cases, it will often help to reduce the general hormone related status of both dogs and castrate the top dog too, with the owners strictly enforcing the the difference between the two and their own ultimate top dog status far more insistently.  All in all, the success rate in tackling inter-male aggression problems is extremely high, but this is not the case when the girls start fighting amongst themselves.

# Inter-female aggression

*Dear Mr Neville*

*My little mongrel bitch, Flossie, is quite happy with the atten-
tions of most male dogs including some of the very big ones in
our local park she seems perfectly capable of telling them when
she's had enough without actually biting them or getting into
fights.  However, she hates our other bitch, a Cavalier called
Jetsam, and attacks her violently on sight.  We have to walk
them separately and keep them apart at home too.  Flossie is
also not particularly friendly with other bitches in the park,
though will tolerate them unless they try to sniff her too closely
or want to play. If a warning snap doesn't deter them, she may
attack them quite severely until they back off.  What we really
want to know is whether we can get Flossie and Jetsam back
together again.*

*Yours sincerely*

*Fiona Wilson*

Fights between bitches, be they fights over dominance status, territory, possessions  or simply clashes between personalities, are always the most difficult to treat.  They are far rarer than fights between males and do not seem to be hormonally motivated other than in rare cases where a bitch may become more reactive around the time of her season. Then some may be less willing to share a home with another bitch who may become a competitor for resources when she will need them most to raise her puppies.  My APBC colleague Dr Valerie O'Farrell has conducted some interesting research into the effects of spaying on the behaviour of bitches and found that there are no improvements to be gained by spaying in treating any behaviour problems except where dominance aggression is already being shown towards the owners, a problem we will look at more closely later in this chapter. Certainly I have only recommended spaying for behavioural reasons when the fights between bitches occur exclusively around the time of one or other bitch's season, or a particular bitch in a group suffers such a major character change at this time as markedly to upset relations between the dogs leading to fights between other bitches, as can occasionally happen. But, usually, in such cases the course of action required is obvious and the owner simply takes the bitch to the vet and has her spayed without any need for a consultation with a behaviourist. There is, however, much evidence to suggest that the pheromones given off by a high-ranking bitch have an effect on the hormone systems of lower-ranking individuals in the group and may suppress the function or 'strength' of their reproductive cycle. Exactly how this is mediated is unclear, but it would certainly help ensure that only the highest ranking and presumably fittest bitches in the packs were able to breed and that the pack did not waste energy producing and nurturing puppies with less fit qualities. However, as with so many such highly evolved influences on social life in the wolf or other wild social animals, such effects are lost or only rarely appear in domesticated versions. Hence our weak subordinate bitches may still cycle normally in the presence of a higher ranking bitch and, by doing so, present an unavoidable challenge and suffer from competitive attack as a result. If this is the case, then clearly spaying of the subordinate bitch is a sensible move.

However, most of the cases of inter-female aggression I have seen have concerned pairs of spayed bitches which seem to have developed as a result of a single incident, rather than from a steady build up of competition suddenly over- spilling into violence, as with the case of inter-male aggression between Merlin and Spritzer. Two perfectly well-adjusted bitches, spayed or unspayed, can suddenly come to blows over possession of a toy, titbit or occupancy of a favoured resting place and thereafter never repair their relationship. This may happen at any age, and is apparently as likely to occur between sisters as it is between two unrelated dogs, though is perhaps more likely with younger bitches. Many of the cases I have tried to treat have contained elements of confusion in the pack status of the two combatants and reinforcing, or creating and enforcing, a dominance hierarchy has been a key feature of treatment. Hormone treatment, using the calming influence of progesterone on the subordinate bitch, (but only if she is already spayed), can help, but really the prognosis is not very good in most cases. Whereas one might expect a 90 per cent plus succcess rate in treating pairs of fighting males, this falls to well below 30 per cent with bitches. Although bitch fights are far less likely, perhaps because they are usually less obviously concerned with rank and generally less pushy in their demands than males, once they start, the fights are often more severe. Fighting bitches rarely give up and, if the owners are not on hand to separate them, they may fight to the death. Fighting breeds excepted, many of the male fights I have witnessed in pet dogs stop if one gains the upper hand and the other submits or runs away. When the two males are next brought together they are probably unlikely to resume the battle immediately and things may simmer for a few days before erupting again, or require a very distinct focus of competition, usually at home, for a scrap to begin. Fighting bitches however, are likely to pick up immediately where they left off wherever they are and, as with Fiona's Flossie and Jetsam, they need to be separated to protect them from each other.

If progress is to be made, Flossie and Jetsam must be brought together and given every opportunity to repair their relationship, but because of the risks, this will have to be very carefully controlled by Fiona, with both dogs wearing trailing leads and muzzles for safety. Fiona must be very aloof and not respond to demands for attention from either of them, and be prepared to intervene quickly in the event of any growling, staring or strutting by one bitch in front of the other. In short, as pack leader, Fiona must not allow any squabbling in the ranks. But if, after all the treatment and several attempts to bring them together on neutral territory, they still become highly aggressive towards each other on sight, then there is very little to be done and separate lives or preferably rehoming of one or other, as far away as possible, is more sensible. While this is painful for the owner to consider, there is little doubt that it will be in the best interests of both dogs, both to avoid physical injury and to save them from living under the stress of having to compete constantly, or live in a house shared with an enemy behind the door.

Many bitches happily share a house with never a growl, and while one may appear to be dominant on certain days over certain resources, the roles may reverse on other days or over other things. Some announce their status by gathering up all toys and guarding them, yet show no other interest in toys at all and don't even chew them. They may bark loudly or stare threateningly to make another bitch give up a single toy so it can be added to their stockpile. We may feel sorry for the underdog, but if this is their way of maintaining the social hierarchy, it would be unwise to interfere by redistributing the toys more fairly, as this would only provoke competition. If, however, the top dog is defending her collection against the underdog by snapping at her, or the behaviour develops to, say, preventing her from leaving the room or being near the owner, it may be time to enforce the hierarchy more stringently and remove all sources of competition, including the toys.

One case I saw of fighting Yorkshire Terrier bitches had proceeded in exactly this manner, with the end result that all toys had been removed and sitting on the lady owner had become the most valued activity in the home. If the underdog approached the lady, the higher ranking dog would leap on her and bite her severely until she ran away. However, the victim continued to try to gain access because once on her owner's lap, she received protection and could sit and growl in safety at the top dog below. Once down again, she would be attacked and the poor owner was caught in a quandary of whether to protect the victim and pick her up again and tell the attacker off, or pick up the attacker and reject the victim. The answer was to pick up neither when they were together and so remove the source of competition while fussing them both as individuals when they were alone. The fighting ceased, the bitches organized their hierarchy and the owner could sit down in peace again. So, if there are particular identifiable situations under which tension or fights occur, treatment of fighting bitches can be successful, providing it is tackled early. Once they are fighting on sight there is precious little hope of a peaceful solution.

## Fragile hierarchies

*Dear Mr Neville*

*We have three dogs of our own, two female Jack Russells and a boy mongrel of similar size who share our home with a regular visitor, another Jack Russell bitch owned by one of our staff who works here full time. All the dogs get along fine, have their own little likes and dislikes and places to sleep. Howver, as soon as the door bell rings, anarchy sets in. They all charge to the door barking like mad, but then, instead of barking at the visitor , they all turn on each other and have the most almighty punch-ups. We've tried separating them with water, rape alarms, rolled up newspaper and even the judicious use of a riding crop but, unless we pick at least two of them up and put them in another room, the fighting continues. Once the door is opened and the caller comes in or goes away, the dogs return to normal again. Some of the injuries from this type of fracas are quite nasty. Have you any suggestions for treatment?*

*Yours sincerely*

*Celia Grant-Smith*

The established pack order in a group of dogs is often only just about as stable as a South American government and, with a little excitement, it can easily fall to pieces. With the knock at the door and the need of every dog and bitch to rush up and defend their territory, they are all much nearer to the threshold of governmental collapse, and subordinate individuals can seize the opportunity to take power while the higher ranking dogs are engaged in foreign policy. The end result in this case was a cartoonist's dream, with a great pile of dogs all barking like mad, some at the door, some at each other, various pairs fighting in turn while the male on the edge rushed about biting all of them on the bum if he got a chance, and mounting the temporarily vanquished before they could dive back into the fray. In front of my eyes there was a veritable explosion of canine behaviour and the enormous increase in sex and violence reminded me of those lurid accounts of the collapse of the Roman Empire!

Treatment involved enforcing a hierarchy between the bitches, and virtually ignoring the male as a simple opportunist of the situation. He was already castrated and generally a very placid little chap; it was the bitches who ruled the house, and the actions of the number two that were the cause of the problem. She would attack number one with the excitement of the doorbell and understandably, number one would try to snap back at her so that she could continue to do her duty at the door. As soon as number two recoiled a little, she was jumped on by number three, eager to take advantage of her temporary defeat and take over her number two slot. So as well as trying to defuse the whole scale of the territorial reaction as described earlier in this chapter, we also arranged to practise keeping number two back from the door, first using a tether, then by training her to go to a corner. This solved the problem, as number three wasn't interested in challenging number one and the male simply lost interest, presumably because there was no-one available to mount! Those owners with lots of dogs clearly may have to be more aware that natural canine behaviour patterns predominate in their packs, compared with those of us with just one or two more human pack-orientated individuals.

## Hyper-excitement – jumping up

We have already seen how dogs may accidently bite us if we get in the way when they are being territorially defensive or fighting one another but the bites are rarely deliberately at us at such times. However, when dogs act more deliberately against us, it is essential to understand why of we are to treat the problem and make our best friends safe to live with.

The puppy that jumps up to greet its owners and visitors may be tolerated and even encouraged to do so when he is small and be easily pushed aside, but when a fifty pound and more adult dog tries to leap up, he is quite capable of knocking one over and inflicting painful injuries with his nails as he reaches up, even if he is only pleased to see you. Jumping up is an interesting behaviour because, while it is easy to presume that the dog is simply trying to get eye contact, he or she may also be attempting to lick at the owner's face. Indeed, if the owner bends down to greet the dog, he may well be licked profusely around the face, and especially around the mouth. This is believed to be an effort on the part of the dog to make the owners regurgitate food for them, as is practised by young wild dog or wolf puppies as they become weaned. Excitable attention at the mother's face is designed to produce a meal, and though this is rarely seen in domestic pet dogs, we naturally encourage our dogs to greet us enthusiastically when we return home and so perpetuate the behaviour through other forms of reward. As the young dog grows up we may continue to encourage that type of greeting and so the dog may try to jump up at us even when fully grown as a friendly gesture. Dogs may also jump up in an effort to reduce their height disadvantage if they are starting to challenge us for rank position in the 'pack', a problem we will deal with in greater depth in the next section of this chapter. But whether dominant, excitable or looking for a feed, the dog that jumps up at us and our friends cannot usually be deterred by being told to get down or pushed off as this only 'rewards' his efforts with extra attention. Even if pushed away forcibly, he may simply bounce back up and still seek to leap up next time we arrive home.

Treatment is better aimed at first ensuring that the dog is never allowed to jump up at its owners, even when they are dressed in their old clothes – after all, the dog can't be expected to know the difference between jeans and a dinner jacket. Once consistency is established, the dog can then be trained out of further jumping with an un-pleasant consequence to his behaviour if he continues to try rather than using threats or punishment from his owner. Best of all, I find preconditioning with Dog Training Discs or a surruptitious and well timed squirt of a new specially designed product called 'Down Dog' at the dog's mouth as he jumps soon makes most such well meaning dogs adopt a new greeting approach on four legs, which can then be reinforced with rewards from the owner.

The dog should also preferably sit on command before being patted or stroked in greeting as it is that much harder to leap up from a sitting position than a standing one if he does get excited again once contact has been allowed. The greeting can be further controlled through offering the dog something, such as soft toy kept conveniently by the door, to grasp in his mouth while standing or sitting, a tactic that works especially well with many gun dogs and those who naturally go off to fetch something to offer to their owners when they arrive.

## Mouthing at hands

*Dear Mr Neville*

*My Pointer, Oliver, is forever mouthing at my hands and wrists. While this used to be fun and I enjoyed a hand to mouth wrestle with him, he will now do this whenever I come home, during other games when he is excited, when I try to stroke him and simply when he wants my attention. Now that he's nearly a year old, his mouthing is better described as biting, though he only puts dents in my skin and hasn't yet drawn blood. If I try to pull my hands away from him, he hangs on and tightens his grip, and if I hide my hands, he simply gets very excited and jumps up in search of them. What have I done and how can I stop him from hurting me?*

*Yours sincerely*

*Alan Fairclough*

If jumping up to get face- to-face contact is a form of greeting and social contact established by the young dog with its mother, it is no surprise to see such contact maintained in social interactions between adults. The excitability of the young puppy greeting its mother home gives way to more controlled and calmer interactions and a similar development occurs between the early dog and its owner as the puppy grown up. As dogs are usually unable to indulge in face-to-face contact with their owners due to the height difference and jumping up is usually discouraged, most realize quickly that physical contact is offered by the owner through their hands and can be initiated by seeking but most accept the right of the owner to initiate all the physical contact for the most part, and only nose their owner's hands occasionally for a reassuring pat and stroke. But a few, like Oliver, are encouraged or learn for themselves that they can demand and dictate matters more by grabbing the hands at every opportunity. Mouthing of hands and wrists by young dogs is a common problem, usually resolved by denying access for a while and offering other forms of social greeting and contact, though a few do try to hang on once the hand has been offered. Once the dog is used to this type of interaction it will, as Oliver has done, often seek to control the owners' hands, hang on to them with increasing strength and be increasingly likely to inflict injury if the owner tries to remove his hands from the dog's mouth. With milk teeth the mouthing may be tolerable but once the second teeth are through, the dog can inflict painful bites without meaning to be anything other than friendly. Mouthing as playful or greeting behaviour in the young assertive pup may also quickly lead to more serious biting of the owner if that pup develops into a challenging young adult dog who seeks to control their interactions. All in all, it is best never to allow such forms of contact to develop in the first place with a young puppy and only to allow calm greetings and physical contact from hand to dog's head or body, never teeth to hand. Once such problems are evident in the young dog or have continued untreated in the adult dog, treatment may be more difficult. Most owners find that verbal admonishment will usually only excite the dog further and heighten his desire to hang on, and trying to give the dog a smack when he already has one hand in his mouth or is likely to grab it on its way down to his backside, is both unreformative and potentially dangerous. Aversion tactics, identical to those used for the dog which jumps up, usually resolve the problem well, especially using theDown Dog spray directed at the dog's mouth as he approaches in search of the owners' hands. However, owners must ensure that they reward desired forms of social contact immediately afterwards so that they replace the mouthing and biting actions of the dog. The dog therefore continues to want to be with the owner on the owner's conditions, rather than becoming reluctant to approach at all because of the unpleasant spray or being unsure of the owner's feelings towards them.

## Aggression towards owners

In looking at the various types of canine aggression in this chapter we have seen many cases where we may be bitten by our own dog, or someone else's for perhaps understandable reasons, excusable ones albeitin many cases unjustifiable ones. We can add to that situations when we might deserve to be bitten if, for example, we were to taunt a dog or physically attack it; situations which are, of course, best resolved by not being cruel to the dog in the first place.

But for whatever reason we may be bitten, it makes us all too aware of the dog's ability to defend itself, grab and kill its prey and, even occasionally, lash out in a frenzy of fear or excitement or without recognizing us at all. It's all part of the risk we must accept in choosing to keep predators with teeth such as cats and dogs as pets.

When we are challenged aggressively or bitten for understandable or excusable reasons, we have the immediate prospect of getting treatment for the wounds and then can deal with the dog and consider his future afterwards. Perhaps we may decide to keep him and view the incident as an unlucky break, or we may be able to reform him for the future, or perhaps he will be rehomed or put to sleep for his actions. The shock of the incident may be largely physical, but when an owner is threatened or bitten by their own dog for less immediately explicable reasons, the shock is not confined to the physical. The emotional trauma of living with a dog that is a pleasant pet most of the time but which may, in a series of different situations, put the owner and his family at risk of being challenged is not an easy cross to bear. The kids may forgive the dog for biting them or their parents and cry at the prospect of their pet being put to sleep. The owner may realize that it is hardly responsible to give the dog to someone else as he may do the same thing to them, and most responsible owners wouldn't dream of taking the coward's way out of simply turfing the dog onto the street. And so the problem may remain in the home, and a decision only made after someone is seriously injured by the dog or the tension simply gets too much to bear.

# Dominance aggression

*Dear Mr Neville*

*My two-year-old Dalmatian, Jones, is rather difficult to live with. He was always a very playful and sometimes quite rough puppy, but in the past few weeks he has started to growl rather threateningly at my wife and me. He will do this if disturbed at any time, when he has a toy or something else he doesn't want us to have, when he has his food and, particularly, when he is told off for any misdemeanours. He raises his lips, meets our stare and growls quite fiercely, though, so far, he hasn't bitten. He is reasonably obedient and fun to take out, but more defiant and unpleasant to be around at home. Strangely, he is very friendly towards visitors for a while and then behaves simi-larly towards them if they stay for longer than a few hours. We probably haven't been bitten because we've taken the hint and backed away from Jones when he is like this, but the problem is getting more and more difficult to live with. If he is on a chair, one can't sit next to him, if he is lying at the top of the stairs or outside the loo, one cannot pass without risk and I'm sure it's only a matter of time before we are bitten. Should I take him on and give him a good beating to show him who's boss in my house? If not, what else should I do to make him safer?*

*Yours sincerely*

*Norman Blakewell*

Jones is presenting very typical signs of the dog who is challenging for high status in the family group, his pack. Often, this is generally referred to as 'dominant aggression' but I tend to find that this type of problem divides neatly into two rather distinct categories, genuine dominance aggression and opportunism. There are certainly dogs like Jones who are truly dominant and aspiring pack leaders but usually they will be male dogs aged about eighteen months to two years old at the time of the onset of real problems. Their character evolves through a combination of genetic predisposition, post natal and early experiences within their litter, hormonal status and then, prior to the onset of social maturity, experiences with their owners and often irrespective of how the owners keep them, they will be slowly but steadily aiming to work their way up the pack in terms of rank.

These are the tough guys, born to lead and a natural part of the canine social set up. Not all dogs can be chiefs and most, of course, will never reach that top dog position because another dog will out-compete them. Others will get so far and then have to wait for the moment when a higher ranking dog becomes injured, sick or dies before progressing further. They are motivated to keep trying, whether in the dog or the human pack, and while there is much that can be done to reduce the risk of being attacked by these genuinely dominant individuals, keeping them involves a degree of acceptance that they may always be rather obstinate, insistent, possessive and sometimes quick tempered, and require a consistent and firm approach for safe co-habitation. Safety for the family is a vital prerequisite for treatment, especially for those viewed by the dog as next up in the system and therefore most likely to suffer from his efforts to overhaul them.

Dogs like Jones are rarely persistently nasty or dangerous, indeed that is the reason why most owners feel able and safe enough to keep them and enjoy their other traits. For Jones, far more so than with subordinate dogs, life is all about status. For the most part, his packmates are viewed as either inferior to him, and, fortunately in some cases, therefore not worth the bother in suppressing with further aggression, or superior to him and likely targets in future that must be overhauled in the pecking order. But Jones will seek to maintain or enhance his high rank only in certain situations or over certain issues. At other times, he may simply expect deference from his packmates and only make the effort to reinforce the demand with a stare, slight prickling of his hackles or change in tail height. If, as often happens, we don't spot the gesture and ignore it, Jones is quite likely to ignore it too. The event simply wasn't worth investing any great show of dominance and is not worth a fight, providing we are submissive or responsive at other times.

Dominant dogs may be especially possessive of trophies such as toys, family objects that they can steal, food, bones, and of resting areas and their bed. To attempt to challenge a dog like Jones over such possessions is usually very unwise, for these are the trappings that he perceives as the benefits and symbols of his status, in the same way as we see fast cars, expensive jewellery and large houses as reflecting human success. He will defend them with utmost vigour and, worse, may even decide to defend them by attacking next time simply as one approaches or passes him, let alone actually challenges him for possession. Jones may be unwilling to be handled closely by his owners, brushed, bathed, have his ears, eyes and teeth inspected or even have his lead put on. A high ranking dog simply doesn't accept that subordinate individuals have the right to investigate him so closely, especially when such handling involves standing over him and staring at him with what he sees as a very dominant gesture. After all, we're only mimicking the behaviour patterns of one high ranking dog towards a rival at these times and he'll use the same tactics to make us back off – a rigid body posture with tail arched, hackles raised and growling. That's initially . . . later, once he sees his rights as established, he may not warn us before biting if we approach with a view to handling him, especially around the socially sensitive areas of the face, neck, withers and rear end.

As a high-ranking individual, Jones will often expect to control key points in the den and control the rest of the pack's access through the house. This usually means that dominant dogs show none of the deference a gentleman would show to a lady, or someone we perceive of high rank, when it comes to passing through a doorway or along a narrow passageway. We would step to one side and allow them through, perhaps even averting our gaze as they passed. Jones will be the one who expects to push through first and have everyone else back away from him, looking away to avoid confronting him. The desire to lead the pack may extend outdoors as well, and is the cause of many such dogs pulling so strongly on the lead and refusing to walk to heel, despite strangling themselves in the process on their collar.

A dominant dog may deliberately sit by doorways so that their packmates won't dare to leave without their permission and, in serious cases I have seen, perhaps even head them off at the door and growl to make them sit down again if they try. As we saw with the marked territory protecting behaviour of some dogs in kennels or cars, if you control the access points, you not only reduce any threats to a minimum, you can control the movements of those inside. One dominant Labrador I saw some time ago had learned to sit in front of the bathroom door at night and deny access to the family with a great show of teeth! When they decided to avoid confrontation and go downstairs to use their other toilet, he decided that he'd been outwitted, and moved to a position halfway between the top of the stairs and the main bathroom, preventing the family from getting to either! Strangely, in the morning he was always delighted to see everyone and, during the day, they could move wherever they liked in their own home!

In monopolizing the stairs, the Labrador was showing the typical awareness of the importance of height to many dogs, and especially dominant ones. If you've ever wondered why so many Yorkshire Terriers and other little lap dogs can sometimes become so nasty when tucked under their owner's arm, or why even a pleasant family pet grumbles when turned off the armchair, it's mainly because by being high up, they can defend their position and perhaps their status against challenge more confidently. It's the same reason why our forefathers built castles on hills, and people on horseback can often appear rather haughty to those on the ground. Most dogs have one distinct disadvantage in the human pack, and that is their lack of height. By being upright on two legs we have a natural advantage. Perhaps this is one of the reasons why dogs usually accept their owners as being higher ranking in the pack, but if the dominant dog can equalize matters a little by jumping up or, more commonly, by getting onto chairs then matters will be more even. If he can get even higher than us by standing at the top of the stairs and so make us mere mortals approach slowly from beneath, with our eyes naturally averted from his because it hurts our neck to peer up all the way, then he has advanced his status still further.

What we are seeing with dogs like Jones is a lack of acceptance of many of the sort of interactions we would expect to enjoy without conflict. This is ever more apparent when Jones refuses to accept being approached or handled and growls to warn his owners away. While this may begin when he is approached while on his bed or resting elsewhere, or when there is a specific aim of handling him, it usually generalizes into any approach with just a few exceptions where there is an obvious pay off for Jones to accept his owners intentions. At other times he may demand attention by mouthing and grasping the owner's hand or wrist. This is an action that can get progressively more painful as the dog gets older. Mouthing turns to firm holding and biting, especially when the owner, then having perhaps accepted the friendly, light initial grasp, 'challenges' the dog by trying to pull his hand away.

Jones may tolerate being patted and stroked while his dinner is being prepared or especially when his owners return to greet him after he has been left at home alone for while. Indeed, it is interesting to observe the mobbing of the top dog that can occur by subordinates in the pack if he returns to the pack after a period of separation. He will tolerate being lept on, nuzzled in all sorts of private places, having his ears tugged and generally allow all sorts of liberties to be taken for a short time, presumably so that his pack get the message that he's back, and still in charge. Then he'll walk away with his position reinforced and then be far less tolerant of such forms of contact unless he initiates it.

A common feature of the dominant dog's behaviour is that he will steadily become less tolerant of any direct approach by the owner, but increasingly expect to demand contact or attention from them. Starved of affection by their pet, owners are usually only too willing to respond to him immediately when he is friendly, unaware that they are reinforcing his perception of his rank and ability to dictate the whole nature of their relationship. Interestingly, there may still be limits to what the dog will tolerate even when he has demanded attention. Owners may be able to stroke him along the back but not handle the head. Dogs like Jones may even roll on their backs in an apparent inviting show of submission, but if the owner then tries to rub their tummy, they may be bitten for being over-dominant and pushing the point home at a time when the dog is really only trying to make a friendly gesture.

If this sounds rather conflicting, it really only goes to show how complex the interchange between dominance/aggression and fear/submission can be between pack mates and how far we are from really understanding it. A dog may behave in a consistently dominant manner most of the time but be physically submissive from time to time or even generally subordinate, making only occasional dominant postures or threats. Dr Abrantes has helped us understand the great interplay between these states, but it remains all rather confusing to any dog owner in the heat of the moment. It is, however, immediately apparent that the dominant dog should be carefully handled, even when ostensibly being friendly or submissive.

Dominant dogs are often very trainable as a result of their often higher than average 'intelligence' or responsiveness to all their surroundings and relationships. This may be especially apparent away from home, but indoors, where rank and status are all the more important, dogs such as Jones are likely to be disobedient, or defiant. Though they may know well the responses expected to basic commands such as 'sit', but they may choose not to respond, mainly because they do not see the owner as having the right or rank to dictate their actions. They may obey quickly when there is an immediate pay off in prospect, such as being fed but, more often, they may ignore the command and just walk away, leaving the owner to command in an increasingly loud or threatening tone before they might respond. Others may take up a defiant posture and refuse to obey, becoming aggressive if the commmand is shouted louder, or the owner advances on the dog in an effort to threaten him into complying. Staring at or leaning over the dominant dog is often regarded as a seriously threatening gesture and provokes an aggressive reaction very quickly. Even gentle approaches at the same level as the dog which can sometimes be tolerated may be at others rejected with a growl and lead to bites if the owner doesn't withdraw.

Jones is likely to be very competitive if allowed to play certain games. Physical strenght can be tested in games of tug of war and wrestling on the floor. The more Jones 'wins' these encounters as a developing young dog, the more likely he will be to use physical tactics such as hand grasping and biting, to establish and maintain his high rank as an adult member of the pack. Try as we may not to play such games, Jones may be particularly proficient at making us; picking up his lead and not letting it go is a common tactic. If the owner pulls back, the competition is on, if the owner gives up possession Jones has won and added another point to his card in the dominance stakes. Aggression of a dangerous kind may not develop even in highly excitable pulling games, but the effects of Jones winning, perhaps because he is physically stronger (and Dalmatians can be extremely strong and tough), or because we let him win out of our sense of fair play, or because we have to go and answer the phone in mid-game, will be felt later. Jones may pick up a toy or a trophy which he will then not give up, and will expect to use his strength to hang on to it, just as he did earlier with something less vital to us. Possession then is reinforcing his right to possess, and the owner can only be drawn into conflict to regain possession . . . and Jones thinks he can win that conflict. Once he has established a rank, he probably can . . .

Visitors may listen is disbelief to the tales of woe from owners of dominant dogs because dogs like Jones are typically delighted to welcome new packmates into their den. They may be noisesomely friendly towards guests, letting them stroke and handle them at will and do things that the owner would be firmly rebuked for. Don't be fooled this is for the short term only! If the visitor stays for any length of time, they too will be brought into line once the dog has weighed them up and decided that they are to stay, and therefore need putting in their place in the pack beneath him.

Jones will maintain his dominance over packmates with occasional threats or displays of aggression in some or all of the situations described. Typically he will also be a rather full-blooded male sexually, and perhaps be a frequent 'flasher', mount furniture, blankets and legs, roam away from home in search of bitches given half a chance, and be a frequent leg-cocker outdoors. We will look at sexual problems specifically in the next chapter, but it is logical that the high ranking male dog is likely to be more active sexually than a lower ranking individual if he is to pass on his success to the next generation. Consequently dominant dogs may also present problems of unwanted sexual behaviour at home, excessive interest and worrying of bitches outdoors and be competitively aggressive towards other male dogs, as if everything else wasn't enough.

While Jones and his ilk may paint a picture of a type of dog that would be better off in a wolf pack and well away from the demands of being a pet, 'dominant' dogs can make the most rewarding of companions. Chiefs may need to be more intelligent and tougher than their subordinate packmates, be more responsive to their surroundings and generally reactive and confident on walks, which are, after all, hunting excursions in the dog's mind. They will often defend the home more vigorously, protect their packmates from attack away from the den, send aggressive dogs packing if they get too presumptious but be independent and unworrying at home and also playful, especially in competitive games with their owners. If they can be made safe, the dominant dog can be exactly what many owners would like, myself included. (Yes, it's that damned Bandit again!)

The person most at risk in the family may not be the child or the lady of the house. If the dog already perceives itself as high enough ranking to be number two in the household behind Dad, then it is Dad who may be most likely to feel the force of his efforts to get the top. Men usually have certain advantages compared with women in the canine dominance stakes because of their more authoritative deep voice, testosterone inspired smell and, I am told by one lady close to home, their occasional lack of patience with the family dog as a youngster. This keeps the aspiring dog more in awe of the leader figure than of the lady of the house.

However, a great many human packs with dogs in them are matriarchal as far as the dog is concerned, and perhaps in the mind of most husbands too! The dog may perceive the wife as top dog and never challenge her, perhaps because their relationship was better defined as the dog was growing up and 'trying it on' with her and the kids frequently during the day. It was Dad who arrived home bad tempered signalling a readjustment in the family social order, with all the kids, if not his wife, dropping down a peg.

But even where, in the past, I have felt that the dog could be made a safe and ultimately rewarding pet after a process of sometimes quite lengthy treatment, I have never advised that the family go ahead if children were at risk. Adults may accept the risk of injury persisting short term during treatment and can usually manage to minimize that risk. Children are more forgiving, may forget about new management plans for their dog and can present untold challenge to the dominant dog if, for example they seek him out when he is is resting under the sideboard. One warning snap bite later and they could be scarred for life, so we take no chances. This was brought home to me some time ago in treating a very dominant Springer Spaniel. I felt that the owner's nine- year-old daughter was most at risk from the dog, but her macho-minded father was determined to 'break' the dog. He would not accept my advice that he was putting his child at risk because we couldn't control the dog sufficiently safely during treatment in the family's particular circumstances. While the dog was reasonably safe with him around, he simply wasn't there often enough because of his job.

I always remember that my first line in writing to him to confirm my diagnosis was 'I advise that this dog be put to sleep without delay by your veterinary surgeon'. When about a week later, he phoned to tell me that he had done so, the only thing he forgot to say was that he had delayed too long. I learned from the dog's vet that his daughter had received twelve stitches in the bite wound to her bottom that felled her, and another six on the back of her head from the attack that followed. Dominant dogs must only be treated under very careful guidelines and with careful assessment of who will be at risk and by how much. If safety cannot be guaranteed for the person in the family who is most at risk, then the dog is better off rehomed to a carefully selected new owner, or put to sleep. Thankfully helping clients make this agonising decision rarely falls to me, mainly because it will already have been painfully obvious that euthanasia was a sensible course course of action and advised by the vet without need for a second opinion from me.

Usually I receive the cases where there is sufficient hope for improvement and the owners are prepared to make the necessary efforts to reform the dog. It goes without saying perhaps, that sending a dog away to be 'trained' out of its dominance is, as with all basic training away from home, utterly pointless. The dog may come back trained to some degree and not at all dominant towards its trainer, but just resumes where it left off with its family when it returns home.

In making the dog safe around vulnerable members of the family, it may have to put up with wearing a muzzle for much of the the time initially, that's if the owners can get close enough to the dog to fit it. Usually the dog will allow at least one member to handle him in such a dominant fashion around the face, so the onerous task of putting it on and off will fall to them. This immediately reduces much of the tension of living around such dogs because, while the dog may still growl and challenge the family, they can ignore the display more confidently if they know the dog can't actually bite. But that's not to give the excuse to then turn the tables physically on the dog and start biting him! The tables must be turned, but more subtly.

As genuinely dominant dogs are often aggressive to other male dogs, and hypersexual, castration is often advisable without delay for the dog of up to about three years of age. Beyond that age there may be little to be gained from castration as his perception of his status will have become learned. The potential for dominance is thought to be established with the determination of sex in the male dog as a fetus and some believe that, even at a few days of age, puppies which will later prove to be dominant are more active, acquire the warmest spot in the nest and ensure that they always get the most productive nipple to suck. As a result they may grow faster earlier and, in playful encounters with their litter mates, find that their brothers and sisters are quickly respectful of them. They learn to initiate games and contact rather than being the recipients of attention from the others and perhaps come to play a little harder later. They may also be more insistent at keeping possession of objects around the nest.

Come the second surge of male hormones, this time self- produced at around adolescence, the motivation behind much of this reactive and self-determining behaviour becomes further reinforced. Indeed, such dogs may be expected to produce more testosterone than their subordinate counterparts. Testosterone levels were tested in different vocations of people in a 1988 study. It was found to be lowest in Christian ministers and highest in professional football players. Levels doubled in tennis players in the 24 hours before a big match and maintained a high level in the winner's saliva afterwards, while dropping in the losers. The suggestion is that competitive creatures have, and need to have, higher testosterone levels. It may also be that while day-to-day behaviour in people with high levels may be indistinguishable from anyone else's, certain reactions in certain situations may be extra violent – the same probably applies to dogs. Hence castration of the even occasionally aggressive male dominant dog may be a sensible first step in treatment. This may yield marked results, although it depends on the age of the dog and how much of his dominance has been learned through success at imposing his will on his littermates, other dogs and, subsequently, his owners. From my own case files it seems that dominant individuals of some breeds, such as Dobermanns, Rottweilers and German Shepherds seem to respond better than others, such as Springer Spaniels and Black Labradors to castration. Contrastingly, with the rarer cases of dominance in bitches, Dr O'Farrell has found that spaying the dominantly aggressive bitch is likely to make matters worse. In her research forty per cent of bitches already showing aggression towards their owners got worse after being spayed and so such bitches may be best left unspayed until problems are resolved.

The most important feature of treatment of Jones, and perhaps the most difficult to apply, is that all his attempts to initiate contact with his owners must fail and especially any efforts to mouth at their hands. The owners must not respond to Jones' stare, his efforts to sit on their feet, brush or lean against them ,nor to the presentation of toys as an invitation to play even to the friendly sidling up with a nose nudging under the hand left dangling over the armchair. Every time the Blakewells respond to Jones' demands they inadvertently re-inforce his right to dictate his and their lifestyle. Faced with no further pay off for his demands, Jones may initially try harder to attract attention, paw at them more enthusiastically, fetch toys or objects like wallets that he knows will provoke a reaction or leap about barking. The Blakewells must try to live through this period, as ultimately, Jones will give up trying and lie some distance from them, looking up with big dark eyes imploring them to respond to him.

At this point, the Blakewells can indeed call Jones to them to receive a short period of attention or simply allow him to sit near them. Then they are initiating the contact and it is Jones, who, starved of affection and feeling a little ostracized from the pack he used to rule, will be more eager to comply with the demands. However, this is not the end of the change round. Prior to receiving the benefit of contact or affection from his owners, Jones must respond to a simple command such as 'sit', and preferably a 'down' as this requires him to adopt a more submissive position near his owners. From the time of the inception of treatment, Jones will learn steadily that 'nothing in life is free'. He must 'earn' his affectionate contact with his packmates, access to his food, to the garden, having his lead put on and earn the right to move from one place to another. With many cases the regime can be slowly relaxed as treatment progresses and the dog becomes less dominant, but with some, this pattern must continue for ever. In many cases, if owners relax their insistence, the dog may perceive his status as having risen again, but success all depends on just how much the dog is motivated to keep trying, even after castration and stricter management strategies. Initially, this treatment may mean that Jones receives less attention from the owners, but the aim is that he will ultimately receive the same amount, or even more, under the new regime and so dog and owner can continue to enjoy that very essential part of Jones being around in the first place.

The next important feature of treatment is to get the dog out of the bedrooms. Many dominant dogs are allowed to sleep in the master bedroom, with all the privileges that go with being able to rest comfortably with the protection of the tougher pack members around. Small wonder that the kids are not seen as having rights to tell the dog what to do when they have to sleep further away from the safe core of the den. Sleeping in the safest or most comfortable place, and sometimes even in or on the bed itself, is one of the prizes of high rank and so will be much sought after and much defended! My APBC colleague John Rogerson finds that owners are first bitten by their dominant dogs in the bedroom in over 80 per cent of cases. My advice always is to get the dominant dog, in stages perhaps, as far away from this firing line as possible and establish a new safe, warm sleeping area for him more at the edge of the den, perhaps downstairs in the kitchen. Rights of access upstairs to the main sleeping area of the pack, and especially in the main bedroom itself, must be earned. People earn them because they own the den, but the dog can never earn these rights unless we loan him the status. If he repays the loan with a bite when we have fewest clothes on to protect us and when we are lying down apparently submissively in bed, then it is time to call in the loan! Of course, used to the comfort and status of the bedroom, he may protest vehemently when moved out,so if the dog is not so dangerous when in the bedroom and with the owners made aware of the continuing risk, the bed can be moved steadily nearer the bedroom door, then out on the landing and finally downstairs and into the kitchen over a period of days or weeks.

Though it may seem bizarre, the Blakewells must endorse their right of access to everywhere in the house at will, and that includes in Jones' bed. From time to time they should simply stand or sit in his 'pit' and be seen to do so, though only when the bed is empty and not initially by turfing Jones out of it, as it may be dangerous to promote conflict. Only later when Jones has been demoted will the Blakewells have developed the right to turf him off his bed, or indeed from the chairs or other vantage points, with a simple word of command and for the prospect of reward.

Things known to promote competitiveness in Jones should be avoided, especially if he is likely to win. His efforts to mouth the owners' hands must be denied any success, so if Jones keeps trying, a well timed spray of Down Dog into his mouth should deter him. This should be immediately followed by inisisting that he sits and then offering strokes or other contact of a more acceptable and less painful and slobbery kind. The simple act of removing all toys and ceasing to play competitive games also can have a marked effect on the dog's desire to dominate in the home.

Outside, Jones will need to be exercised as much as possible to tire him out and games incorporating commands such as the 'sit, wait, fetch, come and drop' routine of throw-fetch games should predominate. Toys can be taken outside for this but, once everyone comes home, the owner shouldkeep possession of the toy and put it away in a drawer or other safe place outof the sight and reach of the dog, so that he can't pick it up and guard it. In short, all the toys are now the owner's, not the dog's and he must earn the prospect of having a temporary share in them through cooperation with his owner.

Gradually the home will become more of a place of rest again and Jones will be much calmer. His toys can be brought out later when the importance of holding trophies has been lost and temporary possession of what have then become the owners' toys can be used as a rewards for doing other desirable things. Tug-of-war games are probably out for all time; instead, Jones must be taught as described earlier to give up any object when told to do so, and receive a reward for compliance rather than being struggled with.

Feeding time is most likely to be when Jones will best fulfil the precondition of sitting, to earn his supper but, as many dominant dogs also show their worst behaviour when the greatest reward is on offer, the Blakewells may have to manage Jones especially carefully at this time. He must fulfil the demands made of him, but if he is already growling with the production of the dinner bowl, or starts to defend it as soon as it is put on the floor, it may be wiser to feed him outdoors for a period and leave this aspect of treating his behaviour to last. We will look at what to do more specifically later in Chapter 8 – Food and Behaviour. Certainly the dog should not receive the same type of food as his owners and never from the table. With the dominant dog, begging is a form of demanding. Feeding Jones from the table is a form of the owners making way at the 'kill' in deference to his high status, which carries the rights of the richest pickings with it.

Owners of a dominant dog especially may benefit from feeding him at a set time from his own bowl. Some behaviourists recommend that the dog should preferably be fed after the family, so that their action in feeding him is more one of abandoning the leftover carcase to the underdog, rather than letting him as a higher ranking dog, eat his fill first, and then come back for more when the family sits down to eat. If he is a nuisance at mealtimes, he should be put outside or tied up so that he cannot interfere. Logical though this may all seem, I am not totally convinced of its usefulness in the treatment of the dominant dog, though establishing and sticking to a regular meal time instead of feeding on demand certainly will help introduce some necessary routine and establish the owner's right to order the dog's life. In extreme cases of dominance, food can be withheld from the dog at all times unless he obeys the demands of the owner. The dog is put onto a dry diet, and portions of the daily ration kept in the owner's pocket and fed 'piecemeal' throughout the day to the dog after he has come when called, sat, etc rather than feeding the dog at set meal times. The food can also be used as a lure to interrupt unwanted behaviour without conflict. Then the owner is also seen as the constant supplier of good things, but on his own conditions. The dog is fed any unearned portions of his diet as a small meal last thing at night as the owner retires for bed. Such a tactic is, of course, not without risk, and so only to be employed with very competent owners under careful supervision.

Once these lifestyle changes have been implemented and tolerated, the owners can begin to enforce their new-found dominance a little more on Jones. By now he ought to be quite a lot more obedient, and regular obedience training to sit, stay, come, down and heel should be practised with him by all the family, with older members supporting the demands issued by children or people previously perceived as lower ranking by the dog. Frequent short encounters, still based on reward techniques, will endorse the owner's right to expect the dog to respond and therefore raise their rank in his mind. Help from a professional trainer on a one to one basis may be useful, but only providing gentle methods are used. Heavy handedness will only provoke a competitive reaction from a dog who already knows he can defend himself if he has to and then push for victory.

Jones can be fitted with a trailing lead to wear around the house to deny him the prospect of resisting commands to come off his bed or out from under furniture and to be able to lead him gently down off chairs or other high vantage points if he manages to sneak up when no one is looking. Having told him to 'come', the owner can pull gently but insistently to make him come out into the open, whereupon he is rewarded. The tactic is identical to that used in treating the Cocker Spaniel who wouldn't leave the car earlier in this chapter, but should only be practised when the lead can be picked up in safety. Additionally, if the dog steals something, he can be pulled towards the owner, asked to sit, and give up the trophy for the prospect of a food reward. Care is needed with this if the dog is already aggressive in defence of his trophy.

Jones should also be prevented from preceding his owners through doorways using the lead, or simply by shutting the door in his face every time he moves forward. The door should be shut in front of the dog, but certainly not with his head deliberately allowed to go across the threshold and hit as practised by one barbaric trainer from Surrey that I once met. After a couple of experiences the dog usually takes a couple of paces back when the door is opened and will allow the owner through. If not, using Dog Training Discs will usually do the trick or a jet of water to startle him if he tries to dart forward as soon as the door is opened can be helpful. Care again is necessary here, as this may provoke a nasty reaction. Jones should preferably be trained not to pull his owners along on the lead, but short term, he can prevented from doing so using a head-collar, assuming he will allow it to be fitted. Used correctly, a head-collar can vastly speed up the process of teaching dogs not to pull and is infinitely preferable to the traditional and cruel methods using choke chains to yank the dog back. Head-collars can also facilitate safe handling of the sensitive head region of the dominant dog, but under the guidance of a behaviourist.

It is essential that the various stages of treatment are only employed at a rate which causes the situation to improve and that the owners are happy to apply. Some dogs can take everything at once and respond well, others need to have their rank slowly eroded away and take some time to respond to treatment. Some even seem to make no progress at all for weeks and then, all at once, fall into line. Dominant German Shepherd Dogs seem to have perfected the art of driving their owners and me to the utter brink and then, just as we were all going to give up, suddenly reforming totally and permanently.

A vital feature of all cases is that confrontation and conflict with the dog is avoided at all costs. It may not be necessary to win every battle to win the war and establish owner dominance. It is always far better and safer to prevent or manage conflict by removing the sources, controlling the dog's access to various parts of the house using the lead etc and to walk away from him if he has already gained the upper hand and is simply inviting competition that the owner has little or no hope of winning. The dog which has taken the wallet under the sideboard cannot really lose so there's no point in trying to 'keep up with the Joneses' (sorry . . . couldn't resist) at every turn. Better to walk away if he growls, or to distract him out by ringing the doorbell or encourage him to come to his owner by rattling his titbit can.

Success will take some time, but can produce an enormously rewarding pet at the end. He may still have specific likes and dislikes, and individual situations, such as getting access to the top of the stairs, may occasionally mean that his old ways come flooding back, so such prospects will have to be managed very carefully or avoided for ever. Baby gates may successfully stop the dog from moving as freely around the den as he used to, and while this may be a pity and restrict his ability to guard the house, it at least means that no further conflict need ever arise when you want to use the bathroom in the middle of the night!

Owners too need careful support during treatment and encouragement to take on the more direct aspects of the process. Some will need to see progress from just one or two simple changes such as the response to castration, removal of toys and making the dog sit for his dinner before they find the motivation and courage to proceed further. Gauging the speed of treatment is a vital feature of any case, but never more so than with the dominant dog.

# Opportunist dogs

*Dear Mr Neville*

*Bella, my Collie bitch of three years of age, has become increasingly tetchy over the past months. She growls at me from her bed or if I try to stroke her while she is next to me on the bed or on the sofa watching television. She's started to snap at me and my daughter if we try to pick up her toys when she wants them, and has even darted across the room to warn us off when we've accidently gone near them. She now won't have her feet looked at or her nails trimmed without growling, and frankly we've become rather wary of her. This seems to have worsened progressively... can we reverse the process and get our nice Bella back?*

*Yours sincerely*

*Patricia Montlake*

Although such truly dominant characters as Jones can appear in any breed or crossbreed, they are rare in my experience. More commonly, and perhaps the commonest problem that I treat in dogs overall, is that of the dog which has inadvertently been afforded a high rank by its human family. Having been raised to a status which it hasn't actually earned, the dog starts to demonstrate similar behaviour to a dominant dog in an effort to maintain its position, or particularly prized aspects of its lifestyle that accompany the privileges of such rank. Such behaviour could occur in virtually all dogs, except those perhaps which are very subordinate, bottom-of-the-pack types who only wish to please and stay out of all trouble. Unlike the truly dominant dog, the artificially high ranking individual is likely to be a bitch as a male, and many bitches like Bella are given ideas above their true station by loving owners. Certain types of owner have been identified by psychologist Dr Valerie O'Farrell as being more likely to suffer these types of problem with their dogs. In particular she has found that owners who desire a lot of love and affection from their dogs, and who feed them human food, are more likely to suffer. The opportunist simply takes advantage of the situation and starts to dictate the pattern under which the desired resources are made available to him.

It is easy to select some individuals from this second category and suggest that they are 'spoilt' and, like a spoilt child, simply bad tempered or demanding when they don't get their own way. While this is true for a few particularly indulged dogs, including one I once saw who had his own bedroom with a four-poster bed in it, the majority have been given an artificially high status unknowingly by their owners. This can occur through ignorance of how and why dogs behave, but again, is equally likely to occur with a family who have owned dogs for years, kept them in a similar fashion and never experienced such problems before. They, probably through no fault of their own, have ended up not with a dominant dog, but an opportunist dog.

Ordinarily, in a dog pack, the opportunist would perhaps be a middle ranker and, lacking the true intent and competitive nature of dogs like Jones, would only move if the opportunity arose to do so easily, rather than actually niggling away constantly for higher status. However, if offered the privileges of rank, they accept them willingly. They can be just as eager to defend those privileges and may defend their rights to dismiss certain 'normal' expectations by their owners as aggressively as the truly dominant dog. The distress to the owners can be even greater than owning consistently challenging dog, as dogs like Bella are often owned by people who only want the best for their pet and bend over backwards in trying to understand and tolerate their pet's aggression or threats. It also comes harder to owners to have a dog who, one minute, is as loving as can be and who will let them take a bone from his or her mouth, yet the next moment growls and even bites them for going too close to a favourite toy. Such opportunist dogs are also often rather confused as to where they fit in their pack. Their whole make-up tells them to be subordinate and non-competitive with their owners, yet the things they would normally not choose to compete for, for risk of being seen as challenging, are readily offered to them or are up for grabs without any protest from the owner. Such dogs are very likely to be unpredictable as a result and, interestingly, are much more likely to look 'guilty' after challenging their owners and temporarily gaining an advantage, or putting the owners down a peg or two. Their expression is, in fact, one of conciliatory submission by a dog that it is all too aware that it has no right to its temporarily raised status. The dog may also fear retribution from its higher ranking owner who may insist on reclaiming their rightful place with a violent counter attack. If I had a pound for every owner who said 'she always looks sorry for herself after she's bitten me', I'd be very rich indeed!

As dogs such as Bella are, in fact, usually well aware of their true position in the group, they are far easier to reform than truly dominant individuals. Indeed many owners manage to do so simply by becoming rather fed up and wanting less to do with the dog anyway. Others, as with a case of a Retriever bitch I saw recently, try to smother the dog with love. This particular owner would throw her arms around the growling dog, look her in the eye and stroke her to pacify her. The dog kept on growling but very slowly became less fierce, lacking the true intent of the dominant dog. A Jones subjected to that approach would most certainly have bitten his owner.

As with truly dominant dogs, treatment of the opportunist never involves taking the dog on with force or confrontation, as they too may use their teeth to try and hang on to their position when challenged. They are especially likely to bite if they have already bitten, rather than just threatened to bite. Instead, treatment involves the same series of measures as for Jones, taking a fresh look at general relations with the family, access to key areas and possessions and control of the dog. Some or all of these may affect how Bella perceives herself in relation to her packmates. By ensuring that she is denied access or opportunity to take advantage of a situation and benefits from behaving in a more subordinate fashion, she can be systematically demoted while still enjoying herself in the group, and being enjoyed as a safe family pet. Dog Training Discs are usually especially effective with opportunists as they give a clear signal to the dog when communication with the owner has usually been rather confusing for it beforehand. Treatment of the Bellas of the world is usually quick, and can be relaxed sooner in more areas after a period of reformation than with a dominant individual and is less traumatic on the owners and dog alike.

# Idiopathic aggression

*'The dog to gain some private ends went mad and bit the man. The man recovered of the bite. The dog it was that died.'*　　Oliver Goldsmith

*Dear Mr Neville*

*My dog , Sebastian, is a terrible Jekyll and Hyde character.*

*One minute he can be sitting by the fire half asleep, the next he erupts into a blind fury and attacks me very severely. This is no joke because he is a huge Pyrenean Mountain Dog and I have to use all my strength to beat him off and run from the room. He never appears sorry for his actions and seems to be in a sort of trance throughout. Afterwards, he just goes back to being as nice as pie. He suffers, or rather I do, the attacks about once a month, and yet at all other times he is a big softy. He lets children climb all over him and has never so much as growled at another dog. Is he mad? Is he safe, not just with me but towards other people? The attacks have always occurred in the home, so I've put up with them for two years now, but after the last one when I was bitten quite nastily, I've begun to wonder about the wisdom of keeping him at all.*

*Yours sincerely*

*Maggie Swift*

While there are many forms of aggression in the canine world which are readily understandable, there are a few dogs which show more puzzling forms. Where there is no apparent cause for a sudden and violent change in behaviour, scientists, in their urge to classify everything, term it 'idiopathic aggression'. Don't be fooled. This basically means 'of no known cause'! However, the consequences of such unpredictable attacks from dogs like Sebastian can be shocking and severe. The condition has also been termed by behaviourists first in America, and then picked up by one or two here, as 'rage syndrome'.

It was suggested that certain breeds of dog, or rather certain strains, could suddenly present such aggression, the implication being that this was an inheritable condition. In America, the problem in the Dobermann, German Shepherd Dog and Bernese Mountain Dog was described as 'noticable' by Dr Benjamin Hart, in 1985, and he pointed also to work in Holland which suggested that the problem was inherited in Dutch Bernese Mountain Dogs at least.

In the United Kingdom, it has been the solid coloured (especially the Golden) English Cocker Spaniel which has been tarred with the 'rage' brush, much to the dismay of the UK Cocker Spaniel Society. Following much publicity about the problem some ten years or so ago, they set about a series of investigations into the breeding and make-up of the Cocker Spaniel, involving, of late, some very distinguished veterinary surgeons. Thus far, they have been unable to pinpoint any problem, nor have investigations in America revealed anything of substance. Despite much clinical examination of alleged sufferers, no neurological or physiological abnormalities have been identified. Some dogs diagnosed as having 'rage syndrome' have been reported to improve under treatment with anti-convulsant drugs more often used for the treatment of sufferers from epilepsy, the implication is that some as yet undiscovered neurological abnormality remains to be found. That, of course, assumes that such a thing as rage syndrome exists, a chronic condition which I and my APBC colleagues feel is very much open to question.

There is no doubt that a trying minority of individuals of some breeds, in particular, in our combined experience, the solid coloured Cocker Spaniels, Golden Retrievers, the Pyrenean Mountain Dog and English Bull Terrier in particular can show highly dangerous and apparently unprovoked tendencies to attack their owners or houseguests. Between us we can also cite single cases in the West Highland White Terrier, Yorkshire Terrier, Jack Russell and perhaps the Bulldog. Several features seem common to these cases and the nature of the attacks. Typically the dogs are otherwise pleasant pets, often obedient and affectionate towards their owners and visitors at all other times. Usually the dogs will be male, and the attacks are more likely to occur in the evening. The alarming and distinguishing feature of the attacks is that the dog apparently gives no warning growl, he simply leaps at the victim and bites savagely, usually at the arms or legs, but also at the face if he can reach. As with other cases of canine aggression, the dog's eyes may appear glazed, giving the appearance of a trance. The attacks can even be life-threatening, especially from a dog the size of a Pyrenean Mountain Dog. Many Cocker Spaniels are owned by elderly ladies . . . an attack may prove fatal not just from the physical injuries inflicted, but from the dreadful shock associated with it. Attacks may be fleeting or persist until the dog is physically beaten off, as Maggie Swift has had to do with Sebastian. Often, once the attack has been halted. the dog immediately returns to his old affectionate self. Others seem confused for a while, rather tired and simply go and lie down to rest.

However, several interesting features are apparent in 'ragers'. The first is that the attacks are always directed at people, and usually at members of the family. No owner has ever come home to find their dog mid-way through a rage attack on the television or curtains. Second, the attacks often occur in the evening when the dog is with the family, perhaps relaxing in the sitting room. they often occur around feeding time for the dog, when we may expect him to be already a little aroused at the prospect of food, or more demanding of a quiet life to digest it afterwards. Ragers are also often likely to be fierce defenders of bones and sometimes other trophies. The implication therefore is that there may be no such thing as 'rage syndrome' and that these attacks may be a pronounced and unusual form of dominance aggression. The rage attack probably occurs at the peak of a cumulative process where the normally subordinate dog generally feels unable to challenge its owners for rank. After a period of perhaps a few weeks of self-control with no hint of problems brewing, the dog goes over the threshold of self-control and attacks the owner in a dramatic and highly aroused manner to challenge for dominance status. Though the owners usually describe the actual attack as being without provocation, it is quite likely that the dog is seething and the attack is triggered by some ordinarily innocuous behaviour by the owner. This may be as simple as shuffling the feet prior to standing up to leave the room, a gesture as we saw with the 'ordinary' dominant dog, that may be seen as a challenge. Equally, the dog may be disturbed by the owners walking past his bed or resting area. Slight movements may also be seen as the first steps prior to a challenge for a toy the dog is lying near, or simply watching on the far side of the room. The attack is obviously way out of proportion to the scale of such challenges and often described as being of low threshold, but I tend to feel that the threshold of attack is in fact very high in such cases if the 'dominance' theory holds for 'ragers'. The dog is basically subordinate in the majority of its relations with the owner, but grudgingly so. The mild stimulus for attack is simply the final straw after a long build up of unrecognized or even undisplayed tension.

Certainly it is my experience and that of Dr O'Farrell, that 'ragers' can respond to sound application, perhaps necessary for the lifetime of the dog, of the techniques used in treating the dominant dog. These tactics would seem to work because the dog is kept much further back from the threshold of rage reaction by being demoted in the group as far as possible. Castration also is an essential feature of treatment for male 'ragers' and has helped many quite markedly, further implying that a rage is a dominance problem, related to the effects of testosterone and accounting for the more likely prevalence of rage attack in males compared with bitches. Recently, APBC members, in particular John Fisher and John Rogerson, have been achieving some superb results with Cocker Spaniels and Golden Retrievers which are alleged to have been ragers. The thoery suggests that these are highly intelligent working dogs which wither do not work to task or only do so in precise seasons (eg. shooting season) and for whom the rage is a sudden explosion of temper apparently in response to the frustration of living an unfulfilling and unstimulating life. This is the presumption because several cases, which have been treated by devising systems of working to task or suitably stimulating alternative activities with the owners, have cured or very markedly reduced the incidence of attach. this is achieved without the use of drugs or hormone treatments which seems to undermine earlier theories based on dominance thresholds or epileptic type conditions. Of course, very few members of these breeds show 'rage syndrome' and so the APBC have rather few animals to work on to test this theory.

However, in many cases, there is no safe prospect for treatment for the rager. Whether dominant or unstimulated, what causes the development of a 'rager' may be a question of semantics for Maggie and her Pyrenean Mountain Dog, or the little old lady and her sweet Cocker Spaniel that has caused her to go to hospital to have twenty stitches in her arm after an attack. There may well be only one fate for such dogs and that is to be put to sleep as soon as possible by the vet.

However, younger, fit owners may be prepared to apply theappropriate treatment and risk the prospect of further attack while they see just how much progress can made. Many are surprised with the results. Some former ragers never attack again, though for many, it is simply the frequency of attack, rather than its occurrence or severity, that is improved.

If the dog is to live, naturally it must be neutered to preclude any prospect whatsoever of it passing on inheritable aspects of the condition to subsequent generations. And herein lies the problem for responsible organizations like the Cocker Spaniel Society in the UK. While its members are cooperating to investigate the problem and willing to neuter or destroy any dog found to show the 'rage syndrome', non-members, perhaps more concerned with success in the show ring, even if achieved by a dog with the condition, may be unwilling to admit the fault, or to lose income by withdrawing the dog from a breeding role. Others, of course, simply deny that any problem exists, or that their dogs could be responsible as they have produced lots of other normal puppies. Therefore they believe that the owners are the cause of the problem. Perhaps they may be, inadvertently, but it would be very hard to maintain a normal dominant relationship with a family pet prone to such reactions, and therefore not suffer attack as a result of ordinary management. The dog, even if just very dominant, may just be too close to being dangerously aggressive in anyone's hands, let alone a little old lady who just wants to spoil her dog.

Hopefully in the coming years we will continue to learn more about dominance and social behaviour generally between man and dog, and discover any cause that may lie behind 'rage syndrome', 'idiopathic aggression' or whatever else we care to classify aggression without an obvious cause.

# Canine aggression in society

*'I loathe people who keep dogs. They are cowards who haven't got the guts to bite people themselves'*　　　　　　　August Strindberg

With all the attention given to the place of dogs in society, and especially the incidence of canine attacks on people and dogs alike around the world over the past couple of years, this chapter would not be complete without a short look at the scale of the problem and implications for the ownership of dogs.

There is no doubt that in some of our city areas, there is a genuine desire to keep a large dog for self-protection. There are certainly many areas of London where I feel decidedly unsafe making house-calls, though it is also true to say that much of that insecurity can also result from the high incidence of large, guarding and sometimes rather uncontrolled dogs in the area, as much as from the prospect of being mugged. High crime areas are not the only places where we feel that dogs can improve our confidence. I recently received a request from a missionary in Tanzania who wanted to make his dogs more nasty to protect him and his mission against robbery! Peace and my guard dogs be with you my son! Naturally, as with all requests I get to make dogs more aggressive, I declined to offer advice.

The number of large dogs being kept, and in often very inappropriate circumstances, is rising both from a genuine need for security and the more insidious desire to own a weapon, or for the insecure to increase their own self-importance through walking with a big dog of a breed with a fierce reputation that makes people back out of our way. In the United Kingdom, it used to be the level and type of ownership of the German Shepherd Dog that caused concern. Every so often there would be a report of children being savaged by guard dogs when they mischievously entered a factory site, or even at home with the family pet who also acted as family guard. Then the Dobermann became the chic looking image dog of the Sixties kept also as a guard dog renowned for a big bark. But both these breeds can often be more nervous than pugilist, both having been developed as guards from more variable, and in the case of the Dobermann, multi-purpose activities for man. Both are, in my experience, more likely to be self-defence biters than dominantly aggressive when there are problems away from their trained or expected guard duties.

I generalize deliberately for a moment about breed temperaments only to mark out the difference between the most popular status guard dogs of times past and the present popularity of a rather different type of dog. The Rottweiler, American Pit Bull Terrier, other Bull Terriers and Bullmastiff (sorry Cassie!) were all originally developed purely for purposes of aggression either in war, or for fighting each other, or baiting rats, bulls, bears and other sad victims in the 'sport' pits of earlier times. When these chaps are aggressive, they are far more likely to mean business than the usually more inhibited, unless deliberately trained to be aggressive, German Shepherd Dog or Dobermann. While all, with the exception of American Pit Bull Terriers, have largely been selected more as docile companions in this century at least, and the bull, or brachycephalic breeds have traditionally made very affectionate pets that usually love children, the capacity for fierce self-defence, and, less usually, attack, remains. These types of dog may attack without any warning growl, threat or bark and sometimes severely in response to very minor challenge, or apparently no challenge at all, from their owners, innocent third parties or other dogs.

Typically the bull breeds 'lock' onto their victims as they did the bulls and bears of old and crush or tear at them. They can be fearless in combat and suffer enormous physical injury without backing down, a feature, of course, prized in the disgusting dog fighting world. Such is the aggressive fury of many that they may even keep attacking their victim long after it is dead. But, most importantly from the point of view of our safety and that of our more docile pet dogs, is that these breeds often do not recognize submission in their victim. Hence, if they attack a person or another dog, their aggression will not be inhibited nor will the attack cease if the victim rolls over, or runs away. Indeed this is just as likely to intensify the attack as contributing to the excitement by screaming or fighting back. With a small Bull Terrier, there is at least a reasonable prospect of an adult being able physically to keep an attack at bay, less so with a 140lb angry Bullmastiff or Rottweiler.

So just how is it that these dogs have been allowed to be kept at all if the consequences of their uncontrolled aggression is so severe? The answer of course is that, despite a fighting background, the bull breeds do make excellent family pets and are no more likely to be the instigators of aggression towards other dogs or people than any other breed. In fact many people would argue that they are safer than many. Others make the valid point that while we expect a Jack Russell to be a punchy confident little so and so, and tolerate or even expect an occasional flash of temper and snap bite, we sound the alarm bells when similar behaviour is shown by a Bull Terrier. Similar, but not identical. A snap bite from a Bull Terrier is more often a case of a crunch, shake and tear and so may be far more injurious.

The crisis point in the UK was really only reached when the popularity of the Rottweiler began to climb. From 2000 registrations made by the UK Kennel Club in 1980, the figure shot up to about 9000 in 1987, though it fell back a little in 1988, probably as a result of all the adverse publicity. Here is a dog of war of great confidence and strength . . . and size. As a result, even though the vast majority of Rottweilers are safe, loyal and exemplary pets (I see more for treatment of separation anxieties than aggression problems!), in the wrong hands or when off the rails, they are far more likely to be highly dangerous in society. Indeed, over sixty per cent of reported attacks are by large dogs (more than 23 kg) which are obviously more capable of inflicting damage than smaller dogs. Sadly, attacks on people by Rottweilers and American Pit Bull Terriers have proved fatal or have seriously injured far too many people around the world to be treated as anything other than exceptional types of dogs. One more death of a person, or for that matter an innocent dog, is one too many if it can be prevented by tighter legislative control.

The way we select our breeding population of Rottweilers, if not American Pit Bull Terriers (they are not a breed recognized by the Kennel Club in the UK and so are not to be found at dog shows) is clearly not doing much to prevent the problems. Indeed, by selecting largely for good looks and with no proper, systematic approach to assessment of character, the 'beauty show' nature of the dog show is more likely to produce a dangerous champion than a dumb, busty blonde as its winner. In the strange, open, largely unfamiliar environment of a show ring, being judged by a strange person while your owner is already a bit excited or nervous himself, a dog rightly ought to be slightly apprehensive. Yet the dog most likely to win will be the one with the combination of good looks and confidence. While this may only rarely have unfortunate repercussions with most breeds, if we are selecting for confidence in already assertive breeds, it's surely far more likely to enhance any disposition for aggression in those breeds. In the controlled conditions of the laboratory it is very possible to breed strains of mice which are notably more or less aggressive than normal by deliberately breeding from selected individuals over several generations. So while the breeding of dogs is obviously less precise, this does show that there is a likelihood that matters may get worse if dogs of some breeds continue to be selected for 'show' parameters only. And worse is that when those show winners are in demand for breeding because of their success, they act not only as the suppliers of confidence for tomorrow's show winners with accompanying rosettes and income for their owners, they are also likely to produce puppies with a greater tendency for aggression, when they are sold as family pets, as most surely are. With a Cavalier King Charles Spaniel, the show world may help produce a confident and good family pet dog as a result of this selection process, however beauty orientated it may be. With the Rottweiler or some of the other large guarding or fighting breeds, it may simply be the roadshow of increasing disaster. Surely it is time to introduce an independent assessment of character based on the opinions of veterinary surgeons, behaviourists, geneticists and responsible dog breeders before any dog is put on the beauty show rostrum? Once a safe, desirable character is selected for, the show people can then have all the fun they like and produce good looking dogs as well as safer ones.

In the United Kingdom in 1989, 84,000 victims of dog bites of all types (predatory chasing, dominant challenge, competition over trophies, etc) were treated by the National Health Service at a cost of £6 million, though the cost isn't as high as it would be if all victims sought medical attention – one study suggested that only 17 per cent of victims seek medical attention. Up to a quarter of attacks reported are against members of the dog's household, with half of all fatal attacks, and almost all of the attacks against children under four years of age, being carried by the family's own dog. The majority of attacks happen in or around the owner's property.

More than 200,000 people are treated in UK hospitals for bite wounds annually, but the great majority are human bites, not canine. Ninety per cent do not require stitches and only one per cent require ten or more stitches. The incidence of dog bites reported to the police in the United Kingdom in 1988 had risen by eighteen per cent on the previous year and the Americans expect a six to thirteen per cent rise per year, but this is mainly as a result of the dog population there increasing generally rather than any change in relative popularity of different breeds. In the USA, Spaniels, Setters and Retrievers and other gun dogs, German Shepherd Dogs, Collies and Dobermanns were all responsible for more attacks than one would expect from their relative popularity with other breeds. Beagles, Afghans and Dachshunds attacked less often but clearly there are differences between strains of the same breeds in different parts of the world. In over five years, I have only ever treated one Irish Setter and two English Setters for any form of aggression against people, but there have been many, many Dachshunds pass through my clinic doors! Other research in America showed that Collies were nearly three times as likely to bite as other breeds, 'beating' German Shepherd Dogs, who were only just over two and a half times as likely as the average dog. No mention of Rottweilers.

As one might expect, three-quarters of all bites reported have been made by uncastrated male dogs, particularly younger ones in the 'competitive' phase of development when, as we have seen, they are perhaps more likely to respond aggressively to challenge or threat. Sixty per cent of all attacks on people are preceded by some form of interaction between dog and victim such as handling, threatening, feeding or taunting of the dog but only 0.003 per cent of dog attacks reported in Britain are of the type one might expect more of the bull breeds and Rottweilers than other breeds. These are described as 'manic' – 'where the dog repeatedly bites or vigorously shakes its victim and there is extreme difficulty in terminating the attack'. Three-quarters of them, it is believed, would have led to the death of the victim had someone else not intervened.

One case reported in the 1980's in the UK led to the death of the Rottweiler which had attacked a policeman. The dog could not be persuaded to release its bite on his leg, so he pushed his truncheon through its collar and twisted it to strangle the dog. Such was the intent of the dog's aggression that it died from asphyxiation before its grip could be released. Even then, the jaws were still locked tight.

Should we judge any breed or types of dog when at their worst? Can we reconcile the need to keep a large dog for protection because of the risk of living in some of the areas we create for ourselves with our own safety? Should I, as an animal behaviourist, even be trying to treat some of these problem cases of aggression when genuine pet owners find that their Rottweiler has gone out of safe control? Perhaps I shouldn't, but somehow I feel that if I and my colleagues are not going to try, the dogs and perhaps society will suffer, and the owners will simply abandon them anyway and get another one. Perhaps it's a case of 'better the devil you know who wants to be treated than the one you don't who doesn't'!

Let's move onto sex, it's more fun.

# 7
# Sex

*'If sex ever rears its ugly head, close your eyes before you see the rest of it'*                                                   Alan Ayckbourn

## Flashing

*Dear Mr Neville*

*We got our crossbred dog from the local animal shelter when he was about eight months old. He was very pleased to come home with us and is generally a very happy little soul without any problems. However, after a couple of days we decided to call him 'Pencil' because almost every time he sits down, he shows everyone what the good Lord gave him. He obviously can't help it, but it is extremely embarrassing to own a 'flasher'. Will he grow out of this?*

*Yours sincerely*

*Mavis Griffiths*

Adolescent dogs can go through a stage of frequent and enthusiastic sexual responses. It is the time when the young dog becomes an adult and the onset of testosterone production in his rapidly developing testes will fuel the development of his secondary sexual characteristics. As well as becoming a little more competitive and starting to test himself against other members of his pack in finding his position in the hierarchy, he will generally muscle up, start to cock his leg when urinating and start to smell like a male to other dogs. Some begin to lift a leg to mark around the house as well but as this may also occur for other reasons, we will look specifically at what to do in Chapter 9.

The rate of production of testosterone in the young male dog is not constant and varies even in adult dogs. When the hormone first comes on stream, its production varies by the hour. Additionally it is acting on areas in the brain which were masculinized just before birth but which in the following months, have had no contact with testosterone. So it is quite likely that the young dog will show frequent and marked sexual responses to his own testosterone and while the effects on Pencil's anatomy may be embarrassing for a while, he should gradually 'calm down' as his testosterone production levels out and he learns how to cope as a young male dog.

## Masturbating

*Dear Mr Neville*

*Our one-year-old dog, Jasper, is a randy little blighter. Even as a young pup he used to mount his blanket, jump on the cat and sometimes even just stand in the middle of the room thrusting into the air. Then it was quite funny, but now the cat has lost her patience, we can't give Jasper a blanket because he wants to mount it rather than sleep on it and no cushion is safe. The only good thing we can say about Jasper's sexuality is that it made us face the prospect of telling our son about the birds and bees well in time! Our vet has suggested castrating Jasper, but this seems a bit drastic as he's still only a young dog. Any help you could offer in treating this problem would be much appreciated!*

*Yours sincerely*

*Adam Best*

Even very young puppies may mount their littermates before weaning and continue to do so as part of their normal development. Play mounting in a non-sexual context is actually necessary for the dog to be able to perform properly when the time comes as an adult dog to mate, and sexual positioning is just another facet of social learning by puppies at a time when they can react in a non-threatening manner with each other. Sexual mounting in immature puppies is believed to occur as result of that pre-natal surge of testosterone though bitch puppies may also show such mounting behaviour. Their brains are obviously not masculinized, but neither are they feminized with a surge of pre-natal female hormones. Their mounting may occur as a result of mimicry of males in the litter or later as a development of mock dominance behaviour, whereby the one on top is playing the dominant role, but in a non-sexual context. Such dominance mounting persists into adulthood, and can occur from dog to dog or bitch to bitch, or much more rarely, between the sexes. We are usually quick to question the sexuality of our dog when he mounts another male, but the behaviour is not the act of a 'gay' dog, it is simply one of the mechanisms dogs use to define their social order. Cows and many other social animals also use sexual postures for similar reasons.

Some puppies do seem to spend more time than might be considered normal in mock sexual behaviour and Jasper is probably one of these. Perhaps he received more testosterone prior to birth than average or perhaps his sexual responses have become an established end pattern of behaviour when he is excited for other reasons. A great many adult dogs look for something to mount when highly excited, almost as a displacement behaviour rather than any urge to mate the whole world. Now that Jasper has started to manufacture his own male hormones, those patterns are likely to become even more frequently expressed when he is excited, and his already testosterone-receptive brain is perhaps now telling him to pass on his genes to anyone and everything as often as possible. Unfortunately Jasper must still learn to direct his attentions onto bitches but, with the usual lack of such opportunity for the average solitary pet dog, he is learning quickly to utilize the availability of readily claspable soft substitutes.

As this is at least in part a learning stage, Jasper may be taught to redirect his attentions if he is 'caught in the act' with a cushion or blanket. As before, there is no point in punishing an already excited dog, as he may become aggressive if challenged at this most delicate of moments (wouldn't you?). But if he can be distracted with a loud noise or by rattling his lead, then he may willingly redirect his excitement onto something more involving the owner.

Offering an alternative such as a walk or game in the garden will usually enable the owners to save face, if as so many young male dogs do, Jasper brings out his blanket to mount in the middle of the living room just when the guests have arrived. The excitement of their arrival and his desire perhaps to keep the attention on himself may provoke his behaviour, therefore the owners shouldn't reinforce it by immediately paying him attention, competing over possession of the cushion or by scolding him. Distraction and alternative opportunity to burn off his excitement is the best policy. The cat is clearly already helping Jasper to learn that some things, no matter how attractive because of their smell, soft feel or movement, are not to be mounted for any reason! With a little help, the owners can continue to teach him and castration almost certainly won't be necessary.

# The dog and the teddy bear

*Dear Mr Neville*

*Our Labrador, Ben, definitely has a sexual problem. He used to try and mount our legs and occasionally try to leap on our daughter but he seems to have calmed down a lot in recent months. However, he has struck up a rather unnatural, if touching relationship with my wife's large teddy bear that normally occupies a chair in our bedroom. When Ben is not to be found downstairs with the family and things have been suspiciously quiet for a while, we always know exactly where to find him. Sometimes he is just lying at the teddy bear's feet, other times he has pulled it down and is in the middle of a very passionate encounter! Away from home he seems largely dis-interested in his own kind and has never once attempted to mount a bitch. We can stop his bear affair by keeping the bedroom door shut but we are keen to know why he should fancy it so much and whether he needs help to overcome his problems.*

*Yours sincerely*

*Andrew Stavely*

It is quite common for young male dogs to 'experiment' with a range of things in discovering about their sexuality. As we have seen, through lack of opportunity to develop more normally through contact with bitches in a pack, a young male may direct his attentions onto other objects, animate and inanimate. Naturally we discourage their sexual advances towards us and as a result, some divert their attentions onto our possessions instead.

The teddy bear is a prime and all too common example, but others form similar close attachments to the family's clothes or towels and one I treated  had what must have been a very painful relationship with his owner's umbrella!  Another, a very fit English Bull Terrier called Winston, fell hopelessly in love with the vacuum cleaner.  My cartoonist friend Russell Jones decided that Winston's obsession was due to 'her smooth, good looking lines, her gentle hum or her romantic shade of avocado green, and her  ability to vacuum right up to the skirting board!'

These things are best controlled by distraction and denying access, but coupled with greater alternative activity. Such dogs often benefit from having a canine companion to react with.  Interestingly, their sexual antics usually don't get directed onto the new dog, or if they are, may soon meet with rebuke.  Simply the company and opportunity for all sorts of social interaction reduces the importance and expression of sexual activity.

## An ungodly relationship with the vicar

*Dear Mr Neville*

*You will not believe how embarrassing it is when your male dog is in love with two men. One of these men is my husband, whom Roger tries to mount whenever he gets the chance, the other, we have only recently  discovered, is our local  village  vicar, of all people. Roger, who is three years old by the way, singled him out at a recent garden party I gave for the Women's Institute. He sniffed at the poor man very intently for a while and then climbed up his leg and proceeded to mount him very enthusiastically.  The unfortunate man was caught between trying to keep up appearances while at the same time trying to shake Roger off.  Roger's grip is extremely strong as my husband can testify and it took four of us ladies to get him off. Despite this, my husband is loathe to have Roger castrated because he thinks it will affect his 'manhood' and make him into more of a wimp, and anyway, he is a lively happy dog at all other times. Can you save us from further blushes please?*

*Yours sincerely*

*Miranda Battley*


Do it, Miranda, do it! While we may all be prepared to tolerate an occasional misplaced or unwanted burst of sexual activity from our dogs, especially when they are young and finding their way in the world, when a more adult dog causes this level of embarrassment, it is most definitely time to have a chat with the vet about that very neat, quick and effective operation.

Of course, many men are worried about the psychological effects of castration on the dog, especially those with large tough breeds who are worried about their declining image if their dog is emasculated. Masculine image-extending breeds such as the Dobermann and Rottweiler traditionally have their tails docked, so all is open to public view, or not, as the case may be after the operation. One Dobermann owner I advised to have his dog castrated agreed that it was a good idea but actually investigated the prospect of having silicon prosthetic testicles inserted into the dog's scrotum as the real ones were removed. Such things exist for men because humans are far more closely linked psychologically to sexual function and appearance, but this owner decided ultimately that this didn't really extend to the appearance of his dog when he discovered that it would cost him well over £150 per artificial testicle plus the cost of surgery!

Castration can have many of effects on the behaviour of the male dog, and most actually make him a pleasanter character and easier to deal with. We have already seen how castration can help treat pairs of fighting male dogs in a house and more generalized dominance aggression. Many dogs become far less competitive and much more biddable after surgery, depending on the age it is performed at and all the other environmental factors and learning aspects that affect any given dog. Castration doesn't otherwise alter the dog and it certainly doesn't make him a less efficient hunter or guard or into a lazier performer of any task in training.

The only adverse effect can be that castrated dogs can put on weight more easily after surgery because their general metabolism is altered and they need less food for maintenance while, at the same time, their appetite may go up. However, there is no need for a castrated dog to gain weight; his diet can be perfectly managed after surgery by his owner. I should say that while two of the three male dogs I have owned have been castrated, I am not one to rush in and recommend castration for clients' dogs unless I am utterly convinced of the necessity for it and even then, usually only after we have seen how the dog responds to behavioural manipulation and perhaps an injection of anti-male hormone treatment. Like many vets, I don't believe in unnecessary surgery if other methods may bring results and can be tried first.

Adult male dogs react sexually in response to their own testosterone and to specific cues, the most obvious being the smell of a bitch in season. Others, perhaps lacking social experience and sexual opportunity may over-respond to the smell of any bitch, or a bitch's urine which contains special scents called pheromones designed to impart messages of her sexual state and perhaps social standing to other dogs. Some dogs may over-react to our scent on clothes, or on us, and perhaps Roger is one of these. His mounting of the vicar may have been triggered in an inexperienced dog by the smell of man, especially as Roger was also prone to mounting Mr Battley from time to time. While this may also have had some competitive dominance component, I think it is only reasonable for us to want such behaviour to cease, and castration is very likely to help.

American behaviourist Dr Ben Hart found that 60 per cent of cases of male dogs of any age that mounted people were helped or cured by castration and a greater success rate would be expected with younger dogs. In my experience, the older the dog is at the time of castration, the less effect the operation will have as more components of sexual activity will have become learned, or be incorporated into other aspects of the dog's family relations, such as the determination of rank.

Additionally, there are a few dogs, including some castrated early in puberty, who cock a snoot at the operation and continue to behave almost exactly the same without their equipment or testosterone . . . enter Bandit once again. Despite being castrated at under a year of age, he will continue to seek and mount bitches in season, even completing the dog tie as the last sequence of the coupling. The dog tie, or dog knot, is that famous bottom to bottom position adopted by mating dogs which looks utterly excruciating! The male is physically unable to withdraw from the bitch due to the swelling of two bulbs on his penis which hold him in until he finally 'calms down'. Some owners confuse these 'bulbs' with testicles and phone the vet accusingly on seeing them after the testes have been removed at castration. One lady I saw had even driven a couple of hundred miles to discuss her young terrier's developing sexuality and these two things which appeared attached to his penis every time he had an erection! For an hour and a half, we discussed the structure and function of a dog's penis...and I didn't go red once!

For owners who are genuinely reluctant to have their dogs castrated for reasons of sympathy or because they would like to use the dog at stud, an anti-male hormone injection will usually dampen the dog's sexual activities for a while and provide an opportunity to redirect the dog's learning and energies onto other activities. Such an injection is usually effective for about three weeks but may decrease the dog's fertility for some months afterwards, a point to bear in mind if the dog is to be used for breeding.

This option is preferable to that employed by the unfortunate owner of a huge, but young Tibetan Mastiff I saw some time ago. The owner, who was well over six feet tall and heavily built himself, was the victim of his dog's developing sexual attentions, but strangely only ever in the kitchen. Whenever the poor man tried to prepare a meal at the table or wash up afterwards, the dog was likely to leap upon him and mount him furiously. The owner insisted that once the dog had him pinned over the table or sink, he just couldn't be shifted. 'What do you do then?' I asked, innocently, trying not to laugh. 'Wait for him to finish' came the long-suffering reply! The dog was given a shot of anti-male hormone injection by the vet and remained controllable while he grew through his adolescence and his hormone levels stabilized. As an adult he became far less reactive sexually and later went on to father many very handsome puppies through the type of sexual contact his owner intended him to have.

Many owners mistakenly believe that hypersexuality in dogs can be relieved by allowing them to mate with a receptive bitch. This is a fallacy. In fact if anything, it is likely to increase their sexual responsiveness and teach them how to perform more effectively. Better to stick to the old adage of 'what you've never had, you don't miss' and deal differently with other forms of sexual problem as they arise.

# Owner mounting

*Dear Mr Neville*

*My Jack Russell is a very sexually aware little dog. He is highly competitive with other male dogs and tries to mount any bitch who will stand still long enough for him, irrespective of how big she is. He seems very hyper-sexed when we are at home too and frequently tries to mount my arm when sitting on my lap, or my leg, if I stand still for too long – especially when I am on the telephone. I feel that dogs have a right to enjoy sex and so I don't stop him, but he has now started to do this to my friends as well, and they are naturally less tolerant. I don't want to have him castrated. Is there anything else that might be done?*

*Yours sincerely*

*Robin Hughes*

This letter is not a joke! I have seen or spoken to many owners who are quite happy for their dogs to mount them in this way in some mistaken belief that they are helping the dog express his full range of normal male behaviour. Try as I have on many occasions to explain the sexual nature of the dog, such owners are clearly confused also as to the nature of human tolerance and the limit to the necessity of fulfilling all the needs of their dog. As consenting owners in their own home, they may be happy to be the sexual target of their dog's attentions, but are usually brought nearly to their senses by the disgust of their friends. The dog's behaviour can be readily halted by the owner not being available to the dog for such attention, redirecting the dog's energy in more desirable pursuits, sudden distraction, a canine companion, anti-male hormone treatment, castration ... anything so far mentioned along with a sympathetic informative approach in explaining to the owner why they needn't or shouldn't worry so much about their dog's sexuality. But if this case makes you wonder about how far the nature of the relationship between man and dog can go, I have also seen several cases where owners have deliberately masturbated their dogs either to relieve their pet's sexual tension or just because the dog was clearly quite a sexy little so and so. Yuk! Bring on the human counsellors, I'll sort out the dog, with a little help from the vet!

# Roaming

*Dear Mr Neville*

*We own a real escape artist of a dog. No matter how high we build our fences or how deep we dig the foundations to them, or put wire mesh across the lawn and keep the doors bolted, Henry will always find a way out. He's escaped through windows, bolted out of the car and scaled ten-foot wire fencing with inward overhangs. We've fallen short of putting up electric fences and control towers, but are getting fed up with having to collect him from the police station. Sometimes he gets picked up many miles from home, other times he simply wanders back expecting his tea after driving us mad with worry. He's now six years old and has been wandering off from the day we got him as a three year old. He's a friendly old rogue when he is at home, but always seems to have a glint in his eye and watches for any crack in the door that he might possibly be able to worm his way through. How can we persuade him to stay at home where we all love him?*

*Yours sincerely*

*Jeff and Teresa Smith*

Roaming is often another feature of the hypersexed dog and seems to be especially controlled by male hormone levels. Certainly castration is the most effective means of control and has been found to cause reduction or cure in 90 per cent of all cases, though again one would expect an even greater success rate with younger dogs before they learn to enjoy the free life and encounter receptive stray or latch-key bitches in season. I remember with great affection a lovely old Labrador called Pest who was owned by the family I lodged with for many of my university days. Pest was an escape artist and well known by everyone in the village. He was traffic wise and rarely went beyond the next village a mile or so away. He was a notorious dustbin raider and seeker of food, as are many of his breed, but Pest also wouldn't miss a chance for action with the girls. My landlord would make a special effort to keep him firmly at home when a Whippet who lived a few roads away came into season. This was no ordinary Whippet according to her owner. This was the fastest whippet ever, and her breeding potential was not to be spoiled by one night stands with the likes of some slobbering, slow but desperate Labrador that found his way to her door whenever she came on heat. Somehow Pest defied us all and always got there! I'll never forget the night when the angry Whippet owner virtually bashed the door down and yelled at my landlord in a broad Lancashire accent 'YON BLUDDY LABRADOR'S BEEN AT MIGH WIPPIT AGIN AND WHAT T'BLUDDY 'ELL ARE YOU GOIN' T'DO 'BAHT IT? Y'OUGHT TO CUT 'IS BLUDDY GRAHPES OFF!!

I saw Peter and Olive Waters, my old landlords, again recently and was sad to learn that Pest had passed on some three or four years ago. But, true to the end, even in his new home in mid-Wales, Pest had been seen, hard at it the day before with some flighty but willing little Collie-type in the town square. He was thirteen then, could barely walk and spent most of his day asleep. One last go, and out. It seemed a fitting way to go for the old trooper!

## Disinterest

*Dear Mr Neville*

*I have what I think must be a rather rare problem with my Belgian Shepherd Dog. Most people seem to have dogs that are always mounting things, legs, furniture and other dogs. Not mine. Tristan, Mighty Baron of Avondale the Ninth, simply won't perform at all. I don't think he's ever had a sexual idea or inclination in his life, which is a real bind because he keeps winning at shows and is in great demand as a stud as a result. He's been presented with all sorts of attractive bitches, and right in the peak of their seasons, but he just goes and lies down. Is there a way of making him more interested?*

*Yours sincerely*

*Philippa Patel*

This is obviously the other side of the sexual coin. Some dogs just don't seem to develop any sexual interest at all, perhaps because of a low testosterone output or lack of receptive areas to it in the brain. Perhaps Tristan didn't receive a pre-natal testosterone shunt, or never had the opportunity to develop sexual responses and sequences with his littermates, as can sometimes happen when only a single puppy is produced.

I have also seen two cases of 'sexless' dogs which had been born without any testicles at all, not even retained in the abdomen as is sometimes encountered. These dogs, one a German Shepherd Dog, the other a Collie cross, both had a functioning penis, but never once cocked their legs nor showed any other male traits. The purpose of testicles descending outside the body is to keep them cooler, as hormone and sperm production occur at lower temperature. Hence retained testicles are often non-functional and there may be an accompanying failure of development of the dog's libido.

A trip to the vet is in order for Tristan to make sure everything is in the right place and functioning but a common cause of failure to perform is that dogs like Tristan may, as well as being inexperienced, be rather subordinate dogs. The presence of other higher ranking males in the home may actually inhibit him from responding to a bitch. He simply may not see himself as having the right to mate! If inexperienced socially, he may also be rather fearful of the bitch, especially as she will be smelling rather different and perhaps 'flirting' in a rather frightening manner for his attentions. Finally, he may simply not have fancied any bitch that has so far been presented to him! While most males will, as Tristan's owner says, mount anything and everything, others may have very specific preferences and only wish to mate with one bitch in their immediate group, or none at all if they are not from their group. A change of venue may help Tristan, and a period of being kept at a different location to any males he is presently sharing with may help him . The chance to live and socialize in a mixed group more constantly may also help him catch up on the learning stakes. The vet may also be able to advise on some appropriate hormone therapy, perhaps administration of extra testosterone may help though I've never had to consider this for any of my clients. Most dog breeders are far better informed than me about the 'mating game' and sort out their problems themselves with various forms of encouragement.

As I'm beginning to sound like one of those radio agony aunts for human sexual problems, we'll move onto the female of the species, with which, as you would guess, there are far fewer sex-related problems.

# P M T?

*Dear Mr Neville*

*Our twenty month year old Bullmastiff bitch, Kirrie, has become terribly depressed both before and after both her seasons. Last time she suffered really badly and we are probably now going to give up our hopes of breeding from her and have her spayed. However, Kirrie is also occasionally a little aggressive towards our other bitch, another Bullmastiff who is already spayed, and we wondered whether spaying Kirrie would subsequently affect their relationship.*

*Yours sincerely*

*Nanette and Robert Monk*

Bitches are not constantly affected by their sexual hormones as are males. Indeed the only time that hormones come into play is when they are helping prepare the bitch's body and behaviour for reproduction and after conception in the development, birth and care of the puppies. The relatively sudden production of the hormone oestrogen as the bitch comes into season may make her more active and 'flirty' even to the point of leaning against her owners invitingly or presenting her rear end for mounting. Some even start to cock a leg like a male when urinating to enable them to mark deliberately and perhaps attract males, while others become more vocal. A few become more aggressive towards other dogs, including males, until they are fully receptive. If this behaviour is a nuisance then spaying would be kinder for her or, if as is sometimes the case, the dog suffers from premenstrual tension (PMT) or becomes depressed after her season because of the production of progesterone, particularly in a phantom pregnancy, then it is probably much wiser to have her spayed. This will prevent all these twice yearly changes and keep her more level tempered. Letting bitches with hormone related behaviour problems have a litter will alter nothing except for the period of the pregnancy and rearing of the puppies. The same problems will be experienced with the next season and so early spaying is advisable, under the direction of the vet of course.

Some pairs or groups of bitches do find it hard to cope with each other if one or more of them changes smell and reproductive profile every season in either or both dogs. Tension can sometimes spill over into fights and there is no doubt that some bitches feel challenged if a lower ranking bitch comes into season and thus competes for males. Then spaying all the bitches in the house can keep things calmer and friendlier. With younger groups of bitches conflicts may arise when one is sexually mature, but socially more immature. In such cases as Kirrie, therefore, it may be wiser, until she has reached social maturity at two-and-half to three years of age to avoid further problems with the other bitch. Until then Kirrie's seasons can be controlled chemically by the veterinary surgeon and her depressions prevented.

We have already looked at how some bitches may collect toys or cushions and treat them as litters of puppies or become possessive over other objects after their season and especially during any phantom pregnancy. Others suffer more innocuous effects such as changes in food preference. A bitch in season can be messy, not to mention the hoards of stray male dogs like Pest that may accumulate outside the front door, all cocking their legs furiously over the gate and howling and barking at all hours to announce their arrival and hopes. Frankly, if owners do not intend to breed from their bitch, it always advisable to have her spayed. Opinion is divided among my veterinary colleagues as to whether this is best done before the bitch has her first season or afterwards. Some believe there is no more need to let her have a season than there is to let her have a litter. The only adverse effect of spaying, apart from the particular case unearthed by Dr O'Farrell's research, is that like castrated males, spayed females may tend to put on weight more easily if their diet is not managed properly by their owners. And that brings us nicely to the second most important thing in life after sex, for the male dog at least, and that is food.

# 8
# Food and Behaviour

*'Bad men live to eat and drink, whereas good men eat and drink in order to live'*                                                    Plutarch

One of the common misconceptions about dogs, and one exploited to no little extent by many pet food manufacturers, is that dogs are only carnivores, or meat eaters. Of course they do eat meat and like it, but unlike the cat, dogs are not obligatory carnivores. In fact, dogs are more like us; they are omnivores and can eat virtually anything. They can also survive perfectly well even on a completely vegetarian diet.

Dogs learn what to eat and what not to eat as puppies as part of the development of their exploratory repertoire. They mouth and chew inanimate objects and develop preferences for then going on to consume certain types of food. Their mother will bring food items back for the litter and regurgitate food for them, while at the same time denying them access to her diminishing supply of milk. Hunger, exploration and increasing demand for certain nutrients, such as protein as puppies enter a rapid growth phase after weaning, all serve to ensure that they experiment with a wide range of potential food items. As adult dogs they will be more scavengers than carnivores and, in the wild, many wolves and dogs will go for long periods existing on vegetable matter such as fruit, grass and roots without any ill effect whatsoever. Indeed, most pet dogs eat grass from time to time and while this may provide a readily available source of roughage and some minerals, it also often causes the dog to

213

vomit. This may have helped ancestral dogs unburden themselves of some of the roundworm load in the stomach and persists as an occasional behaviour in the modern pet dog despite it usually being wormed more effectively with pharmacological preparations.

When a hunting excursion is successful or the chance of a meat meal occurs, perhaps from consuming a lucky find of a carcase, the wild dog will usually take full advantage of the opportunity by gorging himself. In so doing, he can often quickly replenish any deficiencies that have accrued from a preceding period of unsatisfactory diet and build up strength and reserves for the next days or weeks in case the chance doesn't appear again for a while.

Dogs have a great capacity for surviving long periods without suffering physical damage on a sub-optimal diet, both in terms of quality and quantity. Sixty days of hunger strike by a man will usually be fatal and, if not, will certainly have caused irreparable damage and require a very slow return to normal eating habits if the digestive system is not to be shocked further. The dog, on the other hand, can often go straight back to feeding with gusto after a long period of shortage.

Clearly, for all life-forms, food is essential fuel. However, hunting and feeding also carry social obligations. For man or dog, small mouthful size meals can usually be immediately consumed without fear of committing social indiscretions or the risk of having someone else steal them. But formal dinner parties for us can be a nightmare in terms of using the right implements at each course and obeying table social etiquette. Away from small bite-size meals of fruit or vegetable matter and small meals of rodents or dead birds, dogs in packs must also learn the rituals of taking part in the hunt, and then the social etiquette of who has the right to eat first and which bits of the kill they may eat. But even in a pack, where the high ranking dog may well have established the right to eat first and choose its pickings, the scavenging nature of the dog ensues and even weaker or lower ranking individuals will still try to gorge themselves on any large find or kill as fast as possible before reluctantly giving way when the more dominant animals arrive at the scene. Survival depends on the ability to scavenge and stuff yourself as fast as possible and, despite the lashings of food we offer our dogs as pets, this instinct often remains. Hence most dogs can be relied to stuff themselves as soon as the bowl is put down, and to lick it totally clean.

# Food guarding

*Dear Mr Neville*

*Archie, our sweet-natured little mongrel becomes terribly aggressive whenever we offer him his food. He gets highly excited while we prepare it, but remains friendly and will sit on command for as long as it takes us to let go of the bowl. As soon as the bowl is down, he stands right over it growling fiercely, bark-growling if we stray too close, and even jumping slightly away from it to defend it with a snarling flash of teeth if we advance on him. If we stay in the same room, he stuffs the food down like there was no tomorrow, growling all the time but, as soon as it is all gone, he walks straight over to us, wags his tail and is as friendly as could be. We've tried punishing him for growling but this made him ten times worse. We tried speaking calmly to him and edging nearer, but this didn't help much either, so now we just feed him and leave him alone until he's finished. Now he's starting to stand over biscuit treats or edible things he finds on the floor and, as we can't always see them before he does, things are getting a little dangerous. Any suggestions?*

*Yours sincerely*

*Kath and David Sweep*

Food guarding is the most common food related problem that I encounter. It's one of those behaviours that is very understandable to most owners; after all, guarding food would be a behaviour designed to help their dog survive in the wild. As a young puppy, Archie may have growled a little at his littermates to make them back away and ensure that he got the best share of the spoils. With his new human pack he simply carried on with the same tactics, despite learning that if he was nice and friendly, and even obeyed an obedience command as the food was being prepared, it would arrive quicker. Once the food is given to him by the Sweeps or, perhaps as Archie sees it, once the higher ranking pack members have backed away from their possession of the food and allowed him access, he will hang on to his possession and seek to make sure no-one threatens. Possession then is certainly nine tenths of the battle and the previously friendly and obedient dog has become hazardous to approach. Most owners faced with their dog growling at them over his dinner take offence and either tell him off or give him a smack and try to drag him away. To the dog motivated by the desire to survive, this simply confirms his idea that he must defend his dinner at all costs. Archie and his ilk, who can be of any breed, defend all the more at the next meal and even a slight approach or failure to back away by the owner results in a huge display of aggression. Thankfully, this is usually focused around the food bowl, and owners can avoid being bitten by keeping clear or, as the Sweeps have done, feeding the dog in a separate room or outside. However, I have seen have a few food guarders that have become so aggressive at feeding time that they will chase and even bite anyone in the same room in an effort to establish a huge exclusion zone around that most valuable of resources. Typically, any food guarding dog that is challenged once he has possession of the food bowl is likely to increase his defence tactics and become more dangerous.

Unfortunately, the food guarder also teaches himself that as aggressive displays can win the day over food, they can employ similar tactics over other issues, such as t oy possession or occupancy of the favourite chair. Indeed, treatment of the food guarder is as often a case of treating a pointed expression of a pushy dog that is generally challenging its owners for rank in the family pack, as it is an individual problem in an otherwise nice dog like Archie. The pushy dog who is also a food guarder is much more likely to be male than female because of the greater social competitiveness of the male and so the broad treatment for this type is a general canine-style demotion in the pack as discussed for Jones the Dalmatian in Chapter 6.

However, this alone will not inhibit such dogs or the already normally subordinate Archie from guarding his dinner. Specific treatment must be applied whereby the Sweeps' ownership or right of access to all food at any time is endorsed in Archie's mind. This can be achieved initially using a technique taught to me by APBC colleague John Fisher. He calls the dog to him, makes him sit and immediately gives a small biscuit as a reward while, at the same time using the words 'take it'. This is repeated several times and the dog soon builds up a good conditioned response which can easily be emulated by the dog's owners. Then the reward is withheld a little from the dog. If he tries to reach up and take it for himself from the hand, the hand is closed to deny access and the words 'get off' are used in as low a tone as possible and accompanied by a fixed stare at the dog.

Most of course are unaffected and try harder to prise the biscuit from the hand. This is greeted with a mighty roar of 'GET OFF' and a very fixed stare into the dog's eyes. Most dogs, as I did when I first watched John demonstrate this, jump back a few feet and then look very startled and confused. At this point John immediately adopts a gentle tone again and shows the biscuit to the dog while calling him in and making him sit again. The process is repeated, usually only a couple of times, before the dog gets the idea that biscuit is only available from the hand when the release command 'take it' is heard, and that he must sit until he hears it.

The theory behind this treatment is that the owner is mimicking how the dog's mother used to behave when feeding her puppies as they approached weaning. If the puppies sucked a little too hard or their mother had simply had enough of feeding them, she would try to remove herself from them by shifting in the nest. If they carried on trying she would simply utter a low growl which corresponds to John's first 'get off'. If they still continued when small, she would just simply get up and walk away, dropping puppies from her teats as she went. Once they were old enough to pursue her, she would have turned and given the second much louder and more dramatic canine version of 'GET OFF'. This may even have been accompanied by what sometimes looks like an attempt to bite the puppies but is in fact an inhibited bite designed to threaten and frighten but not injure. The bitch's mouth is closed at the last minute and she nudges the persistent puppy with the point of her nose rather than her teeth. The puppies learn quickly that the first gentle 'get off' means what it says and further frightening intervention from their mother is precluded if they respond. It's all part of growing up and getting on to solid food, over which they must then develop their own system of who eats first and in what order.

John's method certainly works for many dogs, though I would not recommend it for the older, seriously and more generally dominant dog without supervision from an animal behaviourist. Withholding access to food, barking and staring at the dog could be seen as a challenge by some such dogs, and put the owner at risk of attack, so as ever, if in doubt, seek professional advice with such cases.

But assuming that this method has established the owner's right to control the dog's access to small readily consumable titbits, it can be extended to small heaps of biscuits offered in a bowl. For most the 'get off' intervention now means 'back away and let the higher ranking owner have access back to the food' to the dog and he or she will do so. But a few, usually older dogs with a longer record of successful food guarding, will not back off and start to growl again when larger amounts of food are presented which cannot be withdrawn by the owner as quickly as one small biscuit.

For these dogs, including Archie, the excitement over food probably begins as their mealtime approaches and certainly when the owner picks up the bowl or goes to the cupboard with the dog's food in it. So for treatment to be helpful, preparations for treatment must begin before these things occur. First, a stout trailing lead of about a metre in length is attached to the dog's collar. He must wear this around the house for half an hour or so before feeding and perhaps even be taken out for a short walk to dissipate any excitement in anticipation of a walk when his lead appears. On return, the lead is simply left on him. Prior to going to the food cupboard or collecting his bowl, the dog is made to sit (for a small reward as usual) some distance away from where his food is to be prepared. If he tries to rush forward, then he should be tied up to restrain him or held back by another member of the family who can also enforce the 'sit'. At this stage, most dogs are accepting that the meal still belongs to the owners and will comply with commands and handling because of the prospect of receiving the ultimate reward.

Once the meal is prepared, the owner can approach the dog, untie him and curl the lead once around a secure fixing such as a table leg. The turn should allow free running of the lead under the force of being pulled by the dog, so chain leads are usually not so good for this as they tend to snag. The bowl of food is then shown to the dog, who must, and usually will, obey a sit command before it is placed on the floor some distance away from the dog and the owner. To get to the food, the dog must pull forward on the lead away from the owner who, as well as having firm hold of the end of the lead, must position himself so that when he pulls the dog gently back from the bowl, he also pulls the dog in a direction away from himself. Hence the point of wrapping the lead around the table, as it will act as a pivot.

The dog is allowed forward towards his bowl of food, but expected to sit on command every so often as he gets closer. If he doesn't, the owner simply maintains pressure on the lead and holds him in position until he responds. If he responds well, he can be allowed access to the food; if he starts to growl, the owner should pull the lead to take the dog back away from the food and reach to pick up the bowl away from the dog to regain possession.

Then the procedure begins again. Conflict is avoided this way and intervention to regain possession of the food is safe for the owner, provided he has positioned everything correctly. The dog's access to the food is governed entirely by the owner, who therefore retains it as 'his food' and only allows access for the dog if he obeys the conditions laid down and stays calm. This system is safer than, say, using one person to control the dog and another to manage the food as, if the dog growls, intervention is not possible without risk or conflict to regain possession when necessary and the whole event can become more and more of a challenge as a result.

Once the dog is eating, he will feel that he has possession of the food and may start to growl again, but the owner can now insist on the right to approach the feeding dog by withdrawing him if he growls using the same technique. At this point it is wise to use a word of intervention such as 'stop' as the dog is physically prevented from eating and pulled back from the bowl. The owner picks up the bowl, gives a 'sit' command to the dog, who is rewarded for obeying with the replacement of the food bowl on the floor and, perhaps after a short 'wait', allowed fresh access to the bowl. Once again, the principle of blocking unwanted behaviour safely while rewarding desired or calm, non-aggressive behaviour can be applied and usually with a good chance of success.

Owners like the Sweeps must as ever remain as calm and non-threatening as possible towards the dog to avoid presenting further challenge and increasing his propensity to guard his food. They should be relaxed and confident, knowing that safe intervention and total control is possible.

Some dogs are also improved in this respect by adding tastier, favourite aromatic items to the food in the bowl in the sight of the dog after the owner has taken it up and while holding the dog back on the lead. Then the dog perceives even greater reward in allowing himself to be interrupted when the owner approaches his bowl while he is actually eating. Again care must be taken with this approach because the dog may be motivated to guard tasty items even more.

## Palatability

*'That's the only dog I know who can smell someone just THINKING about food'*                                        Charles M Schulz (Peanuts)

The nature of the dog's diet has a great bearing on his desire and motivation to guard his food. While it seems an obvious point to make, I don't think I have treated a case of food guarding where a dog wasn't being fed either fresh meat or a juicy, meaty, canned diet. After all, if I were to try to steal your fillet steak from your plate you would naturally be most upset and probably stick your fork in the back of my outstretched hand if I didn't respond to your version of 'get off'. If I tried to steal your bowl of equally nutritious bean curd, you may decide that it's really not worth the bother of defending and perhaps even give it to me if you felt I needed it! The same is true with dogs and, for many food guarders, simply changing their diet to one of the less interesting, blander and less aromatic, complete dry diets stops much of their motivation to guard their food. The whole preparation of the food becomes less exciting to the dog if the 'cues' such as the smell of fresh meat or cooking , the sound of the can being opened and the enticing smells emanating from it are replaced by the sound of a scoop of dry food being put into a bowl and perhaps covered with water.

On the subject of smells, the flatulent nature of many dogs and tendency to produce runny stools may also be improved on less rich diets. Dry food can be bulkier than meat and biscuits and is best fed at two or three sittings so that the dog can consume a smaller size meal comfortably at each. Being more fibrous, such meals also take longer to digest and so the dog is less likely to be ravenously hungry and excited at each of the meals than he is with the approach of a single highly attractive meal.

On the negative side, the feeding of our cats or dogs is one of the most important contact times we have with them as they are often then most responsive towards us. Cupboard love it may be, but we're all suckers for it. By feeding a bland diet in frequent meals, or even on an ad lib (or free choice, constant access) basis as is sometimes possible without risk of the dog overfeeding, we may remove that source of special interaction. Some owners may rather continue feeding meals which excite their dog and encourage a friendly, responsive reaction during preparation, even if the dog turns nasty and then has to be offered his meal outside or in a room by himself to eat it for safety.

# Bones

*Dear Mr Neville*

*Goldie, our three year old Golden Retriever bitch, is the perfect family pet. But while she doesn't guard her dinner, she does turn extremely nasty if we give her a bone. We have now stopped giving her bones as we could never go near her when she had them, and she would sit there for hours defending them long after she'd eaten the meat off them. However, we would like to give her bones as she enjoys them so much. Does she actually need them, and is there a way of giving Goldie bones safely?*

*Yours sincerely*

*Gill Matthew*

Nutritionally there is no need to give a dog a bone as part of its diet providing a proper balanced diet is being fed. But of course, many do enjoy a good strong non-splinterable bone to chew on, and it may help keep their teeth clean. However, while some suffer gastric upset after chewing bones, many more like Goldie are sensibly denied them because of the aggressive guarding reactions they can produce. Bones are the ultimate in slow or non-consumable but highly attractive aromatic items. They often bring out the worst in the usually placid pet dog, and certainly produce the most severe reactions in dogs which guard their usual meals anyway. Some can be managed by being tied up in the garden before being offered a bone and, if they are still guarding it late into the evening long after only that unreachable marrow is left in the middle, they can be drawn away using the tether. As with other food guarders, once possession has been lost, the dog will usually quickly revert to his or her normal friendly self and can be led away, with the owner returning to dispose of the bone safely later. Just a few dogs will continue to guard even old dry bones lying around the garden or those that they have buried (they don't always forget where they've cached them!) and these dogs are best never given bones at all if one is to continue to enjoy a peaceful walk in the garden. Others can be taught to be less possessive about bones and again this is best done as soon as the young dog or puppy is taken on. This is achieved by conditioning receipt of the bone as with its meals, by ensuring that it perceives the owner as having total rights of access to all food using the John Fisher method described earlier and to give up possession of the bone on command as described for helping the dog to relinquish trophies on pages 222-224.

If ever the desire to possess bones was driven home to me it was by a perfectly biddable, affectionate little mongrel bitch named Rula that I boarded while she had her puppies in the Animal Shelter I ran in Greece for a time in the early 1980's. This was a lovely little well-cared for dog that I knew well because she belonged to a lady who lived in the same village as I did. Just a day or so after Rula had her three puppies, some well-meaning but rather silly person came into the shelter while I was out and gave every dog a bone. While she had been delighted to let everyone pick up her puppies and admire them, Rula guarded her bone to such an extent that I couldn't get into the kennel to clean it or change her bedding. Then, when a puppy shifted in the nest towards its mother's bone, Rula attacked it and then the other two with an amazing ferocity. Two were killed and the other, despite being well cared for by Rula after I managed to remove her bone, did not survive to be weaned. Away from bones and spayed before going back to the village, Rula was for ever more her normal pleasant self.

# Food stealing and scavenging

*Dear Mr Neville*

*Phantom, our Dandie Dinmont is a dreadful thief. We simply cannot leave any food out where he might find it and have to tie down our kitchen waste bin to stop him raiding it. He knows not to do it when we are with him but, as soon as our backs are turned, the cake, dinner or crisps are gone, the bin is turned inside out or there is a loud crashing as he pulls down plates from the table in search of something to eat. He is fed twice a day and is not in any way starved or thin. We've tried giving him a good telling-off and showing him the empty plate or mess he's made in the kitchen but nothing seems to stop his scavenging. Is there anything to be done?*

*Yours sincerely*

*Roy and Beth Grayling*

It is always surprising to me that more dogs are not opportunist scavengers like Phantom; after all, the wolf ancestor and all wild canids survive partially at least by scavenging and taking advantage of any feeding opportunity that comes their way. Perhaps most dogs do perceive all food as being the property of their higher ranking owners and that their opportunity to eat only ever occurs when the owners let them have access to the food bowl. For a few, however, the problem of scavenging can lead not only to stolen food and a turned-out bin, it can also lead to gastric problems for the dog if he eats anything and everything he can find out on walks as well. Some dogs will only steal food when hungry and providing more frequent bulkier meals may help even out their appetite and reduce the scale of the problem. Others may steal food because of an increased appetite caused by a medical problem, so a check up by the vet is always advisable before embarking on any behaviour-modifying treatment.

Some breeds, such as Labradors, are especially noted for scavenging and gluttony in general. Breakdowns in performance in Guide Dogs are rare, but with Labradors it is often caused by the irresistible discarded sandwich lying in the gutter. The dog darts for and gets the sandwich, the poor unsuspecting blind owner gets swung out into the road – rather a dangerous situation and one requiring a period of retraining back at the GDBA centre to sort the dog out before he goes back on duty.

For the ordinary pet owner, food stealing and scavenging can be nearly as much of a nightmare and require constant vigilance and control of the dog when food is around. Punishment of dogs like Phantom after the deed is done is, as always, pointless, and does nothing to prevent him raiding the bin or stealing from plates the next time he gets the chance. Sometimes the problem can be successfully treated by the owners setting up the situation and, lurking behind a door, watching through the keyhole while the dog is left access to a tasty morsel on the table. As soon as he takes the food, they then charge in on him, repossess the food and make the dog sit on command. The dog is really conditioned by the startling nature of the intervention which is associated with the act of stealing the food because he is 'caught in the act' but, in many such cases, all this does is to make the dog more subtle and quick about his thieving.

I recently reviewed a book on dog training by an American author whose advice on dealing with 'garbage or trash can raiders' involved getting into the bin and dangling an attractive piece of chicken out of the lid. When the dog comes to steal it he advised one to leap dramatically out of the bin and, no doubt covered in tea leaves and potato peelings, frighten the life out of him. Smelly, but at least advising the right principle of startling the dog with aversion techniques . . . but don't expect me to climb into your bin!

Instead, for any sort of stealing or raiding I would use more straightforward aversion therapy which is seen by the dog as having no connection whatsoever with the presence of the owner. Remote ambushes can be set up, the best being to leave an irresistible piece of chocolate cake on a low table in the living room for the dog to find and retire out of the house altogether. Under the cake, or for bin raiders, just under the lip of the kitchen waste bin, is placed a cap banger, which is set to go off instantly the pressure is taken off it as the dog dislodges the lid. These bangers are obtainable from all good joke shops and are reusable simply by buying more exploding caps. The dog will associate food or bin-raiding with the unpleasant consequence of a loud startling explosion, which is otherwise totally harmless. The owners can rush back in on hearing the explosion to calm the dog and comfort him. Sometimes after only one such experience, the dog will only ever take food from its owner and from the safety of its bowl. This method should of course never be used with dogs which, in addition to being food stealers, are also gunshot or sound phobic or of a nervous disposition or which suffer from heart conditions.

# Polyphagia

*'Gluttony is an emotional escape, a sign something is eating us'*
Peter de Vries

*Dear Mr Neville*

*My Black Labrador is very appropriately called 'Pig'. He eats just about anything and everything he can find and he looks for food all the time. He has already been to the vets twice to be operated on to have various things removed from his stomach. One was a foil pie dish that went down with the pie he stole from the table, the other, less explicable, was a roller skate wheel belonging to my son. Is there anything we can do to switch off his appetite, bearing in mind that he is already a little over-weight?*

*Yours sincerely*

*Gordon Allen*

A friend of mine who lived on a farm once told me of how her Black Labradors periodically disappeared, but that after a few excursions searching around the entire farm, she learned to go straight to the cattle feed store to find them. There, lying gorged and fit to burst, she would find her 'pigs' in that post-prandial satisfied state that only Labradors who have achieved their life's aim of stuffing themselves to the state of immobility, can radiate.

Polyphagia, or excessive eating, can lead not only to the ingestion of potentially dangerous items but also, of course, to obesity. It is believed that about 30% of pet dogs in the UK and USA are overweight, and diet clinics for dogs are now commonplace in modern veterinary practice as we continue to stuff our pets full of high quality food and titbits in much the same way as we ourselves over eat.

Unlike cats, which are very good at regulating food and energy intake according to requirements, the dog is usually programmed to take advantage of any food that becomes available and gorge itself in case it subsequently has to go through a lean period. It is usually up to owners to manage the dog's intake at mealtimes if obesity is to be prevented. A veterinary surgeon can advise about how to provide a correct balanced diet for the different phases of a dog's life and certainly if the dog is overweight. From the behavioural point of view, dogs such as Pig can be helped by being frequently fed a high fibre, low calorie, balanced diet. This can be achieved using one of the complete dry diets or perhaps by adding fibre in the form of bran or vegetables to the dog's usual diet, but again under veterinary supervision.

Some dogs tend to eat more when under stress of some sort and I myself have put on over 10 lbs so far in writing this book, due to the pressure of meeting the publisher's deadlines, 'snacking' on high calorie foods together with a reduction in day-to-day activity! There is some suggestion that we may actually feel better and less stressed through eating because it causes the release of endorphins in the brain, even when we eat beyond genuine requirements and despite the pains of breathlessness due to being overweight when walking up the hill with the dogs at the end of a day's writing!

So the old idea about 'getting the dog into a routine', which may help reduce stress, and defining his pack position more clearly in canine terms as discussed earlier in this book may also help as part of Pig's weight loss programme. Bored dogs too, may tend to over-eat and become obese as a result. Greater activity and stimulation generally will obviously help with such cases.

Regarding the ingestion of non-nutritional items such as skateboard wheels, needles, rubber balls and the thousand and one other things that vets get called on every year to remove from dogs' stomachs, specific aversion tactics using the same remote approach as for food stealers can be applied to known favourites, and training to 'drop' on command will help when the dog is 'caught in the act'. Otherwise it's a case of keeping a close eye out and perhaps even muzzling the dog short term to prevent consumption of dangerous items when close supervision is not practical. It is important not to stress the dog at such times by constantly standing over him. This may inadvertently encourage him to pick up other objects and consume them quickly in an effort to attract attention and avoid loss of possession. Owners should be relaxed and, as always, reward the dog with praise and the greater reward of a titbit or toy to hold for good behaviour in ignoring previous inappropriate targets.

# Inappetence

*Dear Mr Neville*

*Sadie, my King Charles Cavalier Spaniel, is very reluctant to eat all her meals and is also a very fussy eater. My vet has done all sorts of tests on her but can find nothing wrong with her. She seems fit and healthy but will sometimes go nearly two days with hardly a thing to eat. Is this a psychological problem or am I worrying too much?*

*Yours sincerely*

*Miss Sheila Ford*

As well as having the potential to be complete gluttons, dogs can also go for long periods on a poor or insufficient diet without suffering harm. Water should always be available of course but, providing the dog remains in good condition and there is no medical cause for any inappetence, owners like Sheila shouldn't worry too much about occasional missed meals. After all, it's a rather human feeding habit to expect to eat at certain times of day, every day. Some dogs will happily fit in with our routines, but we shouldn't be too quick to sound the alarm bells if they don't.

Dogs can go off their food for a variety of reasons, including temporary loss of appetite during the first days at a boarding kennel when the owners go on holiday. Indeed, any change of routine or emotional upset may temporarily put a dog off its dinner. Sometimes the dog can be encouraged to eat again by feeding more aromatic attractive food than usual, warming it up or hand feeding it. For traumatized dogs such as those suffering from grief after a bereavement in the human or dog pack, a short low dose course of Valium prescribed by the vet can relax them and stimulate their appetite. However, it is important to wean the dog off the drug, or off being hand fed so that his feeding behaviour doesn't come to rely on this type of support. When hand feeding the worried dog, care has to be taken not to encourage learned helplessness in the same way as one has to guard against over-dependency in the treatment of nervousness and phobias.

Other dogs can be encouraged to eat by making feeding generally more of a competition. Providing there are no fights, two dogs can sometimes be fed together so that the competition posed by one to the other will stimulate the reluctant one into finding a ravenous appetite. This can be mimicked by reducing the time the single dog has to eat his food – all food uneaten after five minutes is taken up unless the dog is still eating. Equally, the owner can pretend to challenge the dog for its food to encourage it to consume it more rapidly, but this must be done carefully so as not to produce a food guarder of the worst type . . . one that doesn't even eat his food!

Other dogs simply don't see themselves as having the right to eat their food when the owner is present, rather the opposite case to that of the dominant food guarder. Such dogs are simply so subordinate that they don't wish to be seen as presenting any form of challenge to their superiors by daring to eat in their presence, even if the owner has given way and provided food for them in their own bowl. The natural tendency is to worry and try to encourage the dog to accept food from the hand. Really what the owners need to do is leave the dog totally alone so that he can eat without offending anyone.

# Devotion-to-duty anorexia

I well remember one rather unique case of apparent anorexia in a large and perfectly well trained German Shepherd Dog called Max that I saw in Manchester. Max was owned by a family who ran an 'open all hours' corner shop in quite a rough area and was kept partly as a pet and partly as a guard. He spent his day behind the counter keeping a beady eye on the customers but generally went un-noticed unless some unruly or drunk customers came in. He would then stand with his paws on the newspaper counter and just look at them with his ears pricked. Only once had there been trouble and Max had leapt over the counter and headed off the thief at the door. The wretch dropped his spoils, and the proprietors then took over from Max without so much as a tooth having been bared or a growl snarled. No one had ever taught Max to be like this, he just did it naturally. He was quite the nicest German Shepherd Dog I have ever met, but he had a problem. He just wouldn't eat. The owners could just about hand feed him with tiny portions of choice steak or chicken but even this was a battle. In desperation they had even left the ham, chocolate, cakes, in fact everything in the shop out on the counter for him to help himself to, but he didn't so much as sniff it. When I saw him, he looked in reasonable condition but was starting to lose weight under his great coat. His owners were getting desperate and so I went through all the usual treatments, but they'd all been tried. In the end I suggested one of those inspirational hunches that just appear sometimes when you need them, if you're lucky. It seemed that because Max was so devoted to duty he simply wouldn't eat when the shop was open. That was a problem because it was open from 6.00 am in the morning until 10.30 pm at night. All the owners' efforts to feed him had occurred when they were eating their meals at breakfast and dinner time in their living room immediately behind the shop. I suggested that instead, they should only try to feed Max after the shop was completely closed for the night and give him dog food in his own bowl just outside the back door. It worked. Max wolfed his dinner down like any normal dog under these conditions. A remarkable case of devotion to duty that I will probably never encounter again, but it gives me one more idea up my sleeve if I do, thanks to Max!

# Fussy eaters

*Dear Mr Neville*

*Pepe, my eighteen-month-old Poodle, simply won't eat his usual tinned food. We've tried giving him all sorts of different things, but even when given best steak or chicken, cooked carefully just for him and mixed with biscuit to try and give him a balanced diet, he will simply pick out and eat the best bits of meat. I know he should eat the biscuits to get a balanced intake and help keep his teeth clean but he seems to be getting ever more fussy. Is there anything I can do?*

*Yours sincerely*

*Annabelle Carswell*

Fussy dogs are not uncommon and many do indeed fail to receive a balanced diet as a result. The smaller lap dogs such as Poodles and Yorkshire Terriers are particularly noted for this, but many larger dogs can also be very fussy eaters. Usually there is not much link between the type of food offered and the dog's behaviour, though some may have specific likes and dislikes. More often, small companion dogs especially receive a lot of titbits between meals and simply aren't hungry when anything is placed in front of them as a meal at dinner time. The owners may then start to fuss around the dog who then learns that, by refusing food, it receives a lot of extra and compassionate attention which, in itself, may be more rewarding than the meal. In most cases, fussy eating can be treated by offering a balanced well-mixed, or even blended meat and biscuit diet or a consistent formulation diet, such as one of the high quality dry diets. Alternatively, increasing the fat content of the diet by stirring in a little margarine or corn oil, or perhaps adding a tasty stock cube, can increase the palatability of any food if there is a genuine acceptability problem.

Once an attractive balanced formulation is found, the owners should stick to offering it and not panic if the dog refuses it on a couple of occasions. The rule of thumb is that providing the usually active dog looks healthy and is otherwise normal, don't panic until no food has been taken for three days, and then call the vet straightaway. Also check that the dog hasn't simply located an alternative supply of food, such as at the compost heap, or found a way to get to that most prized of foods found only in the cat's bowl!

Whichever normal diet is offered, it must be highly palatable and offered on a restricted access basis to encourage mock competition as described earlier. If the owner is more ambivalent, the dog can be left access constantly to food to pick at as often as it likes, provided that it doesn't over-eat and risk becoming obese. This free-feeding tactic may suit smaller active dogs especially, as they may burn off energy more quickly and need to replenish it more often than a larger less active dog. The free-feeding option also detaches the owner from influencing the dog's feeding behaviour through too much attention at mealtimes but, as discussed earlier, may also remove what they may expect to be one of the high contact points of the day with their pet. As ever, if in doubt over the dog's feeding habits, consult the vet as most problems, especially sudden changes in eating habits, may have a perfectly reasonable medical cause and be readily treatable.

# Strange eating habits

*'As a dog returneth to his vomit, so a fool returneth to his folly'*
Proverbs 26:11

*Dear Mr Neville*

*From time to time my dog is sick, especially after eating grass. My vet has found nothing wrong with him and it doesn't really occur very often. The nasty thing is that he then goes on to guard his vomit and then eats it again. It's really disgusting but we can't get him away from it to clear it up and stop him eating it. But why does he do it in the first place?*

*Yours sincerely*

*Robert Mungle*

This type of behaviour is probably another of those hangovers from the days in the dog's ancestry when regular dinners were not provided by nice pack mates. As a scavenger, the dog's intake, even as a modern well-fed pet, will include many things of apparently low nutritional quality and in some cases things which are quite disgusting to us. In the wild, survival may depend on that gorge policy, so anything and everything may be consumed by our dogs irrespective of its quality or substance. The dog's vomit may be one of the more nutritious items it encounters and will contain elements that the dog has already decided are edible. It's really a case of not letting anything go to waste, especially if the dog is hungry.

A higher fibre diet can help reduce hunger, but dogs which bolt their food down especially quickly may also be prone to vomiting bulky meals straight back up again and then have to reconsume it all. If it all seems rather distasteful, we should remember that puppies of wild dogs and wolves survive to a large extent on the regurgitated stomach contents of their mother for some time after weaning and until they are able to hunt or catch food items for themselves. Epimeletic vomiting, as this is known, is an ancestral behaviour that has largely been lost in our pet dogs (Chows are a notable exception), though the worrying behaviour by puppies at the mouth of their mother, her owners and sometimes their eventual family owners is initially designed to force regurgitation of a meal.

Later, as we have already discussed, it may become incorporated into the puppy's repertoire of attention-demanding behaviour because of the rewards of fussing or excitement (including being pushed away!) that it receives as a result.

## Coprophagia

*Dear Mr Neville*

*As a young dog my Irish Setter was forever eating sheep and horse dung when out on walks over the fields near where we live. We presumed that this was simply a phase that he would grow out of and , as it seemed to do him no harm, we ignored it, especially as friends' dogs seemed to do it to some degree as well. But Clancy didn't grow out of it. He now eats not only every pile of animal dung he can find, but also other dog's mess and his own. It's totally foul and quite apart from feeling sick watching him, his breath is just horrible. We are thinking seriously of having him put down as we really can't live with this much more. Can this obsession be treated?*

*Yours sincerely*

*Klaus Artmann*

Coprophagia, as this behaviour is known, is actually one of the most common causes of behavioural complaint that owners have with their dogs, yet because of the whole disgusting nature of the problem, few people will mention it to their vet or behaviourist. When one UK company established a series of veterinary help phone lines offering advice for dog and cat owners, the most frequently dialled number was the 'Coprophagia' line. The anonymity of the system proved just how prevalent the 'problem' really is. Yet, for the dog, coprophagia is usually not a problem. It is simply a case of a scavenger maximizing his intake and taking advantage of a nutrient source. Faeces usually contain undigested or semi-digested material which can provide some nutrients at least for the dog. Nursing bitches naturally, and more acceptably perhaps, consume their puppies' faeces. But to us coprophagia by dogs is quite disgusting and obviously a major source of dissatisfaction of owning a scavenger as a pet. There are probably very few dogs which haven't taken a mouthful of animal manure from time to time if they have had the chance, and this, to dog owners in the countryside at least, is usually more acceptable than the dog which eats other dog's faeces, or its own. Of course there may be increased risk of gastric upset or parasite ingestion for dogs which engage in this behaviour but otherwise the main danger is that owners may reject their dog as a result of it. Some dogs seem to become obsessive about the whole idea and spend their walks 'hunting the stool', while others, including one Dobermann I saw some time ago, turn and eat their own faeces while they are still warm. He was a real stool eater's champion stool eater, having learnt to spin round extremely quickly while squatting to defecate and catch it almost in mid air!

Treatment of the coprophagic dog involves several different features. First, if the dog consumes only its own faeces, these must be cleared up immediately to reduce the dog's access to them. Next the dog should be trained to defecate on command. This is not as difficult as it may sound and many service dogs are taught this as part of their formal training. It's a case of building on being with the dog when he naturally wants to defecate. As soon as he gets in position, the owner should use the word 'busy' or other simple word of his own choice and reward the dog with praise and a titbit as soon as he has finished. After a few such experiences, the dog learns that 'busy' is associated with the act and position of defecating and he can then be denied opportunity to defecate at other times, within reason of course. Coinciding with the times when he would normally need to go, he can be taken to a desired place and given what, if he needs to go, has then become a release command to be 'busy'. The poop should be 'scooped' immediately and the dog taken on for exercise.

Bored dogs, particularly those kept inactive or kennelled for long periods, may become coprophagic, and so greater exercise and stimulation generally may help relieve some of this behaviour. But for dogs which eat only their own faeces, attention to diet is most important. Some veterinarians have suggested that coprophagia in some dogs is caused by a deficiency of some of the B vitamins and vitamin K, which are usually manufactured in the gut by bacteria and, for the most part, lost into the faeces. While most dogs still absorb enough of these elements, the coprophagic dog may be less efficient at it and simply be trying to maintain supplies. While it is therefore worth supplementing these vitamins in the diet under the direction of the veterinarian, all coprophagic dogs should, in any event, be fed a consistent, balanced diet in two or three short meals per day rather than a single one. Again, the higher fibre diets may reduce any hunger motivation to eat stools, though the drawback is that there will obviously be more faeces produced on such regimes. Feeding several meals may also make the timing of the dog's need to pass them less predictable and training to go on command more difficult.

Meaty diets tend to produce more aromatic stools containing either higher amounts of undigested protein or other attractive waste compounds, so a dry diet will usually produce less desirable faeces. Certain things can also be added to any diet to make the stools less palatable. An iron tablet (available from the pharmacist) can help, as can a few chunks of acidic fruit such as pineapple, according to APBC colleague John Rogerson. Sometimes treating faeces after they have been deposited by coating them with unpleasant tasting substances such as chilli powder or pepper can deter some dogs but, in my experience, dogs will learn only to avoid the treated stools after investigation and will still find all others attractive enough to eat. Others simply like the fact that someone has gone to all the trouble of adding condiments and flavouring to the menu of the day and consume them even more quickly!

Direct punishment of the coprophagic dog 'mid-mouthful' is usually too late to modify the dog's behaviour for the future and, even if successful on one or two occasions, will simply make him consume them faster before the owner can stop him at the next opportunity, or make him into a secret faeces-eater!

Instead, aversion therapy can be practised with dogs that eat their own faeces, or those of other dogs and other animals. As with all aversion tactics, timing is the key to success. The dog is led deliberately on an extending lead and collar towards all faeces on a walk or towards some of its own deliberately left uncleared in the garden. The dog should be allowed to go forward on the extendable lead to investigate the stools. Simple sniffing is normal and shouldn't provoke any reaction from the owner. If the dog then walks on, he should be rewarded with praise from the owner and perhaps called in to receive a titbit. If, however, the dog attempts to take a mouthful, the owner should react instantly by applying the brake on the lead and pulling the dog gently away while at the same time sounding a rape alarm, sounding a set of John Fisher's Training Discs (especially effective if the dog has been preconditioned to stop on hearing the sound) near the dog, squirting the dog with water, or bitter spray; in fact anything that startles the dog. It may even be possible (for the stout hearted) with the slightly more approachable horse or sheep dung, to booby trap faeces with the cap bangers described earlier for treating food stealers.

As with the other situations where aversion therapy has been suggested, it is important that the dog associates the startling with the unwanted behaviour, in short, that the noise etc is a consequence of attempting to eat stools. After such intervention, the owner must always be reassuring to the dog and perhaps then distract him with a short period of more interactive play before allowing fresh access to the stool. 'Repeat as necessary', as the prescription goes, and introduce the dog to several piles per walk. With practice, the dog should soon become more wary of attempting to eat stools, though again it is important that during treatment he doesn't have opportunity to consume any stools at all. So if allowed off-lead in any place where he may encounter some, he should be muzzled or preferably only allowed off-lead in 'stool free zones', that's if there is such a place!

# Psychodietetics

*Dear Mr Neville*

*My Staffordshire Bull Terrier, Tyson, is a highly excitable little dog like many of his breed, but is also prone to drastic changes of mood. One minute he can be resting, the next he is rushing and leaping around like a madman and then suddenly rather depressed and quiet. Of late, he has also tended to become aggressive towards my wife and I when he is excited for other reasons and, as we are expecting our first child in a few months, we are worried that Tyson may have to go. We've tried all approaches from increased obedience training to distraction and punishment and extra loving when he is excitable, but all to no avail. Is there anything more psychological that might make him more predictable?*

*Yours sincerely*

*Geoff Stobbart*

'You are what you eat', so the saying goes and we are now only just beginning to discover how diet affects our own behaviour, let alone that of our dogs and cats. Reactions to particular food items are now being investigated following the discoveries that children especially may be sensitive to certain food additives, in particular, some of the 'E number' colouring agents, and some chemical preservatives. Many people and animals are allergic to certain types of food, such as lactose sugar in milk and other dairy products including chocolate, wheat protein, or some types of seafood. These allergies often manifest themselves in man with skin reactions such as rashes and blotches and pruritus. These are actually over-responses of our immune system to the allergen but other types of reaction to elements of our diet are now being recognized, such as neurological disorders including fits in some rare cases.

As I am not a nutritionist I work very closely with my veterinary colleagues on cases where I feel the dog may be responding unusually to its diet in some way. It is very easy to extrapolate from a few recorded, individual cases and anecdotes where a dog's behaviour has been markedly helped by altering its diet and be tempted to presume that, as a result, some diets are problematic or more likely to lead to behaviour problems. It is important to realize that, providing a balanced diet is being offered which is appropriate to the dog's requirements regarding its lifestyle, activity and age, veterinarians and nutritionists believe that there will be only a very tiny proportion of the canine population who will suffer any adverse behavioural reactions to any constituent of any diet. It will probably occur at about the same very low level as genuine reactions are encountered in man. Reactions that do occur will generally be due to one of four reasons. Dogs may indeed be genuinely allergic or hypersensitive to some component of the diet and show an immune mediated reaction to it. Perhaps a little less likely is that individual dogs may be physically intolerant of certain components because they lack a particular enzyme or lack the ability to break down those components completely, or even at all. Others even more unusually may have what is described as a food idiosyncrasy. This is a reaction to a food or a component in it that may appear similar to an allergic reaction, but which has not arisen as a response of the immune system. This will be rare and most likely to be a reaction to a particular artificial chemical in the food and probably occur as a result of direct effects of the substance on the nervous system.

However, one of the older and persisting explanations, though largely unproved by any scientific investigation, is that red meat protein or high protein levels in prepared dog food may cause many dogs to be aggressive or nervous, or increase the scale their reactions if they are already prone to being aggressive, excitable, moody or jumpy. Of course much may hinge on just what is a balanced diet for any individual dog quite apart from any sensitivity that that dog may have. But it is generally true to say that most pet dogs are fed a diet far in excess of their requirements for the more sedentary lifestyle we now offer compared with the more active lifestyle that their digestive systems evolved to process food for. Thus it is logical in many ways to expect some reaction to high protein intake in the dog as he has evolved to be a scavenging omnivore and consume larger amounts of fibre in the forms of vegetable matter, hair and gristle and less protein on a regular basis than we offer. Also, being less active as a pet than as an active scavenger/predator, his energy requirements and perhaps the relative proportion of nutrients in the diet will also be altered. In recent times the food manufacturers have started to appreciate this and now offer special puppy foods and 'active dog' foods with, for example, higher protein levels than the average adult dog maintenance diet. There are also special recovery formulations for convalescing dogs and regimes more suited to the less efficient digestive systems of the older dog. There are even specialist prescription diets available from the vet to help with the treatment of certain medical conditions, such as kidney disease, so clearly our knowledge of the effects of what our dogs eat is now ranging far beyond simply wolfing down a standard diet.

To reduce the likelihood of sensitivity to the protein level or the possibility that a meat and biscuit diet is not being given in a balanced mix, I usually recommend that the dog is weaned on to a dry complete food gradually over the course of a week or so by exchanging the canned food or fresh meat increasingly for the complete food. Remarkably in some cases similar to Tyson's, and with many cases of nervousness or low threshold aggression, this is the only treatment that has proved necessary. In many more cases of aggression, particularly dominance aggression towards owners, a diet change seems to have helped make the dog less reactive, and easier and less risky to apply the rank-demoting treatment to.

## After-meal madness

One case I saw not long ago concerned a Bulldog which attacked its owners' feet at 7.30 pm precisely every evening, exactly half an hour after its meal. If the meal was delayed, so was the attack, which occurred whether the owners moved or not. The dog would be very active after its meal, sit down to rest and then start to tremble before looking up and targetting its owners. During the attack, which would last only a few moments, the dog had a glazed expression and was undistractable. The owners simply had to leave the room or sit it out. Afterwards the dog was always rather confused and very tired and would sleep for the rest of the evening and night without incident. No problems were experienced during the day, but then the dog only received one meal of what the owners thought was the best canned meat and biscuit that money could buy.

The owners' vet had tested the dog for many ailments, without success. To test the diet sensitivity theory, the dog's diet was changed to the usual bland diet employed in the treatment of diarrhoea, chicken and rice. As soon as the change to this regime was complete, the attacks ceased. Neither I nor the referring veterinary surgeon have any idea how this reaction was occurring, but the owners didn't care – now they can watch the television in peace for the entire evening!

# Staring at walls

*Dear Mr Neville*

*Our nine-year-old Airedale dog, called Robert, periodically gets trembling attacks and seems to stare at the wall. Sometimes he focuses on a picture or the ceiling and simply cannot be distracted with food, kindness, being yelled at, ringing the doorbell or anything else. He simply stands and stares and trembles. All we can do is to put him in a dark room for a couple of days as this seems to help relax him. After a couple of days when he simply won't eat or drink and has to be dragged out to the garden to relieve himself, he snaps back into his usual self. This has been going on for some time, but seems to be getting worse in recent months. Is this some strange mental illness?*

*Yours sincerely*

*Susan Painter*

While some bizarre behaviour, including fits and trances, can be managed and prevented with anti-convulsant drugs, this is very much the territory of the veterinary specialist. In this case nothing specific had been identified by Robert's vet. I decided to follow my usual routine of trying to eliminate any diet-related problem, no matter how unlikely. In this case, it seemed that Robert's body could have been metabolizing whatever it was that caused these strange reactions during his two-day withdrawal from family life. Once that element had all been processed and excreted, he returned to normal, presumably for as long as it took that agent to accumulate again to some critical level, whereupon he would start to behave strangely again. The increasing frequency of his staring bouts was perhaps a function of his age in that his liver was becoming less and less able to deal with the substance. It was worth a try.

Robert was actually being fed according to the suggestions on the can with a recommended mixer and so it seemed unlikely that his reactions were due to excess protein intake or an imbalance. We weaned him over onto a high quality complete dry diet and, just to remove any chance of sensitivity to dairy products, the Painters were asked to ensure that Robert was not fed any cheese, milk, chocolate etc for three weeks.

Robert responded totally and has never demonstrated his bizarre reactions since. He can tolerate and enjoy dairy products now so we presume that these were not the cause. His reactions were almost certainly due to some allergy, intolerance or idiosyncrasy regarding his canned food but we shall never know exactly why he behaved so strangely. The Painters are understandably reluctant now to carry out any tests on him that involve challenging him with the old diet as they prefer him as the pleasant, normal tough old soldier that he is without his old problems.

As a result of these occasional bizarre cases and many more improvements achieved through dietary management of dogs referred for aggression or excitability problems, I now tend to look closely at diet in most cases. This is especially the case where sensitivity to canned food, difficulty in ensuring a balanced diet or, more scientifically perhaps, where other possible dietary effects, such as skin reactions, are observed. I usually recommend one of the higher quality processed complete dry foods offered wet or dry, with fresh water always available of course, ask the owners to ensure that the dog is fed nothing else for a week, and then review progress. Sometimes there are difficulties in getting dogs to accept this type of food when they have been used to highly palatable meat meals, and so cooked chicken, fish or breast of lamb (one third by cooked volume) and rice, pasta or potatoes (two thirds) is used to test the theory in a more palatable way. The veterinary surgeon is subsequently asked to advise how to supplement this diet to ensure that the dog receives the correct vitamin and mineral intake and to achieve a balanced regime if the dog's behaviour improves but he simply won't accept a pre-formulated complete food.

Of course, there is no hard scientific data to support this type of treatment, simply the working experience of myself and others, but I am delighted to say that research is now being carried out into this new area of psychodietetics by some of the larger responsible pet food companies. Hopefully we will learn much in the future about about why and how our dogs 'are what they eat'.

# 9
# Messy Problems

*'Is there any point to which you would wish to draw my attention?'*
*'To the curious incident of the dog in the night-time,'*
*'The dog did nothing in the night-time.'*
*'That was the curious incident,' remarked Sherlock Holmes*

Sir Arthur Conan Doyle

What goes in must come out and it certainly does. The 7.3 million dogs in the United Kingdom deposit over 1000 tonnes of faeces and 4.8 million litres of urine every day! We are now rightly concerned about the quality of our environment and there is little more unpleasant than stepping in dog faeces on a pavement or having your kids slide through it while playing football in the park. Local authorities are busy all over the country instigating anti-fouling laws and controlling the access dog owners have for their pets in recreation parks. And few things have ever inspired such activity in local authorities or for that matter, stimulated the mind of so many amateur inventors than trying to produce the ultimate poop scoop. The fact is simple, responsible owners clean up after their dogs in public places, irresponsible owners don't and there's a lot of them, so legislation is required to try and make them do so.

Most dogs are, of course, clean in their own homes after an initial period of house-training as puppies, but problems can occur subsequently, chiefly as a result of medical conditions. However, failure to learn in the first place and other behavioural reasons can perhaps just as often lead to a messy, smelly problem and very quickly dissatisfied owners. As ever, the treatment required to tackle the problem may vary according to the circumstances and accurate diagnosis of the cause is required.

## Indoor marking

*Dear Mr Neville*

*Since my husband passed away last year, Mack, my three year old male mongrel dog, has frequently cocked his leg around the house. He's done it up just about every piece of furniture I have. I keep telling him off and keep cleaning it all up, but every day it's the same. How can I stop him from messing like this?*

*Yours sincerely*

*Mrs A Redbourne*

This is clearly not a toileting problem *per se* but one of territorial marking going on indoors in the same way as most male dogs cock their legs to anoint lamp posts and trees when outdoors on walks. Normally they don't need to do so indoors because the home is their den and a place so secure that there is no need to waste effort marking to identify it further. Typically, indoor marking problems are presented at adolescence by young developing male dogs and afterwards by some adult males which are particularly territorial, very high-ranking or even rather dominant. They will mark around the house all the more if a bitch comes into season nearby. The mark usually comprises a smaller squirt of urine than the flow normally released when the dog is genuinely relieving itself and some dogs seem to have such an enormous capacity that one wonders if their insides contain anything more than a huge bladder. How a dog can go for a three hour run without a drink, marking every bush, and still go round the garden when he returns defies the imagination!

This behaviour is often largely under the influence of testosterone in the un-neutered male and may reliably be resolved by castration in over fifty per cent of cases. But, as with much other testosterone inspired male behaviour, a greater success rate is expected if the surgery is carried out soon after puberty. An anti-male hormone injection prescribed by the vet may help resolve the problem in a dog which has suddenly begun to mark around the house or does so from time to time in response to fluctuating male hormone output during adolesence rather than marking consistently. It may also help to treat dogs who decide to lift a leg to endorse their presence in other people's houses, or as sometimes happens, on other people. The dog's response to this treatment will usually give an indication as to whether castration may resolve the problem more permanently. Interestingly, in such cases, the dog may still mark just as frequently outdoors, and in the vet's waiting room where others have preceded him, indicating that the scent of other dogs' marks stimulates the response to some extent.

In some cases, neither surgical nor temporary chemical castration will help much. These are the cases such as Mack where the behaviour has occurred in response to insecurity in the home. Mack is trying to endorse his presence and protect himself and his owner by identifying their occupancy to any passing potential threat. He may also be trying to boost his own feelings of security by surrounding himself more with his own smell and at anointing posts which he passes frequently or recognizes as key points in the geography of the home.

Typically the dog cocks his leg up vertical objects such as furniture and curtains rather than just onto the floor, as they hold the scent at nose level, for the perpetrator at least. Keeping a close eye on the dog and the application of a little discipline may help, though preferably in the form of a startling 'NO' followed by reward and reassurance for not doing it. This may help condition him, and other startling or preconditioning tactics described in previous chapters may help with the pushy marking male because they can increase the owner's status and reduce the dog's feeling that he has the right or the necessity to leave his mark around when the boss is in.

So, there are greater complexities to indoor marking than simply the territorial reactions of male dogs, though interestingly it is rare to encounter a bitch spot-marking with urine or 'lifting a leg' as many do outdoors especially after spaying. Even when indoor marking is more the reaction of a nervous dog, or one for whom home security has collapsed somewhat perhaps after the death of a family member, human or canine, the reaction is usually only found in males.

Most indoor spraying cat cases discussed in *'Do Cats Need Shrinks?'* also concern male cats, neutered or un-neutered, but there are also female cats which spray when they or their home are perceived as being under pressure. A bitch may sometimes mark indoors when in season as a mate-attracting or nest-defining behaviour but this is only short-lived and will cease if she is spayed.

With such marking in dogs, treatment may only be successful if the cause of any insecurity can be identified and the dog helped to learn to cope with it, as described in Chapter 5 under nervousness. With the loss of a family member, time and tender loving care from the rest of the family, and perhaps a better social structure of more canine definition between Mack and the family will help. However, as this is sometimes least practical to apply when the family need the dog as a companion more than ever, sometimes treatment with mild sedatives or alternative medicine (prescribed by a vet with a special interest in this area) can help the dog settle quicker and not be so anxious as to need to endorse his presence in this way.

The smell of the dog's own mark indoors may also cause him to overmark it, so thorough cleaning to remove all traces of previous efforts at all marking posts must be carried out whatever the cause of the problem. This is best achieved with a warm solution of strong biological detergent, followed by a rinse with cold water and a spray with alcohol such as surgical spirit. Curtains and chair covers etc should be dry cleaned. All cleaned areas must be left to dry thoroughly before the dog is allowed access back to them, and initially this should only be under supervision. Feeding the dog at particularly favourite spots or placing his bed there may also add a feeling of greater security to that region and reduce the need for him to mark it.

Without doubt, some male dogs also learn to lift a leg indoors as an attention-getting behaviour and others do so when excited or when feeling vulnerable. Redefining social relations and ignoring the behaviour rather than scolding the dog as it happens may help diminish the frequency of it in such cases. Punishment often contains elements of reward for the attention-seeking dog and may only compound the problem. If the dog only marks when he is left alone, it is probably symptomatic of separation anxiety as discussed in Chapter 5 and require a similar approach to treatment. Other cases contain elements of all these possible causes!

# Competitive marking

*Dear Mr Neville*

*We have four male dogs, none castrated, two Fox Terriers and two English Bull Terriers. At night we separate them with the two Fox Terriers sleeping in the kitchen and the two Bull Terriers in the adjoining living room. During the night, every night, one or both of the Fox Terriers cocks his leg up the dividing door. We've cleaned up, punished and put pepper dust down to deter them but all to no avail. What can we do?*

*Yours sincerely*

*Janice and Martin Standen*

When I went to see this case I was astounded that four young full-blooded males of such strong minded breeds could live peaceably together, yet there they were, all curled up in a heap together by the fire. They all played highly competitively together with lots of growls but there had never been a fight or even a snap. They had a perfectly stable hierarchy with the two Fox Terriers obviously numbers one and two in the pack and the Bull Terriers happy to accept positions three and four. The owners reinforced this perfectly in their behaviour towards the dogs . . . except for one thing. At night they made the underdogs (the Bull Terriers) sleep nearer the safe core of the house and pushed the top guys (the Fox Terriers) to the more vulnerable kitchen with its door to the outside. They protested by marking up the door. We simply swopped the sleeping arrangements around to give the Fox Terriers their rightful access to the favoured living room area and put the Bull Terriers out to the kitchen and the problem disappeared overnight.

# Involuntary urination

Young puppies are initially unable to eliminate without physical stimulation from their mother, but soon learn to control the passage of urine and faeces. Control has to be learned if the nest is to be kept clean and dry and the dog is not to soil itself. Later urine becomes an important communication device for the social dog as he or she grows up. While most do learn quickly and respond to our efforts at conditioning them not to eliminate in our homes, a few may continue to lose control at certain times. Providing there is no medical reason, this loss of control is involuntary and occurs because the various sphincters that hold the urine in the bladder or the ureters become relaxed when the dog is aroused in certain circumstances or when relaxed during sleep. It usually improves with age and a little management from the owners.

# Excitable urination

*Dear Mr Neville*

*Whenever my husband and I return home our lovely little eight-month-old West Highland White Terrier dog bounds up to see us and then rolls on his back and wees all over his own stomach. We've had to put an ugly plastic sheet for him to roll on by the door to avoid spoiling our carpet any further. We'd hate to be unpleasant to him when he's so pleased to see us but how can we stop this from happening?*

*Yours truly*

*Evelyn Robertson*

The sheer excitement of owners returning home is just too much for some young dogs and causes this type of involuntary reaction, typically from that submissive position that the dog has adopted as a further sign of his joy that the pack is back to look after him. As well as generally restructuring relations with the dog so that all social contact is better defined and conditional upon the owners' initiation, it is important that they are cooler towards him when they return from being away. They should certainly not respond to the dog if he is lying on his back and should keep their initial greeting to a short verbal acknowledgement that he is there. They should then resist the urge to bend over him or fuss him and walk coolly past into the house, perhaps letting the dog outside into the garden to relieve itself if it is only just hanging on after having been left for some time. When the excitement of the moment has died down, they can call the now calmer dog to them, gently make him sit and then fuss him around the head, rather than encouraging him to roll over to receive attention. Steadily the excitement of the owners' return will be reduced in the dog's eyes without any loss of affection time for him. It simply occurs later when he is better able to manage it and less likely to urinate through lack of control.

## Submissive urination

*Dear Mr Neville*

*We have a timid rescued Dachshund called Heidi. We're sure she was badly treated by her previous owners because if have to tell her off, or simply ask her to move, she rolls on her back and urinates all over the floor. It seems as if she's just unable to control herself, though as the urine comes out in pulses, I presume she is trying very hard to keep it it. We know she can't help it, but can we convince her that we intend no harm?*

*Yours sincerely*

*Beryl and Richard Robinson*

Heidi is perhaps an unfortunate case of a dog who is either naturally very submissive, or one who has indeed been made to suffer by previous owners continuing to punish or tell her off when she had already shown submissive or appeasing responses. She has perhaps learnt as a result that the normal submissive responses she can make may not defuse the threat to her and is therefore fearful as a result. Once again control is lost and she urinates, though as the Robinsons have observed, she is probably aware that indoors this may lead to further trouble and tries to hold on, but just can't. Many other dogs, usually submissive bitches, also urinate involuntarily from the same position when approached by other dogs in the park. Treatment may be difficult for those where the behaviour is the result of previous maltreatment or lack of understanding but most will respond to social redefinition, and a calm gentle approach. The Robinsons should never have need to get cross with her and simply calling her to them from a distance, to move her if she is in the way or if she is misbehaving will be all that they need to manage her. They should certainly ignore any totally submissive response of lying on her back as any further attention at this point will make her afraid and likely to urinate. That type of total submission is Heidi's way of saying 'I agree to your every demand' and she will learn through gentle experience that nothing further will happen to her once she is in that position. Ideally she also come to show her deference without such total capitulation later as she settles into her new home.

# House-training

Some breeds of dog are notoriously difficult to house-train or more prone to relapses than others. Just as Persian cats comprise the bulk of my feline toileting cases, so Poodles and Bichon Frises are most often referred for toileting problems. Despite being the most frequently referred breed overall in my practice, I don't recall ever seeing a German Shepherd Dog for this type of problem and most of the gun dog breeds seem to be very easy to house train and rarely suffer breakdowns. Some do suffer a loss of toilet control when left alone as a symptom of separation anxiety, but this is more of an involuntary response to being anxious and usually responds well to the treatment outlined in Chapter 5.

*Dear Mr Neville*

*My Bichon Frise, Charlie, has never been really house-trained despite our best efforts in training him to go on newspaper as a puppy. He is now nine-months-old and while he will remain clean on some nights, he will sometimes defecate and urinate even though he is walked last thing to relieve himself. He only uses the paper we leave out for him sometimes. He will also do it in the daytime and occasionally even while we are in the same room. We've tried to be nice to him and also punish him by showing him what he's done and telling him off, but he doesn't seem to learn. What are we doing wrong?*

*Yours sincerely*

*Sonia and Clive Marksham*

Treating the problematic Bichon Frise or Poodle is the same as for other toileting dogs, but with far greater attention to detail. Even then, individuals of these breeds have still proved difficult to house-train so that mistakes never occur and owners may have to accept that there will always be some risk of finding mess to clear up some mornings. Most do improve generally as they get older, but then slip back into old ways as they enter old age. For most toileting problems the main principle of treatment is to re-offer the same opportunity to learn where and where not to go as one does with a young puppy.

Many owners house-train their new puppy by training him to eliminate on newspaper initially, moving it nearer and nearer to the back door and then finally expect him to go outdoors in the garden. While this is often a reasonably effective way of house-training, I find it can take quite a long time and there is no real substitute for making more effort in the early days with the puppy. By encouraging him to use paper overnight or when left alone when he hasn't yet learned to hold on for very long, if at all, owners are really just saving themselves the bother of getting up in the night and being with him to ensure he is taken to the right place. In some cases, the puppy may learn that it is acceptable to go on any newspaper, including the ones that arrive on Sunday before anyone has got up to collect them from by the front door! But generally, by signifying that it is acceptable for the dog to eliminate anywhere indoors, paper training may only delay the process of teaching the puppy only to go outdoors away from the den.

I find there is no substitute for getting up every couple of hours with a young pup and taking him out onto the grass or wherever else he will ultimately be expected to relieve himself. It may be as inconvenient as when a new baby first arrives, but at least it's for a shorter period and the puppy will soon pick up the idea not to soil in the house at all. It's also, of course, the best time to start training him to toilet on command as discussed earlier. In doing this we are really teaching the puppy to adopt grass or soil as the substrate for toileting and so identify it as his latrine, especially if he is always taken to the same spot where he will be stimulated into urinating at least by the smell of his previous efforts. It also makes sure that he is always in the right place at the right time when he needs to urinate or defecate. This may even lead to the environmentally friendly action of having the dog only willing to toilet in his own garden, or perhaps only on command on a surface where faeces may be cleared up easily when deposited in public places.

Similar tactics apply to treating the older dog with a house-training problem, though one can usually expect quicker progress and a quicker tail-off of such intensive management because he will already have greater capacity to hold on than a young pup, whose bladder fills quickly and whose passage time of food is much quicker. During the day, the puppy or problem adult should also be taken outside frequently, perhaps even every hour or so initially, and walked up and down vigorously to stimulate movement of the bowels and urinary system. As soon as he passes anything at all, the owner should heap praise on the dog to reinforce his actions positively. Only then can the dog be allowed to play or run free. In that way, he will learn that the first job on going away from the den is to empty himself and this is likely to bring reward from the owner and the opportunity to enjoy himself. Both the puppy and older dog will be more likely to want to relieve themselves on waking or after meals or any excitable activities indoors and so should always be taken outside immediately after these events. On return indoors after toileting, they can be kept with the owner for a while without risk of accident before being put back into their den or bed for rest.

Older dogs which have a long history of house-soiling problems may sometimes benefit from being allowed to sleep next to the owner's bed at night so that they can ask to be let out. If the owners are deep sleepers, a line can be attached to their wrist so that the movement of the dog in standing up to go to a corner or trying to leave the room to eliminate will wake the owner and enable them to get the dog to the right place. Demanding, yes, but usually effective because the dog never makes a mistake. Care must be taken not to over-bond the dog to the owner and make him dependent on their presence as this may lead to separation anxiety problems later, which may include toileting problems of a different nature!

## Indoor kennels

It is important during the early stages of treatment, or when house-training a puppy, that any early learning not to soil the den is built upon. This is best achieved by giving the dog his own den in a quiet, draught-proof corner, usually best in the kitchen, in which he spends his resting and sleeping periods. Ideally this takes the form of an indoor cage, just large enough for the dog to be able to stand up, turn round and perhaps stretch in as an adult.  The base should be completely covered, initially at least, with soft warm bedding.  He should be acclimatized to being enclosed gradually so that the cage is seen very much as his den. Alternatively and sometimes equally as successful, the dog can be tethered to a secure fixture to restrict him solely to his bed area.  This is helpful for the dog which is reluctant to be enclosed in a pen. Providing he cannot hang his bottom over the edge of the material, the length of the tether may define a safe, non-toileting zone, especially if the dog is restricted to the protection of a corner and perhaps under a table.  The dog should have learned as a puppy to move away from his bed when needing to relieve himself and so is likely to try and hang on if confined there. The secret is, of course, not to leave him there so long that he is unable to  hang on, because having been forced to soil  his own bed even once, he is more likely to continue to do so afterwards, quite apart from the distress he will experience.  So, when getting up every hour or two and attending to the dog, one will be taking him from a place where he is trying very hard not to soil to one where he is actively encouraged to do so and rewarded for it. Gradually the dog can be expected to remain clean for longer and longer periods and finally stay  clean  all night.  Having established that his latrine area is outdoors, most  soon  learn  to indicate to their owners that they need to go out if 'nature calls' at times other than their usual walk or outdoor play times. They can also steadily  be allowed freer unsupervised access to rooms in the house other than where their den is situated, especially if the dog is expected to guard the property when alone or at night, but this is best offered very gradually, one room at a time.

The process of house-training is one of errorless learning, and by extension, it is logical that punishment of any form will not help house-train a puppy or dog with a problem. The old wives' tales about 'rubbing his nose in it' or taking him to it to show him what he's done and telling him off after the event are utterly pointless as the dog will only become fearful of the owner's presence and be extremely unlikely to associate their earlier actions with the owner's displeasure. Guilty they may look, but this is simply a submissive reaction to the owner's mood or threats at the time. Catching the dog 'in the act' should also not meet with punishment from the owner. The dog can be startled into stopping by clapping hands, but then he must be calmly taken outdoors to finish and should still then be rewarded for getting it in the right place. Any mistakes indoors should be seen as accidents or the fault of the owner in not getting the dog out frequently enough or failing to recognize the signs that the dog needed to relieve himself. However, there is no need as is sometimes quoted for the owner to give themselves a good telling off, as this too may alarm the dog!

Cleaning up all mistakes very thoroughly is essential if the dog is not to be attracted back to the same area next time he needs to relieve himself. The dog's sense of smell is far keener than ours, which is too easily fooled by strong masking odours in many proprietary cleaners. Cleaning is best carried out using the approach outlined earlier for indoor marking problems. Cleaners which contain ammonia are probably best avoided, as this is a constituent of urine and may only serve to attract the dog to urinate in the same place again, even though it may smell clean to us.

Predicting when the dog needs to relieve himself and ensuring that he is in the right place at the right time is half the battle, so timing of feeding and access to water can help, especially with older dogs. Many will benefit by being fed in the morning so that they are empty by bedtime and will not feel the urge to go in the early hours of the morning. Similarly, access to water can be denied in the early evening to make sure the bladder is not totally full during the night, though naturally care must be taken with larger breeds, overweight dogs and young puppies, or during hot weather or in well-heated houses, or with any dog suffering from a medical complaint. To be on the safe side, the veterinary surgeon should be consulted before manipulating feeding and drinking times for dogs.

The nature of the diet may also affect the dog's eliminatory habits. Higher fibre regimes may make passage times more predictable but also lead to a greater stool volume and a larger mess to clear up if accidents do happen and so a lower residue diet may suit better.

Once clean indoor habits are established, many owners, particularly of little dogs, find that their pets will use a dog flap in the back door. Larger dogs need larger flaps of course and these may represent a risk to household security as dog size burglars may easily force their way through. One case cited in the courts in 1991 in the west of England concerned a small burglar who managed to squeeze into a house through the cat flap (he must have been very supple!). Unfortunately, as well as the cat, there was a large quiet dog waiting for him when he got in and he kept him pressed to the wall until his owners returned.

# Substrate attachment

*Dear Mr Neville*

*I have recently acquired a four year old Jack Russell via a dog rescue society. Gertie was previously owned by an elderly lady who died not long ago. Gertie is a perfect little dog in every way, but will not relieve herself on anything other than newspaper, which has to be put down at night and periodically in the day for her to use. I spend a lot of time at the local stables tending to my horse and riding, and Gertie simply loves to come along. But despite having total freedom around the stables and in the woods all day, she simply will not go, and waits until we get home before she will pass anything at all. In trying to break this I have stopped giving her paper for a whole 24 hours but she went without so much as asking to go and without any apparent discomfort. I was loathe to leave her any longer for fear of causing internal damage. While her devotion to newspaper is a little inconvenient, I also worry that I will have to take lots of papers for her every time I go away for a weekend because I fear she will not go anywhere else. Can she be retrained into using anything else now?*

*Yours sincerely*

*Margaret Farley*

Once dogs are bonded to using a particular range of surfaces for toileting, it is difficult to change them as adults onto anything else or extend the range. The secret is really to get them used to a variety of substrates as puppies if the intention is to take them to a wide range of places as adults. Puppies kept in concrete floored kennels for too long may never make the change to using grass when finally homed at the age of several months – yet one more consequence of 'kennelosis'. Dogs like Gertie which are trained to use only paper, will often simply not change to using anything else, no matter how apparently suitable or convenient. Many dogs will go for ages in kennels without relieving themselves through the stress of isolation from their home and perhaps lack of opportunity to get to the right place or onto the right substrate. One kennel owner friend I know has boarded several dogs which, while eating and drinking normally, would simply not eliminate at all for three days! With Gertie, we still tried all sorts of tricks to make her use grass, even to the point of penning her in the garden, feeding her and leaving her access first to newspaper on the ground, then to shredded newspaper and then diminishing the amount available to her. She used the paper, and she used the shreds but only until they covered an area about the size of a quarter of a page of the larger newspapers and only if they were several 'layers' thick. We left her in peace, we stood by and rewarded every use, we tried all sorts of things but still we could not bond her onto using the ground. In the end we gave up and she now has access to a litter tray with paper in it at home, which the owner takes with her if she plans to be away for more than eight hours. So the answer in the end for Mrs Farley, is 'no' but that we couldn't extend Gertie's range of acceptable substrates did show us just how well trained a dog could be in its toileting habits and so gave hope to others with the opposite problem in their dogs!

# 10
# Noise Problems

*'Tis sweet to hear the watch-dog's honest bark*
*Bay deep-mouthed welcome as we draw near home*
*'Tis sweet to know there is an eye will mark*
*Our coming and look brighter when we come'*          Lord Byron

Recent investigations by the UK private health insurance organization, BUPA, have shown that the sound that drives people most to distraction is not a pneumatic drill, heavy traffic or aircraft, but the sound of a constantly barking dog. It irritates because it is loud, sudden and unpredictably intermittent and, while most of us can learn to tolerate the yaps and barks of our own dogs, we often forget how enormously disruptive they can be to others.

Of course, vocal communication is very much a part of the natural repertoire of the social dog from the cries of a puppy which stimulate a protective response and even milk flow in their mother through to the warning barks of the adult dog when protecting its territory. The various sounds a dog can make enable it to communicate information about its emotional state, health, sexual status or to attract the attention of its parents or pack mates, or reject them. Most excited dogs bark or yip and frightened or injured dogs may yelp, but every dog's voice is unique. By and large we can pick out our own dog from the barking crowd and a mother dog can probably identify individual puppies by their voice only a few days after they are born. Whines and whimpers, be they attention demanding, expressions of discomfort or pleasurable moans, are largely the preserve of puppies, though many continue to use the same sounds when communicating with us. This is because we encourage them to behave as puppies long into adulthood when they would otherwise develop other forms of vocalization to communicate with adult dogs. By behaving as a puppy towards us, the pet dog, especially if one of the smaller 'mothered' breeds, learns to get our attention, affection and food because the sounds invoke the same protective feelings in us as does the cry of a baby or mew of a kitten.

Between themselves, adult dogs are more likely to bark, howl, growl or grumble except when a subordinate dog or loser in a fight whimpers while retreating from the higher ranking dog, perhaps in an effort to invoke that same more placid response. Growls tend to be accompanied by obvious body postures indicating threat or fear, as do barks. However there are many types of bark as every owner knows. The short repetitive single bark of quite high pitch indicates more of an alarmed state and is perhaps designed to alert packmates and attract their support, whereas the more continuous and often deeper alarm bark is uttered by the dog who is more confident at defending his patch and is more directed at the threat he perceives than to attract support. Other barks are produced when the dog is excited, perhaps at the onset of games or the prospect of a walk. This can be one of the most irritating barks of all, being high pitched and repetitive . . . spaniels and Bandits are famous for it but, fortunately, once the walk or game begins, they usually stop and so the noise is tolerable because it is short lived.

While the larger breeds, especially those selected by us for guarding purposes such as the Dobermann or German Shepherd Dog, generally have deeper barks, frequency is often the preserve of the smaller breeds such as Jack Russells and other terriers. Some such as Greyhounds and Basenjiis rarely make a sound, others are sometimes more locally famous for their bark than anything else.

Interestingly, most pet dogs bark far more frequently than their wolf ancestor, though the wolf of course, is famous for his howl. Most wild canids, and hounds in particular of our pet dog breeds, also howl. Howling is the great long-distance form of communication for canids and is used as a rallying call between pack mates prior to hunting or as an alarm to gather themselves together as a pack to face any threats. It may also be used as a short excitable greeting behaviour when pack members do get together and in celebration of the discovery of the scent of the prey when hunting or after a kill.

An individual isolated from the group may howl to try and gain a

255

fix on the position of his packmates from their response so that he may rejoin them and this explains the separation anxiety howling of some dogs when left at home on their own. Their howls go unheeded and so they keep howling, perhaps ever more desperately. Such is the long-travelling and invasive nature of the sound that anyone unfortunate to live next door to the owner of a persistent howler is very likely to complain, perhaps even quicker than if the dog barks when left. Owners of kennels dread the arrival of a howler, indeed some even ban some of the hound breeds or particular individuals of other breeds because once they howl, all the other dogs in the kennel often join in the chorus and make life utterly unbearable.

Wolf researcher Dr Fred Harrington of Mount St Vincent University in Nova Scotia has come up up with an interesting theory about the howling of wolves following analysis of a pack's response to the sound of a recorded wolf howl. A chorus of wolf howls starts with one wolf and builds up steadily as the others join in. The chorus lasts about a minute and is designed to tell any rival packs nearby to stay away from the howlers' territory. The time between the choruses of individual howls shortens until they overlap and individual wolves are no longer recognizable. However, as the chorus progresses, the howls also start to vary in pitch and intensity and give a more confusing picture to the listener. The direction of the chorus is also confused by the behaviour of the wolves when howling. Typically, they move around in close formation and in amongst each other, and this itself seems to stimulate further prolonged howling. One might think that the larger the pack the greater the cacophony but Dr Harrington discovered, using recordings and radio tracking data about the relative positions of the wolves, that there were few differences between the sounds produced by small packs compared with large ones. Indeed, small packs of only a recently bonded pair or just three individuals produced the longest and apparently most confusing howls in response to the howls played to them by Dr Harrington. Neighbouring packs are therefore probably unable to distinguish between howling packs that might be strong in number and able to defend their territory and smaller, more vulnerable ones because of the confused acoustics of their howls. Those howls are also distorted further by echoes and degraded by passing through trees, around rocks etc. So while a large pack may have no need to sound any larger, a smaller group will need to sound bigger and therefore less vulnerable using these tactics which appear to have evolved specifically to confuse the competition. This is exactly how the famous French Legionnaire Beau Geste in P C Wren's novel fooled the enemy into thinking his fort was well protected when he stood his dead colleagues at the ramparts and rushed around firing their guns in turn. The deception works because it isn't worth the risk to the opposition in testing the real strength of the howlers even if they themselves may practise the same tactic against their own rivals. The system functions because, like us, the amount of auditory information a wolf can remember is probably limited to about five to nine voices at a time. This indicates that there would be enough wolves to put up a fight if they were attacked and could inflict serious injury on their aggressors even in defeat. Wolf packs rarely attack each other and so must rely on howling to space themselves across a range because when they do meet, fights can be extremely fierce with many individuals being seriously injured or even killed. This system of bluff gives the new packs a chance to get started.

While the treatment of the howling dog is usually less risky from the behaviourist's point of view, vocalization problems in dogs can often be the most difficult problems to treat, especially with the noisier breeds such as the Dobermann and many of the hounds. The alarm bark of the dog defending our home is often welcome but many pets take their role over-seriously and simply won't shut up when asked. In some cases, they may continue to bark even after the caller has gone away or sometimes after he's been welcomed inside. Once excited for any reason, our dogs may bark incessantly and be difficult to control. Many dogs also bark or whine to gain our attention and do so ever more vehemently if we ignore them.

The tendency with any form of excessive or unwanted vocal behaviour dogs is to shout at them to shut up and literally out bark them. This threat bark from us may be successful with the less excited dog or even with some loud individuals because it causes a mildly submissive reaction which is unlikely to include any vocal responses. But, for most, our yell simply tells the dog that we are excited at the same thing as he is. Consequently, he barks louder and longer and we just get more and more frustrated.

Many owners are victims of their own efforts in teaching their dog to bark on command, an easy thing to condition most dogs to do for the prospect of a titbit. Unfortunately, having learned that barking brings the rewards of a titbit and extra attention, the dog then learns to apply the same technique without being asked, and owners wish they'd never bothered to encourage him in the first place.

# Excessive barking

*Dear Mr Neville*

*My Dobermann Jordan is a great guard dog but barks at every slightest noise and just will not shut up when told. I've tried telling him off but he doesn't seem to hear me, I've tried squirting him with a hose but he doesn't seem to notice and when I've walloped him he's simply run away out of range and carried on barking. He's not interested in biscuits or other bribes once he's barking and I'm at my wits' end to know what to do. Any ideas how to help before I go deaf?*

*Yours sincerely*

*Andy Thrower*

Treatment of the incessant barker can be difficult but certainly the same techniques as described for the over-zealous territory defender in Chapter 6 should be applied for dogs like Jordan. Preconditioning 'stop and look at me' reactions with Dog Training Discs and then predicting the dog's reactions and being ready for them will enable the owners to gain better control of the dog at the door and perhaps train alternative responses.

Physical proximity to the barking dog is often an essential feature of treatment as this will infer the higher ranking owners right to defend the territory or, as is perhaps more often the case, enforce his right to have the dog behave according to his wishes through enforcing his dominance and right to lead. Hence a trailing lead on the dog will enable swift intervention and close proximity when the dog barks, be it as an excitable or attention-getting behaviour or as an overdone territorial reaction. Dogs like Jordan, and those which yap for attention have usually learned long ago to maintain that flight distance from their owner if they can to avoid physical restraint or unpleasant repercussions. Denying this is sometimes all that need be done to stop the barking. Others can be startled into silence using a jet of water or an unfamiliar loud noise and this will enable the owners then to intervene, calm the dog and take control of the situation. Alas, such tactics may only work for the moment and not retrain the dog long-term. For excitable dogs in particular, such interventions may simply give them something extra to bark at and an alternative approach must be used.

To achieve lasting results, it is essential that owners stay calm and don't join in the barking by yelling at the dog. Nor should they punish him once he is close by and under control as this will be perceived as a consequence to the threat or incident that caused the dog to bark in the first place, and simply make him bark harder and longer and, most annoyingly of all, at some distance next time. The owner must instead relax with the dog and reward silence with calm praise, perhaps after encouraging a 'sit' command for the prospect of a food reward or holding a toy, which the dog will be more likely to accept once he is under control. These rewards also usefully keep his mouth occupied! The 'down' response should also be trained at calmer moments as many dogs are less likely to bark when lying down, perhaps because they are then in a slightly more vulnerable position and don't wish to draw attention to themselves. Nervous barkers will be far more likely to be quiet if they can be helped to deal their fears and rewarded for calm acceptance as outlined in Chapter 5. But whatever the cause of the barking or noise, it's always a case of practice and being prepared. The aim is always to calm the dog down as quickly as possible, and not excite him more by yelling at him or chasing him with threats of punishment.

Anti-bark collars which release an unpleasant scent when the dog barks are tempting as a 'quick cure' to barking problems, though in the UK they are very expensive. Whether they are effective in the short term rather depends on the dog's perception of the smell being unpleasant enough to make him forget what first aroused his desire to bark and, in the long term, the dog may simply grow used to the scent and carry on barking regardless. But more importantly, it is essential to consider the frustrations and possible alternative and more problematic behaviours that could arise through causing the barking dog to shut up when he has a very good and natural reason to bark, such as at an intruder or in trying to rally his pack to protect him. And it hardly seems fair in a two dog household that the barking of one dog nearby might cause a well-behaved quiet dog to receive an unpleasant pong from his collar and thus be 'punished' for being near a bark. It's all down to responsible use no doubt, but of great concern to me as a behaviourist is that while the smell may inded stop some dogs barking after a first bark, there is nothing in the collar that subsequently rewards the quiet. In short, the desirable behaviour is not reinforced, while vestiges of the 'punishment' linger in the air for the quiet dog. The dog may, at worst become confused and mildly distressed when treated in this way, and the problem of barking remain, but in the USA, Japan and some countries in Europe, bark-limiting electric collars, based on a similar but painful method, are commonly employed for treating noisy dogs. As soon as the dog barks, he immediately receives an electric shock which inhibits further barking. Personally, I have great reservations about using one of these, though a friend who lives in a London apartment with a lovely German Shepherd Dog did use one to excellent effect in that his dog now barks once at strange noises or a knock at the door, but thereafter shuts up and is not a nuisance to the neighbours. However, the ethics of using this treatment are highly questionable as, in my experience and that of my APBC colleagues, most noisy dogs can be made quieter using patience and controlled rewarding techniques. Nervous barkers especially could suffer with one of these collars by getting into a spiral of bark-shock-anxiety-bark-shock . . . with dreadfully cruel results, and I am not convinced that the bark of a nearby packmate could not set off the electric shock in the collar wearer and lead to all sorts of problems. That all said, I confess I did borrow my London friend's collar to use on one persistent barker, a Rhodesian Ridgeback with which we had made very little progress using the usual techniques and where the owner's wife had genuinely threatened, 'it's me or the dog'. Fortunately, the collar malfunctioned and the dog never received the treatment because the owner took up a new appointment overseas and rehomed the dog before it was repaired. In its new home the dog hardly ever barked, which underlined the importance of considering the whole family's relations with the dog and its home lifestyle in all canine problem cases.

Debarking a dog by surgical removal of the vocal chords and surrounding tissue is practised in some countries even after very little attempt to modify a dog's bark using behavioural techniques. Fortunately in the UK the veterinary profession are reluctant to carry out this type of surgery and will usually do so if the only genuine alternative is the destruction of the dog because of complaints from the neighbours or local authority. Even after debarking, the dog may retain some voice with a throaty cough, which the neighbours may complain about even more on welfare grounds when they discover the cause and, of course, any desirable aspects of the dog's bark as a guard or alarm will be lost to the owners. Rehoming the genuinely unbearable unalterable barking dog to a remote home where his bark may be more valued would seem kinder than de-barking.

Prevention was never so obviously better than cure with such a difficult problem. Control of barking is best taught to a puppy as he starts to bark around 12 to 18 weeks of age, though the techniques can also apply to the older dog in many cases. The first guarding or excited bark is usually impossible to prevent, but immediately afterwards the owner should give a soft voiced 'sssh' and reward the dog with calm praise and a titbit to reinforce the silence.

For less excitable or naturally rather submissive dogs, even a 'NO' after a bark may be frightening and a soft reassurance that all is well is really all that is needed to prevent the dog entering a loud anxious spiral of barking. If he does, then the intervention tactics described earlier may be needed and, as with most remedies, are far more likely to give quick lasting results with a young impressionable dog than an inveterate howler.

## Nervous barking

*Dear Mr Neville*

*I have a sixteen-month-old Springer Spaniel called Becky who is forever rushing up to every dog, and some people out on walks and barking furiously at them. This she does from a few feet away, but with her tail down and a worried expression on her face. If I call her, she may come back apologetically, or just carry on barking as if she hasn't heard. Strangely, she doesn't do this at training classes where she is doing extremely well. It's all rather embarrassing – is there anything I can do to stop her?*

*Yours sincerely*

*Lavinia George-Smith*

This is quite a common reaction for unsocialized or rather nervous dogs. They learn to dispel the prospect of attention from other dogs or people by charging in first with a loud display, but conducted from a safe distance to ensure that escape can be effected if the 'victim' ignores the barks. When that distance cannot be maintained, or where the owner has a more positive protecting influence as with Becky at the training classes, or when other owners move their dogs out of the way anyway, the dog may then be perfectly relaxed and quiet. As with dogs that use similar but more serious aggressive behaviour to preclude close investigation (see chapter 6) the aim of treatment is to achieve greater control and influence at distance using an extendable lead so that initial barks can be interrupted immediately. Startling interventions or preconditioning with Dog Training Discs can be used as before to gain a short period of silence which is then rewarded, as are any calmer approaches that the dog makes towards the other dog or any quiet retreats. With practice, preferably in a variety of places meeting a variety of dogs, Becky and her ilk will usually improve in their social competence and can then be allowed off lead again.

Dogs which bark and howl when left alone are best treated with the suggestions outlined in Chapter 5 for sufferers of separation anxiety, along with sudden intervention tactics for those who start barking as soon as the door is closed and they are left behind. Rather than returning to scold the dog, which simply rewards the dog's efforts in trying to keep the owner with him, the door should be suddenly opened, the startling tactic of rape alarm, jet of water, or Dog Training Discs employed and the door closed again. In other words, the unpleasant reaction is seen by the dog as a consequence of his barking. Once he is quiet, these dreadful things don't happen. It's the same principle as the electric shock bark limiter but without the physical cruelty, and with practice, it usually works. Similarly, attention getting whining and barking must be ignored if it is not inadvertently to be reinforced, even by punishment. Persistence can be met with the dog being pulled within range by the owner (most keep that flight distance when trying to attract attention) and conditioning based on reward for calm, quiet behaviour, with distractions used only if the noise becomes unbearable. But for many barking dogs, the best way to teach them to be quiet is to teach them to bark on command first and then to 'sssh' on command and then reward for being quiet. The 'sssh' can then usually be transferred to other noisy situations where the dog has chosen to bark independently.

# 11
# Bizarre Problems

*'Like a dog, he hunts in dreams and thou art staring at the wall*
*Where the dying lamp flickers, and the shadows rise and fall'*
Alfred, Lord Tennyson

Thus far we have concentrated on the usual canine behaviour problems that are referred to me for treatment. But, of course, in dealing with dotty dogs, there are always bound to be the odd and sometimes very odd cases that crop up and which are either so unique or bizarre as not to fit into the previous categories or so extreme that they deserve a special mention of their own. Some might think that what follows would be the typical caseload of a dog shrink but it is not so. Only the final chapter of this book concerns the inexplicable and the hilarious dogs that occasionally have passed through my doors with their sometimes bemused, amused, worried or long suffering owners.

## Stress

Stress is a little understood word that has so far largely been avoided in this book. Everyone knows what is meant by stress and virtually all of us suffer from it at some time in our lives. Dogs, too, can suffer from stress and many of the problems I treat could be said to be reactions to stress of one sort or another. The relationship between environment, behaviour and physiology is very apparent when we or our dogs suffer from stress, and scientists are only slowly unravelling the complexities of it all.

Startle reactions and developmental learning help the dog cope with challenges and stay alive. Discretion is often the better part of valour for the dog, which may run away from danger quickly if the threat isn't discouraged by his defensive growl or muted by a submissive crouch and tail lowering. More assertive individuals may actively repel living threats – a common example is that of the dog which has learned to deal with other over-friendly dogs by standing its ground and growling back rather than running away. More nervous individuals may rush and hide in safe corners, behind their owner's legs or under bedclothes if unable to cope with challenges at home. Whichever method is adopted, the behaviour changes are designed to reduce the conflict of the moment.

Physiologically the dog is able to respond because adrenaline is released into the bloodstream from the adrenal gland, situated above the kidney. Adrenaline primes the dog for 'fight or flight' by causing the heart to pump faster and send more oxygenated blood to the muscles, while at the same time preparing the body to deal with increased carbon dioxide waste which will result from the activity of running away or fighting off the challenge.

Stress is a very common cause of behaviour changes in dogs. Situations that can lead to stress include alterations in owner routine and lifestyle, retention in an unfamiliar environment, such as at the vet's surgery, being forced to share a home with an aggressive rival or being locked indoors accidentally for a long period. Overcrowding and prolonged exposure to worrying stimuli such as high frequency sound can induce stress, as can grief following the death of a companion.

When our behavioural responses to challenge don't succeed in reducing it, the adrenaline continues to flow in order to keep the body prepared. Stress is often the result, and in human terms is manifested by irritability, tiredness, anxiety and depression. Heart disease and stomach ulcers can also result from the very mechanism designed to help us cope with the risk of injury, when we are unable to avert stressful challenges. Many of us adapt to stress and 'toughen' up both physically in coping with the rigours of, for example, sitting in a city traffic jam every day en route to work, and physiologically as our nervous systems evolve to be less sensitive to the adrenaline coursing through our bloodstream. This 'toughening up' is comparable to the learning by habituationi described in Chapter 5 in the physiological sense, and is a vital process in the adaptation to changing environment for any species. If the stress of moving from favoured forest shelter across an open plain was too much for a deer to the extent that it stayed in an old area with insufficient food rather than risk moving to a fresh area, then it would probably die out as a species quite quickly. That it can overcome the stress of moving across open land where it is temporarily more vulnerable by physiologically adapting to its body's usual responses to such challenges, is what enables it to make the move and survive without suffering any harm from the stress itself.

Some people clearly enjoy being constantly in a state of readiness and, although stressed, do not suffer from any physical or psychological consequences. The difference between those who revel in such a state and those who are anxious, insomniac or get stomach ulcers seems to lie in the biochemistry of their respective nervous systems. Their individual sensitivity at the neurotransmitter level, determines how they react, tuned by 'stress immunization' from exposure when young. Such an explanation, if true, at least helps us understand why everyone differs in their ability to cope with stress and, of course, why each dog will also vary. Bandit seems to enjoy constantly being in a state of readiness and reactivity, while my other dog Cass gets very worried if life is too hectic in anything other than occasional short doses. Bandit is more than enough stress for her, and me for that matter!

While there is no evidence of stressed dogs developing stomach ulcers or heart disease, clearly many do exhibit behaviour changes and responses under stress which are similar to our own. The effectiveness of the immune system at combatting infection may also be reduced with prolonged exposure to stress in man and dog. Low threshold aggression or irritability, depression manifested by secretive or inactive behaviour and pronounced attention-seeking all seem common. Indeed, canine responses to stress of any kind are similar to those of other mammals and generally fall into one of two categories: excited reactions or inhibited ones.

Less frequently reported in the dog and perhaps only observable in the artificial confines of the experimental psychologist's laboratory are convulsions, hysteric epilepsy, excessive salivation, panting and colic. Anorexia, pronounced sensitivity to touch, diarrhoea, hair loss and even psychological neutering have also been reported. Hair loss is seen as a common reaction in stressed or worried dogs. Check out some of the more nervous individuals at dog training classes or those receiving a hard time from the trainer or their owners and you may see hair falling out with every move.

Alleviation of any stressful influence when the dog's reactions have failed to achieve their aim is one of the main features of treatment of many behaviour problems referred to me. The influences may be environmental, if the dog's security in the house is not defined and it is always being competed with for resources of food and shelter. They may be social, if the dog does not get on with other dogs that it has to share its house with, or with one or more of the family. But whatever the cause, treatment of stress in the dog is largely achieved by removing or modifying the stressful influences or controlling the dog's exposure to them physically so that it can 'toughen up'. Most cases involve a combination of both approaches and this treatment is usually far more successful than attempting to diminish the physiological reactions of the dog solely by using stress-relieving tranquillizer drugs. With these, the stressful responses may disappear for the duration of the prescription, but if nothing has changed when the treatment is withdrawn, the dog will become stressed again and the problems will recur. The temptation is simply to keep the dog on drugs constantly to prevent stress reactions but this is obviously only masking signs of the problem and not getting to grips with the real causes. However, used properly, tranquillizers can help in the treatment of stress in dogs, though many respond quickly and well if the stressful influences can be identified and successfully manipulated without using tranquillizers long term.

# Self-damaging behaviour

*Dear Mr Neville*

*Sadie is a very sensitive dog. She is now four and was spayed when about six months of age. I have no other dogs because, much as I would like one, I don't think Sadie would ever accept another one and would be jealous. She is generally rather a nervous little soul and although she enjoys going out, won't go far from me. Sometimes she will not eat for a few days and simply hide herself away if I have friends to call. She can also be rather snooty at times and ignores me if I have been away for a while or won't respond to her demands for affection. While*

*I love her enormously and can accept that she is a very sensitive dog, I am worried because when many of these problems coincide she will nibble and lick at her forepaws repeatedly in a trance like state. Subsequently she has a nasty purulent wound on one paw and a hairless inflamed area on the other which requires veterinary treatment. My vet says that the problem is largely psychological and so I am writing in the hope that you may be able to help.*

*Yours sincerely*

*Lyn Gordon*

Diet sensitivity, particularly to preservatives and artificial flavourings and colourings, or lack of certain fatty acids, are suspected as causes of many self-induced skin conditions. Allergy (especially to fleas) and post-wound over-grooming can all set up skin irritations such as dermatitis and eczema. Sore areas on dog's forepaws where they have constantly licked them are perhaps the most common signs of self-induced trauma in response to stress of one sort or another that are treated by veterinary surgeons. However, I suspect that many similar stress-related conditions also arise which owners do not consider serious enough to warrant veterinary attention, and so they go unrecorded.

The normal adult dog grooms itself rather little compared with the fastidious cat to remove dander, parasites, matts and loose hair, which possibly also reduces the risk of parasite infestation. Dogs kept in pairs or groups may groom each other more than as individuals, as grooming helps re-enforce social bonds between friendly animals and, of course, much of our relationship with the dog centres on his or her acceptance of our grooming-like activities of stroking and tickling. The tactile self-stimulation of grooming by licking, scratching or mild biting is also therapeutic in helping to relieve tension, as we too experience through scratching or combing ourselves when nervous.

A dog may also suddenly start to lick itself for no apparent reason. Perhaps it is responding to a minor irritation of misaligned fur or, as is often seen in the face of obvious stressful influences, as a diversionary displacement activity which is more comforting than facing up to the problem. Dogs such as Sadie, which are sensitive to change or stress, or those constantly challenged by unresolvable threats of one sort or another, may lick or nibble themselves more often and more rigorously

267

in an effort to avoid exposing themselves to the perceived risks. This nervous self-interest is often the cause of serious lick granulomas on the forelegs, usually near the back of the paws as an easily reached target when lying down.

I tend to see such cases only after all medical potential causes have been eliminated and the possibility of psychological influence is all that remains. Often those dogs are very similar in general disposition to Sadie and, as with most nervous problems, treatment is usually a combination of modifying the dog's exposure to the stressful influence(s) as far as possible while providing opportunity to learn to cope under controlled circumstances. For many, a short period of wearing an Elizabethan collar worn around the head is a sufficient distraction and prevents paw licking long enough for the injury to be treated and to break the habit. In fact the slowing factor in treating the self-mutilation is often the treatment of the injury itself, which can be severe, take ages to heal. Such wounds can also recur very easily whenever the dog becomes worried or upset in the future and turns to chewing or licking himself for solace. The frustration of wearing an Elizabethan collar and the original 'psychological' cause of the licking are sometimes treated temporarily with a tapering dose prescription of sedatives or tranquillizers, similar to those used in treating more general nervous conditions, accepting that this may slow the dog's rate of learning to cope. But, even as I write, the same drug cocktail developed by Worcester veterinarian Robin Walker for the treatment of nervousness and phobias in dogs described in chapter 5 is proving mightily successful in trials with certain canine self-mutilation cases. This is especially the case where the underlying cause is insecurity due to an unresolvable threat or a post-traumatic or generalized nervousness. Again Robin is quick to underline that in all cases the drugs are an assistance to appropriate behaviour therapy, not a cure in themselves. The drugs enable the owner to address the causal factors in the dog's lifestyle and help him learn to cope with life without chewing or licking himself repeatedly. Then the drugs should be gradually withdrawn, however tempting it may be for the dog, the owner and the vet to mask the signs of the problem and maintain the dog on the drugs for life.

# Other self-mutilatory behaviour

*Dear Mr Neville*

*Our Dobermann, Cleef, is constantly licking at his flank when in his basket. Not having much fur there anyway he has made the whole area red raw and now bald. We've tried coating him with pepper dust and even hot curry powder but this has only given him a taste for Indian take-away food and he now dribbles and begs every time we have one! Telling him off only stops him temporarily and he will do it when he is with us or on his own. Is there anything we can do to stop him licking himself to death?*

*Yours sincerely*

*Arthur Bingley*

Self-inflicted damage to the flank area is an inherited disposition in many strains of Dobermann, particularly in America and many Dobermanns elsewhere will suck their own flank in an uncomfortable position when resting or worried. Flank sucking will often cause eczema to develop as a result of the skin being frequently damp, and a few cases go as far as self-mutilation down through the flesh. Some I have heard of have even undergone exploratory surgery by the vet in an effort to find some underlying physical abnormality, but there is none. Beyond distraction, topical treatment of any lesions or inflammations caused by the licking or subsequent infection, and an Elizabethan Collar and the inadvisable long term use of Robin Walker's drug cocktail in severe cases, there are no safe permanent answers for this problem at present. Perhaps Dobermann breeders may take steps in future to identify sufferers and avoid breeding from them but with such a popular breed, it is unlikely that sufficient control of breeding could be achieved to eradicate the problem.

It is clear that the pain of any self-mutilation is over-ridden by the activity itself as a reliever of any stress the animal may be under, yet the sufferer usually remains just as sensitive to other painful stimuli. Powerful nervous blocks must therefore be released in the brain or central nervous system during self-mutilation which prevent pain avoidance responses. This in turn usually indicates how strong the animal's motivation to avoid the stress of solitude, enemies or other influences must be at the time it begins to mutilate itself. However, with flank-sucking Dobermanns, there often seems to be no trigger to the behaviour, it just happens. But with this exception perhaps, it appears that self-inflicted damage is preferable at the neurological level to merely the risk of damage from an outside influence. The continuation of the behaviour is probably connected with the brain's release of endorphins which gives some pleasurable reward to the action, and other natural opiates released as relievers of pain when the dog is injured. These chemicals mask the sensation of pain to such a level that the therapeutic angle of self-interested, self-directed behaviour continues. It is here at the micro-concentration level of neurological chemistry that the best hope for treatment lies. At present we can only try to remove stress and offer usual sedatives in treatment, although the use of the morphine antagonist Naloxone is being investigated in studies on horses in America and cats in Holland and may be researched at my Bristol University clinic in the future.

At my Bristol clinic I always try to see cases of self-mutilation with veterinary surgeons who have a special interest in skin conditions. Hopefully, between us we can get to grips with these problems using a combined veterinary/psychological approach to treatment. They get the skin and I get the stress, but hopefully not to the point of giving myself a lick granuloma!

# Stereotypic pacers and chasers

*Dear Mr Neville*

*Our Border Collie, Shan, paces around our garden for hours and has now worn a track. She follows the same route in the same direction, but can easily be distracted and will come in when called. The problem is that after a while indoors she sets up a route around the furniture in the living room as well and will soon wear a track in the carpet if we don't treat her. When not on her hikes, she is a perfectly normal and happy dog and a fun pet to walk and play with. Can we stop her ?*

*Yours sincerely*

*Belinda and Richard Blackburn*

Repeated cycles of behaviour such as pacing, circling and even tail-chasing, a particular favourite of Staffordshire Bull Terriers and some German Shepherd Dogs, fall into much the same category as the self-mutilators. The apparently motiveless, unvarying and rewardless behaviour patterns of pacing up and down or round and round is seen especially in Collies and, of course, in many zoo and confined farm animals. In the past such stereotypies, as these behaviours are known, were regarded as symptomatic of poor welfare and indicative of an unstimulating lifestyle and boring environment. Symptomatic they may be, and strange and even disturbing to look at, but scientists now seem to agree that these behaviours are not necessarily the responses of an animal that is suffering. Indeed, it is likely that by engaging in such behaviour, a pacing dog, bar-chewing tethered sow in an intensive pig unit or circling caged Echidna in a zoo is actually receiving some positive feed-back. Such repetitive actions are also believed to stimulate the release of endorphins which provide a more pleasurable state of mind for the animal than its normal circumstances. When confined zoo or farm animals are deprived of the opportunity to express much of their normal behavioural repertoire, such activity perhaps enables them to derive the same amount of stimulation as would be experienced foraging for food, seeking mates etc in a 'natural' environment. So, while stereotypies make for poor zoo exhibits and lead to complaints from the public, they may be an inevitable and not particularly harmful activity for some individual animals of certain higher species in particular, unless it develops into self-mutilatory behaviour or the act of pacing for long periods causes injury to the feet, for example. Zoos are naturally more motivated to reduce the problem than the farming industry for whom income is derived from production and not the visible spectacle of animals, and many are now engaged in researching programmes of environmental enrichment for their animals. New ideas will hopefully give the animals more to do, make them 'happier' and reduce the incidence of stereotypic behaviour. Simple ideas seem to work best, such as making Chimpanzees forage for their food of fruit and vegetables in great mounds of shredded paper or hay in the same way that they would use on the forest floor, rather than simply plonking the food in troughs or on the floor for them. Such enrichment programmes, as one might expect, seem to work better with younger animals rather than older ones, who may be so entrenched in repeating fixed patterns of behaviour as to fail to notice or respond to the availability of new opportunities.

Similarly with dogs with pacing or tail chasing problems, treatment involves perhaps some initial distraction to break the self-reinforcing cycle of their actions. Any breaks, however short should be rewarded with the opportunity to play equally exciting but more constructive games with the owner and then providing the dog with a greater level of stimulation generally. This may be achieved simply with some dogs by offering more frequent exercise and structured contact with the owners or even providing a second dog as a companion and playmate.

With working breeds such as Border Collies like Shan, it is logical to presume that she is is a highly intelligent dog without any outlet for the role she has been developed to fulfil. When friend and cartoonist Ralph Steadman was finally persuaded by his daughter to get a Border Collie, he felt that Flop simply wasn't happy as an ordinary pet because of all those unfulfilled natural instincts. So he bought Flop a small flock of sheep to keep an eye on and work, under his direction, a couple of times per day in the field at the back of his home. Flop is now an immensely happy dog, but while Ralph's option may be open to only a few collie owners, it does indicate how important it can be to match a breed of dog to one's circumstances. A minority of individuals of certain breeds or types of dogs will always need rather more stimulation and attention than others if stereotypic or other undesirable 'alternative' behaviour patterns are to be avoided.

# Psychogenic vomiting

*Dear Mr Neville,*

*I have three dogs, two girls and a boy, all neutered. All are very different and all have their likes and dislikes. However, they are all very affectionate with each other and towards me. The problem concerns the boy, Ben, who vomits quite frequently when indoors, but only when I am with him and the other two dogs. It started when he was ill some time ago – he is now completely well. I have tried feeding different diets, provided at different times of day, but to no avail. Could the vomiting now be psychological?*

*Your sincerely*

*John McInleys*

This is a very unusual case of attention-seeking behaviour. During Ben's illness he learned that as soon as he vomited, his owners rushed to clear up the mess and heap attention him. Now, when seeking individual attention from them in competition with the other dogs, he vomits and is guaranteed success. Naturally the behaviour doesn't occur when the McInleys are absent. All the owners must do is to ignore Ben when he vomits (unless they suspect genuine illness of course) and Ben should soon stop vomiting. It will also help, no doubt, to restructure the owners' relationship generally with all the dogs and especially Ben as described in the treatment of so many other dog/owner relationship difficulties in this book.

# Parrot-induced stress

*Dear Mr Neville*

*We have a very unruly Springer Spaniel who we are forever yelling at to behave and calm down. He is always on the go, but recently seems to be even more jumpy than usual. He cowers whenever we raise a voice to him and I must confess that we have given him a clobbering in the past for being naughty. The problem is that he seems to be stressed and is constantly ducking even when we want to be nice to him. How can we reassure him without making him totally unbearable?*

*Yours sincerely*

*Simon Brooker*

Life with a zesty Springer can be very trying, certainly until they get older and, sadly, many owners do reach the point where they are forever smacking the dog in their frustration for lack of any other success. When cowed through punishment, the dog may be quiet for a while, even if it doesn't reshape his general behaviour. So I went to see this case to assess how bad things were, how much the relationship between Simon and his family and the dog would need to redefined or rebuilt from scratch, how much attention to training may be needed etc. The Brookers were certainly a loud family and it was no surprise that an already hyperactive Springer would always want be on the go and would nearly always be in the way. But, as we went through a programme of things to do and things to stop doing and how to direct the dog's energies in a productive or enjoyable manner, it seemed that here was a dog far more on edge than even a mad Springer in an excitable home environment might normally be.

As the consultation went on I became more and more convinced that there was some additional factor that the Brookers weren't telling me about. Suddenly it all became clear. With an ear-screeching yell, the words 'SIT DOWN' from the kitchen drowned us all into silence. The poor dog was being yelled at constantly not only by the family, but even all day while they were at work or at school by the Blue Macaw ) in the kitchen who had learned the phrase probably most frequently used around him. Poor dog! We had to teach him to sit on command for rewards using a different word, 'quick', which was only to be used when the door was shut on the parrot. And while things did indeed improve in the dog's general management and control, I suspect the parrot never gave up yelling at the dog, and the dog never really got over that damn bird!

# Trauma

*Dear Mr Neville*

*My Jack Russell Terrier, Bomber, was recently hit by a car outside my house. Thankfully he suffered only minor cuts and bruises which my vet has treated very well. However, since the accident, Bomber has simply not been the bomber that he used to be. All his old chirpiness and toughness seems to have disappeared and he is now reluctant to go out and even more reluctant to be walked near the road. While I can understand this, and accept that it may take him some time to get over the shock he went through, his behaviour indoors is causing us great concern. From time to time and for no apparent reason, Bomber will simply stare into space, or at a wall or other static object. If not distracted by one of us saying his name quite loudly or picking him up, he can keep up the staring for ten minutes or more, and seems to be oblivious to everything around him. On one occasion we came home to find him in one of these trances which he could have been in for several hours.*

*Now we tend to take him everywhere, which isn't too conven-
ient. Any suggestions for help?*

*Yours sincerely*

*Adrian and Vera Greenhough*

Traumatic incidents, almost by definition tend to come as a surprise.
The body's startle reactions to being attacked are swiftly by-passed
and there is no opportunity for the flush of adrenaline to be put to use
in helping the victim escape as the damage is done before the victim
is aware of what is happening. Instead, adrenaline can cause the
after-effects of shock; lowering of body temperature, increased heart
rate, raised blood pressure, causing hair to erect and muscles to
contract involuntarily producing nervous shaking. Dramatic yes, but
thankfully rare as a cause of long-term behaviour problems in dogs.
They either die at the time from the physical trauma of a road
accident, for example, or soon after from the effects of physiological
shock.

The psychological effects of that one short accidental incident are
far-reaching and could be permanent in many ways. However, with
long term 'TLC' and permanent company for as long it takes, Bomber
should make a reasonable recovery. He will need controlled
introductions to known problems like traffic and just being near the
road, and perhaps a little drug assistance as outlined in the treatment
of many nervous conditions. But if Bomber didn't make any progress
or, worse, started to get morose and inactive, or developed other
fixated behaviour patterns after a few weeks of trying, some owners
would not try to repair the damage for too long and instead would have
the dog put to sleep by the vet. Perhaps this is a more humane option
in some cases, especially if the patient was previously a highly active
and confident character. However, Robin Walker's drug programmes
now offer a much greater chance of recovery when used to support
appropriate behaviour therapy and TLC.

# Shadows and lights

All dogs have their likes and dislikes. However, just as some people
get up to the most bizarre activities (why anyone should want to crawl

down a wet dark hole in the ground in the name of potholing is one example I have never fully understood!), so do our dogs in the pursuit of their own enjoyment. These obsessions usually have strong elements of learned behaviour and may involve either bursts of great activity or simple staring at certain objects. While Robert the Airedale's picture staring obsession (see chapter 8) occurred as a result of some peculiar response to a component of his diet, similar behaviour has been recorded in other dogs, with Bull Terriers and Rottweilers being the most frequent exponents in my casebooks at least.

## Shadow chasing

*Dear Mr Neville*

*Our two year old Rottweiler, Cassius, chases shadows and light reflections with an intensity that is hard to believe. He leaps from his bed to pounce on shadows especially, darting frantically across the room to keep up with them. We used to play using a torch beam for him to chase, but things got too boisterous to continue. Now he's almost obsessed by hunting streams of light on sunny days, or chasing shadows in the evening. If we tell him off now he gives us a rather nasty look and we are rather worried that things are getting out of hand.*

*Yours sincerely*

*Lionel Raymond*

These type of obsessions are not uncommon in young dogs because shadows and light beams are attractive moving targets to chase. Most lose interest as they grow up because there is nothing of substance to 'kill' at the end of the chase, and they get bored with the activity because the world seems full of moving lights and shadows. However, for those who are perhaps more interested than most and more reactive with their surroundings generally, it seems only to need a little encouragement from the owners for the behaviour to continue into adulthood and become an obsession. Peaks of activity naturally tend to occur when there are more lights or shadows to chase in the morning or evening, or on sunny days when occasional clouds pass in front of the sun, but the chasing often only occurs when the owners are present because of the attention-getting aspects of the behaviour. Initially encouraged by them to chase beams and having shadows pointed out to him, Cassius now continues to chase both as a form of learned self-amusement when life is too quiet for him and to attract his owners' attention. As with so many dog problems, telling him off or punishing him also contains elements of reward but, while he may stop momentarily in the face of threat from the owner, Cassius is clearly a dog now right on the point of defending his rights to chase shadows.

Shadow and light chasers can seem to withstand very heavy punishment from their owners and continue to chase their quarry with great gusto at every opportunity. With such dogs, physical intervention or threatening verbal discouragement is clearly unwise and usual sound, bitter spray or water squirt distraction techniques are unlikely to startle him out of the behaviour for long. Indeed these tactics may be seen as confrontations or challenges and put the owners at risk of a self-protecting attack from their aroused obsessional dog. So it is usually a good idea to enhance their general status with the dog as described elsewhere so that they be seen more as having the right to control the dog at anytime. However, this is probably only necessary with large and assertive shadow chasers like Cassius. For most, treatment hinges on being able to divert the dog's attention onto something he perceives as being at least as rewarding to do and, preferably, more so. This is probably best achieved by the owners first conditioning Cassius to focus much of his other activity and contact with the owners around a single favourite toy as described in chapter 5. This toy can then be used to distract him for the prospect of a game or greater reward of affection from them, but only after he has complied with a 'sit' command. This re-establishes contact and control without confrontation. Others may be best treated with alternative forms of intense distraction as were employed in the unique case of Pontius . . .

## Staring at walls

*Dear Mr Neville*

*Our English Bull Terrier, Pontius, has a habit of staring at light beams on walls. He started this as a puppy when we noticed he chased a torch beam along the floor and up the wall as we used a torch and then put it on a table. The beam stayed on the wall and Pontius stood with his nose a few inches away staring intensely at it. The dog could not be called away, in fact we don't think he hears or sees anything when he's staring at torch beams. He became extremely upset when we pulled him away as a puppy on even that first occasion, now we daren't even try as he turns on us nastily if we grab his collar. Once we've backed away, he goes straight back to the beam. Obviously we used to just make sure that he wasn't around when we needed the torch but the obsession has now developed to the point where he stands just as transfixed in staring at where a beam used to be! This can occur if a shaft of sunlight comes through the window and hits the wall, though not if it only lands on the floor. If we draw the curtains, Pontius will stand, sometimes for an hour or more just staring at where the light was. He will do this mainly when we are at home, but we have also come home on occasions to find him 'parked' nose to the wall and have no idea how long he's been there. Ordinary sunlight outdoors and lamps indoors don't seem to interest him. He seems quite mad and getting worse . . . is there anything we can do?*

*Yours truly*

*Amanda and Derek Briggs*

Pontius most certainly could not be dragged safely away from those walls where lights were or had been and certainly showed all his bull terrier tenacity at resisting any efforts by his owners or me in trying to remove him. Even if he was put on a lead and then shown a beam, he would advance at the person on the end of the lead 'in a major manner' for a few moments until he realized who it was, then he would scrabble desperately to get back to the source of his delight. A short walk after some interruptions sometimes meant that he would forget all about the light but, increasingly, Pontius would remember and return to the wall once back from his excursion. There seemed to be no attention-obtaining rewards to the behaviour by the time I saw Pontius, as he would indeed start to stare at lights without the presence of anyone in the room (we shone a light through the window!)

and he would not lose interest if the owners left the room if he had started staring at the wall while they were there. Eventually the problem was brought under control by offering Pontius the powerful distraction of a favourite toy to play with. Though this sounds rather easy, what it didn't stop was his desire to stare at light beams on walls, but it did enable the owners to interrupt him successfully every time. A rubber toy with an unpredictable bounce called a 'Bobo' was established as the key to very rough and active play between Pontius and his owners. He was conditioned to respond to it by taking it in his mouth and then trained to release it to them on command, and this was made the pre-cursory behaviour for all the good things of life for Pontious, such as being fed, having his lead put on etc. All other toys were removed and no other contact was permitted for him with the Briggs for a couple of weeks.

Now the same techniques of controlled exposure were employed as for the second part of treating Cassius the Rottweiler in the last case. Torch beams were shone deliberately at the wall and, as soon as Pontius started to fixate on them, the toy was brought out. Usually he would respond to the owners if they were just talking to him and picking at the rubber toy to make a distinctive popping sound that they usually made to attract him. But the more into his trance Pontius became, the more likely it was that the toy would have to be rolled in front of him. If he came to them in response to being called or hearing the popping, he was made to sit as usual and then encouraged to play a throw/fetch game with the toy for a few minutes. If the toy had to be rolled, he would switch extremely violently from staring at the wall to a full blown attack on the toy. He would chew it and snarl at it, drop it and dive on it repeatedly for a few minutes and be just as unaffected by his owners' calls. But after a while he would wind down and eventually bring it to them on command for the throw fetch game to begin. Life with a Bull Terrier can sure be interesting!

## The enemy within

*Dear Sir*

*My Staffordshire Bull Terrier is a real scrapper with other dogs and gets into a real frenzy if he gets the opportunity to fight. As we live in a fairly remote area, this isn't too much of a worry as we rarely meet any other dogs. Capone is allowed to wander around at will in the garden and in one small field of our farm which is enclosed, so that he can't get out. However, on our last trip to the vet's for his annual booster injection, Capone unfortunately got into a scrap with a Jack Russell in the waiting room. Quite how it happened we don't know, it was all too quick, but having separated the dogs I was amazed to find that Capone, having mistakenly grabbed his own back leg in the fight, continued to stay locked onto it and snarl and bite it as intensely as he would another dog. He seemed to feel no pain at all from what he was doing to himself and it took myself, the vet and two nurses about five minutes to break his hold on his own leg! Help!*

*Yours sincerely*

*Matthew Vergara*

The intensity of a fighting dog's aggression is fortunately rarely witnessed but, of course, the fighting or baiting breeds have been deliberately selected to be fearless, extremely pugnacious once aroused and perhaps less sensitive to injury than other dogs. In some of the disgusting descriptions of dog fights produced in days past or even now, as evidence from animal welfare inspectors during the prosecution of the nasty individuals who organise dog fights today, it is apparent that even severely injured dogs continue to fight. They are apparently even more strongly motivated to fight on than to retire and lick their wounds. So, if you're a scrapper like Capone, even from one of the present day usually more benign ex-baiting and fighting breeds, and you get into a fight and misdirect your bite, I guess its only to be expected that you'll keep on biting, even if it's your own leg. If it did hurt, I guess that would only stimulate Capone to keep on attacking the source of the pain. Stay away from anywhere that Capone might ever meet any dogs, Mr Vergara, and try to keep him to being a gangster around his own farm only. The sight of another dog may be all he needs to 'put a contract out' on himself and pull himself to pieces!

## The enemy without

*Dear Mr Neville*

*My Fox Terrier, Drift, attacks our back door whenever it is opened. It is all bitten and scratched at the base where he has assaulted it, and nothing we do seems to be able to stop him, short of tying him into his bed. If we punish him, he attacks the door all the more, though he is friendly with our cat, other dogs and has never so much as growled at us. How can we stop him?*

*Yours sincerely*

*Mrs K Ewer*

Excessive territorial guarding reaction? No. Direct challenge to home resources or dog's bed or possessions? No. Protective reaction towards owners? No. Predatory reaction towards moving target? No. Dog deterred by aversion tactics of loud noises, water ,Dog Training Discs? No chance. Running out of ideas to test? Yes. Damn and blast, kick the door shut in frustration. Drift goes to bed and lies down and never attacks the door again! Guess: door seen as a pack member moving or approaching Drift and the core of the territory without permission and needing to be put in its place by the human pack leaders. By attacking the door, we had established that it had no right of approach, so the dog knew that all people, after the owners had kicked the door shut as well, had it under control and there was no need for Drift to defend his position in the pack against the door. Any further suggestions gratefully received!

## The enemy above

*Dear Mr Neville*

*My three year old Rough Collie, Lassie, seems to hate light bulbs for some reason. We think one may have popped over her head some time ago, but whatever the reason, she now seems to want to get in first. She used to jump up onto tables and chairs and take a leap at them, bursting them in her mouth, amazingly without causing herself any injury. So naturally, we moved all the furniture away from under the lights and put all the table lamps away. But she is a clever dog. Lassie now waits until one of us or an unsuspecting visitor is standing close enough under the lamp to take a run up their back and chomp the bulb over their heads. Winter is coming, we don't want to live in darkness and haven't dared test her reactions to candles! Any ideas for treatment gratefully received!*

*Yours sincerely*

*Clare and Tony Watterson*

Surely this is a unique case! The dog was ultimately desensitized by being fed and played with ever closer to light bulbs and lamps and, preconditioned with Dog Training Discs, interrupted with their sound on a couple of occasions in the initial stages of treatment when she tried to bite light bulbs. This seemed to make her think twice about the capacity of light bulbs to defend themselves! Happily this was a case where the dog finally 'saw the light' and stopped reacting to it. Lassie responded totally to treatment, but imagine the disasters her behaviour could have caused in a stately home full of chandeliers!

## The enemy on the street

*Dear Mr Neville*

*My scruffy old mongrel dog, Roger, had a most unfortunate experience when out for a walk some time ago. He has always insisted on cocking his leg on just about every tree and lamp-post. But unfortunately he recently received a nasty electric shock to his nether regions from a lamp-post just a few yards along the street from our house. He was really burned quite badly, but though the vet has done a wonderful job and he is now fully recovered and the local authority has checked and mended the lamp-post, Roger is now terrified to go out past any lamp-post for a walk. To get him out to the park, where he does relax and enjoy a run again, we either have to walk in the middle of the road well away from all lamp-posts, or take him in the car. How can we reassure him that this really was an unlucky unfortunate incident that is unlikely ever to happen again?*

*Yours sincerely*

*Theresa and John Threesome*

Poor Roger! This is a typical and very understandable example of how a single traumatic incident can lead to a phobia which, like many phobias, is then very difficult to treat. Roger should respond to desensitization treatment as outlined for the treatment of any phobias in Chapter 5, but it will take time, I suspect, to bring him nearer and nearer to lamp-posts. Robin Walker's drug aproach may also help and an enormous amount of gentle rewarding encouragement from the Threesomes will also be needed to help Roger to overcome his fears. Ideally he should first be taken to perhaps more countrified areas where there are fewer lamp-posts on the streets and less traffic to worry about. Steadily he should be walked in as normal a fashion as possible by the owners, being encouraged all the way. A headcollar may give better control, especially if Roger panics, and giving him something to hold in his mouth may help comfort and distract him.

# The moon starer – a real lunatic

*Dear Mr Neville*

*Molly, my Spaniel X Collie has a strange obsession. As soon as the moon is full, she will stare at it in trance-like state, both through the window, and in the garden at night. Though she is very obedient, Molly simply won't come in at all at such times and I have to go and fetch her. She won't settle on these nights and scrabbles around in the kitchen until the early hours . . . is she a benign werewolf?*

*Yours sincerely*

*Joan Cartwright*

The effects of the moon on our biorhythms, physiology and behaviour are probably far greater than we realize or can measure. For estuarine and shoreline life in particular, the gravitational pull of the moon in causing the tides is the single major influence on their distribution and behaviour. Menstruation in women is also believed to occur on a twenty eight day cycle because of some original association with the twenty eight day cycle of the moon. The effects of the moon, presumably through gravitational or magnetic influences were well recorded in the asylums of the nineteenth century. At the full moon, patients became extremely active and sometimes delirious, while they were manageable, if disturbed, at other times. Indeed this is where the term lunatic arose, though there is really no scientific explanation of how and why only some individuals should be so responsive at the time of the full moon.

Molly is the only dog I have ever encountered with such a marked response, and certainly the only one who seemed to have identified the moon so obviously as the cause of her distractions, though some owners have reported restlessness and even occasional howling by their pets at such times. Werewolves are, famed for their transformation and activity at the full moon, but none of us believe that that sort of thing could have any basis in truth . . . do we?!

With Molly, I checked out whether it was simply the large round lit shape of the moon that was attracting her, but it wasn't. She also showed no real interest in the moon at other times, even when it was almost full and very bright in the sky, but she was always very restless even if a full moon was obscured by cloud. Though Molly's behaviour was more an interesting phenomenon than a problem, I was left with the feeling that here was something well beyond the scope of a mere animal behaviourist to understand.

## Alcohol addiction

Addictions are really best described as physiological dependency on something, usually, in human terms, a chemical such as the nicotine of cigarette smoke or on certain drugs or alcohol. Some dogs may give the impression that they are addicted to certain diets or foods because of their enthusiasm when given the chance to indulge themselves or their refusal to eat other types of food. But there are few cases of addiction recorded in animals simply because they are unable to manipulate their access to anything sufficiently to become dependent on it. Any addictions are probably only possible because we allow that access, though again, few dogs are sufficiently interested in the sort of substances we get hooked on. Beagles forced to breathe smoke filled air in laboratories excepted, I have never encountered a dog which would tolerate the foul smell of cigarette smoke (okay, okay, so you've guessed, I'm one of those boring reformed smokers of the world!), especially given their great sense of smell, though doubtless many might become partially addicted without realizing it if they spent a lot of time in smoky environments such as in pubs. Equally, most dogs will shy away from alcohol, though many pubs can boast a dog which enjoys a lap of beer, that's if they're not pretentious enough to have banned dogs on health grounds because they serve what they often euphemistically describe as food. Check some of their kitchens to see what a health hazard can really be, and then decide if you'd rather eat with your dog in the front room at home! For some dogs, the enjoyment of booze can become what appears to be an addiction, judging by their behaviour if their beer is withdrawn suddenly!

## The dog and the beer

*Dear Mr Neville*

*When our local pub sadly closed and the landlord and his wife retired, my husband and I took on their German Shepherd Dog, Max, as our pet. He is seven years old, a perfect companion and guard for us but unfortunately seems to have grown used to getting a pint of beer or the drip tray slops every evening after closing time from his previous owners. When 11.30 pm arrives, he comes and stares at us if we are still up and paces up and down ever more irritated if we don't give him what he wants. If we are already in bed, he scratches furiously at the kitchen door and barks incessantly until one of us goes down and gives him his beer. He laps it up greedily and then settles down in his bed for the night. How on earth can we break this habit?*

*Yours sincerely*

*Janice and Paul Grayson*

Such regular features of a dog's life are indeed hard to shake, though often a change of home and lifestyle causes the demands to disappear. Not so with Max, for whom a beer before going to bed is clearly an important feature of life. His behaviour is typical of the frustrated dog though not necessarily one of the addict being denied his favourite addiction. As the amount of beer expected and being consumed was of some concern, we decided that drying Max out slowly by reducing his alcohol intake as a first measure was the best course to take, leaving the regular demanding aspects of his behaviour till later. Steadily he was offered more and more dilute beer though treatment did reach a point of offering about a four to one mix of water and beer, below which Max would not go. So, having got him onto lowish alcohol beer (he wouldn't touch genuine low alcohol beer and frankly, I don't blame him!) without side effects, we gradually brought the time forward when he was given his tipple to the early evening. A happy compromise has been reached without 'cold turkey' setting in for Max and, as far as I know, he continues to enjoy his beer to this day without causing so much disruption to his owners' lifestyle. And their dog beer bill has been cut by 75 per cent!

## Racist dogs

*Dear Mr Neville*

*My Black Labrador, Buster, is an utter racist. He only has to see a West Indian or Asian person and he growls and lunges at them. I can assure you that as a vicar, I am most definitely not racist in any way but I am extremely worried about my dog's behaviour. I have owned him since he was a puppy and to my knowledge, he has never been taunted by anyone coloured. How can we teach him the ways of racial harmony?*

*Yours sincerely*

*Rev. Basil East*

While the human-like boozy habits of Max were due to opportunity provided by his original owners, there is nothing quite so embarrassing as the dog which behaves in such an apparently human bigoted manner of his own accord. Sadly many human racists do actively encourage their dogs to dislike and even attack members of other races, and particularly other colours of people than their owners. And, of course, dogs are well capable of distinguishing between different types and colours of people. But it can really be difficult to reassure the dog's intended victims when, as the owner, you are totally unprejudiced and have never trained or encouraged your dog to distinguish different peoples . . . especially if you are a man of the cloth! Treatment will involve as great a degree of control of the actual lunges as for treating any aggressive reactions in dogs, using a head collar to control the dog and appropriate reconditioning. A better defined relationship between the Rev East and Buster must be developed so that the dog can be more relaxed and learn to take a lead from his owner when out on walks. But most of all, the Rev. East is going to need a supply of willing coloured volunteers to introduce Buster to who will be kind and rewarding to him so that he comes to associate good things with meeting coloured people generally. So Buster's actions may actually lead to a little more co-operation between the various local communities and religions than the Church might sometimes go in for in some areas.

While on the subject of religion, the Lord moves in mysterious ways, not the least of which concerns those people who feel the need to go knocking on people's doors to tell them all about it and enlist them in their particular brand of worship. Many are spotted early by the faithful family mutt, and if your polite 'no thank you' doesn't keep you agnostic or aetheist or safely in your own Church, then the prospect of the less polite canine version of 'go away' may encourage the doubtless well-meaning individual to try elswhere. Colonel, my old Dobermann, was one perhaps heathen dog for whom the arrival of a person of religious persuasion on the doorstep posed a special threat. Such proseletisers induced, for some reason, a marked guarding reaction, while most other visitors were usually welcomed. The difficulty in treatment for Colonel was in finding enough religious callers to take part in his rehabilitation! Having seen Colonel in full bark, they decided that he was probably the 'Prince of Darkness' and became suddenly less interested in the salvation of his master. Most wisely decided that here was a house where the Lord could do His own work and, frankly, I was glad of Colonel's protection, heathen or not!

# In the mire

*Dear Mr Neville*

*My Red and White Setter has a really disgusting habit of rolling in any farm animal manure he can find, especially great runny piles of cow dung. He also rolls on top of any dead animals he finds in the fields, even on little dead mice. I am tired of having to hose him down and bath him on return. Why does he do this and how do I stop him?*

*Yours sincerely*

*Mrs Yvonne Willow*

Yuk! This may be a continuing ancestral behaviour whereby the dog is trying to disguise his own smell with that of another animal to enable him to approach his prey later and perhaps upwind with less chance of detection. There may be an added bonus in appearing successful to your packmates through smelling like the prey itself, hence the behaviour may become particularly directed at rabbit or sheep dung if, for example, the dog lives in rabbit or sheep country, or at any small dead bodies if the dog sees itself as a general predator of smaller things. Quite why some dogs seem to favour runny cow pats is not really understood, but it is also possible that by rolling in anything it can find, the dog is actually reinforcing constituents of its own normal scent. Hence some dogs head for the nearest cow pat as soon as they have had a bath! While aversion tactics may help treat some dung rollers, this seems to be such a deeply ingrained 'natural' behaviour that it is usually difficult to reshape, and walking the dog away from the dung of other animals may be the only way to avoid a smelly walk home to the bath.

# Reflective behaviour

*Dear Mr Neville*

*My dog Bella, who is a sweet natured Cavalier, will not look at herself in the mirror.  Other dogs I have seen go mad when they see themselves .  Is Bella different?*

*Your sincerely*

*Susan Ryder*

There is little so vain as man in the animal kingdom. Though we are unlikely to suffer the fate of Narcissus who, in Greek mythology, was turned into a peacock for his obsession with his own looks, many of us spend far too long in front of a mirror admiring ourselves or adjusting our appearance than is good for us! While chimpanzees and budgies may also spend long hours gazing at themselves, it comes of something of a shock when our dogs react to their own image in a mirror because we may regard it as  such a  personal event that dogs ought not to be worried about it. While most dogs don't seem to notice themselves at all in the mirror, there are a few who stare apparently longingly at themselves given the chance. There are a few more who bark furiously at themselves, probably in  an effort to make that rival who dares to show them the same intent with eye contact and body language, back away. The more assertive the dog gets, the more the rival  responds . . . very frustrating!

Most common, however, are dogs like Bella who avoid making eye contact as a submissive gesture when they see themselves in the mirror.  They catch sight of a dog staring them in the eye and, being gentle natured souls, give a show of deference and look away.  Just how well a dog can see a mirror image will depend on the quality of the reflection (hence most don't stare at themselves in water reflections as did Narcissus), the nature of the dog's eyesight and proximity of the mirror.  If the dog is short sighted like many Pekingese, or stands too close to the mirror if he is of a long nosed breed, he may not be able to define the image well and may not recognize it as a dog at all, just a blur. Few seem to learn that the image is of themselves. After all, they probably don't know what they look like in the first place!

# Television tastes

*Dear Mr Neville*

*My three year old Flat Coat Retriever, Bangle, loves to sing along with certain television programme theme music. She especially likes the soaps such as Neighbours and East Enders and will come charging into the living room to howl and sing along whenever she hears the music. She also likes some songs on the radio but they have to have long notes for her to join in. She can also be encouraged to sing if we start and wave our hands at her to conduct her. Is all this musical activity performed because she likes the music or wants to out-compete it and make it go away? And how do we get her to shut up when the programme starts and we want to watch?*

*Yours sincerely*

*Margaret Barnes*

Many dogs are very responsive to certain notes or sounds and, with a little encouragement, we can enhance and continue their singing. My old Dobermann would happily howl along if given a note and conducted, especially with his equally vocal friend, a singing Setter from Surrey. So it's not surprising if a few dogs learn to sing along if triggered by perhaps similar sounds that they hear on the radio or television. After all, as we saw in chapter 10, the sound of one wolf howling will usually soon set his packmates off. But if Bangle has any taste at all, she won't be singing along to the soap themes because she enjoys them. It's usually simply due to the fact that the whole family rush madly into the living room to watch the programme when they hear the theme music, which raises the whole level of excitement for the dog as well. But whereas with other programmes, perhaps only some members of the family dash in to watch the television and there is always someone left to play with or respond to the dog's increased excitement, everyone in the family watches the soap, and so the excited dog follows them and starts singing. She's guaranteed to get some attention, and initially fun and fuss but, later, even being told off is better than being let down by your pack who have all suddenly become mindlessly inactive and are all sat staring at the television ignoring you. So perhaps the dog comes to recognize certain tunes as being competitive for the family's attentions and sings along as soon as she hears them to make she sure gets her just rewards for being the family dog. Perhaps others are just happy minstrels!

## Bones or puppies?

*Dear Mr Neville*

*My Staffordshire Bull Terrier bitch, Beefie, has recently pro-duced a cracking litter of puppies but although she nurses and cares for them well, from time to time, she has taken them out into the garden to bury them! We've unearthed them about half a dozen times now and have had to adopt a policy of escorting Beefie's every trip to the garden and keeping the doors shut at all other times. I am a vet but neither I nor any of my practice colleagues have ever heard of this behaviour before. Any ideas? Will it last?*

*Yours sincerely*

*Robert Stevenson*

Many dogs bury bones and a few bury even more readily consumable items such as biscuits, presumably as food caches to utilize later when they are hungrier. A few dogs also don't like the position of the bed when whelping and move their puppies one by one to a preferred area in the house, though this is a far more common behaviour in cats than in dogs. Beefie may have been showing a combination of food caching and puppy moving when she took them out to the garden ... or perhaps she didn't like her puppies very much and was burying them with the intent of digging them up later when they had grown up and were less of a strain to look after! Who knows? But after those few attempts and early unearthings for the puppies, and with continuing supervised access to the garden, Beefie stopped trying to bury her litter and ultimately raised all five puppies very successfully.

# Contraceptive dogs

*'He was formed for the ruin of our sex'*                    Tobias Smollet

While Chapter 7 was devoted entirely to the sexual extravagances of dogs, it seems fitting to plumb the depths once again for the final words in this book on canine behaviour with the notable case of Gnasher, a wonderful character I saw a couple of years ago shortly after his owner got married.

> *Dear Mr Neville*
>
> *I know you deal with animal behaviour problems so I hope you won't mind that I am writing to ask for your help about our sex life. I'd better explain. Elizabeth and I were married a month ago. She moved into my house with me and Gnasher, my four year old Jack Russell. Gnasher knew Elizabeth of course, though he was and still is very much 'my' dog. The problem is that Gnasher simply won't let Elizabeth get into bed with me at night. He's used to sleeping in his basket at the foot of the bed but when Elizabeth tries to get into bed, he leaps onto it growls fiercely. I've tried to put his bed in the kitchen and shut him out but he simply cries until I get up and let him back in, whereupon he marches up to Elizabeth and starts growling at her in bed. No amount of bribery or telling off from either of us improves his anger, in fact if Elizabeth so much as looks at him, he gets really nasty. I have to say that he was never like this with anyone who stayed before I knew Elizabeth (a long time ago of course!!). What are we to do? Our sex life is in ruins because of Gnasher, but I don't want to get rid of him.*
>
> *Yours sincerely*
>
> *Elizabeth and John Fisher*
>
> *PS You could save our marriage!!*

And so we have come full circle to saving marriages again, not to mention the newly weds' sex life! And no, I didn't conduct the consultation *in situ!* Instead a combination approach of restructuring relationships between Mr and Mrs Fisher and Gnasher was applied so that they were both more in control of his actions and he had to earn all the privileges of living with them both for a while. This was especially targetted towards Elizabeth who had both to establish her presence in the pack and then her closer position to John than Gnasher's. Of course this meant demotion for the dog, but he was rewarded all the way by Elizabeth, who also took over the main duties of feeding, exercising, training and brushing him for a while. A little Dog Training Disc therapy was applied initially and the dog was tethered to his bed at night, which was allowed to remain at the foot of the Fisher's bed. Gnasher was thrown titbits by John as Elizabeth got undressed and went to bed, and soon Gnasher 'the contraceptive' as he was known (name changed to protect the delicate) became far less disruptive and returned to being a much loved family dog. The treatment must have worked because I got a card about a year later to say that Elizabeth and John had produced their first baby, a daughter called Carole, 'a playmate for Gnasher'!

*'You think dogs will not be in heaven? I tell you, they will be there long before any of us.'*                                    Robert Louis Stevenson

# Epilogue

From time to time in the writing of this book my own dogs, Cass and Bandit, have suffered from lack of attention, shorter walks, shorter temper from me and must wonder what on earth I've been up to. If I can tell them that even one owner has managed to resolve a problem with their dog, or now feels that help may be possible after reading this book and are happier as a result, they will feel much better. Or at least I will feel less guilty. Perhaps the two of them will get a human shrink in to have a look at me, restructure my relationship with them, make sure I earn any pleasures of life and that any attempt to indulge in unwanted activity is blocked with appropriate preconditioning with rewards for good behaviour. Time to behave by the sound of it!

'Let Hercules himself do what he may
The cat will mew and the dog will have his day'
William Shakespeare (in *Hamlet*)

# Help for Pets with Behaviour Problems

Some of the suggestions outlined in this book for treatment of canine problems require careful application, especially when dealing with aggressive dogs. Accurate diagnosis is also required for treatment to be successful, so please seek help if you have any doubts at all about how to tackle your dog's problems. In the first instance seek the advice of your pet's veterinary surgeon. If he or she would then like to refer you, one of my colleagues in the Association of Pet Behaviour Counsellors will be pleased to help.

## Association of Pet Behaviour Counsellors

My practice is one of the founding members of the Association of Pet Behaviour Counsellors (APBC). The APBC now comprises many professional member practices nationwide so if your pet has a behaviour problem, a member may be able to offer help in your own area. Please contact the most convenient practice, or write for further details to the Honorary Secretary, APBC, 257 Royal College Street, London NW1 9LU